JAMAICA CRICKETERS

1894/95 - 1994/95

compiled by

Philip Bailey, Bill Lane and Philip Thorn

Published by the Association of Cricket Statisticians and Historians, West Bridgford, Nottingham
1996
Typeset by Limlow Books
Printed by Tranters, Derby
ISBN: 0 947774 59 9

INTRODUCTION

The Island of Jamaica is in the Western Caribbean and has an area of 4,207 square miles thus being slightly more than twice the size of Lancashire. It is about 144 miles in length and 49 miles at the greatest width and in shape has been compared to a turtle. The island was originally inhabited by Taino Indians known as Arawaks.

The Arawaks called the island Xaymaca, meaning 'well-wooded and watered'. In May 1494 Christopher Columbus, on his second voyage, sighted the island on his way from Cuba (some 90 miles north) and having landed on the northern shore declared the island to be part of the Spanish dominions. He christened the island St. Jago after St. James, the patron saint of Spain, but the new name did not last long and Xaymaca came in time to be called Jamaica.

Columbus visited the island again in 1503 but there was no permanent settlement until 1509 when some 70 Spaniards landed at St. Ann's Bay - little is recorded of this period of Spanish occupation but the Arawak Indians were largely exterminated. Spain showed little interest in its Colony and in 1597 Sir Antony Shirley took and plundered Spanish Town. In 1635 a Colonel Jackson headed 500 men from the Windward Islands and overpowered Port Royal.

After the English Civil War, Oliver Cromwell wanted to fix public opinion elsewhere and decided the Spanish colonies were an ideal target. After an abortive attempt to invade Hispaniola a party of English troops, mainly Royalist soldiers, took Jamaica in May 1655. The Spaniards made several attempts in the next few years to recover the island but in 1670 the Treaty of Madrid endorsed British occupation. In the years that followed, the island was settled from England, from Nevis, and from other sources such as America and Barbados.

Jamaica became a haven for buccaneers and one such, Sir Henry Morgan, became the Lieutenant-Governor. But after he was sent back to England it was not long before the first Assembly, consisting of thirty persons, met in January 1664.

Cocoa, indigo and hides were the most important products but sugar soon took over and along with coffee, bauxite and tourism remains so to this day. The island is divided into three Counties and fourteen Parishes and the latter are named in this publication, where known.

Turning to cricket in Jamaica, this is recorded as being played by the pupils of St. George's College in Kingston in 1850. Both the St. Jago and Vere and Clarendon Cricket Clubs were founded in 1857 but neither lasted very long and the next major event was the foundation of the Kingston Cricket Club in January 1863. The Kensington Club was founded in 1879, the Melbourne Club in 1892 and the Lucas Club in 1898.

Due to Jamaica's distance from the other West Indian cricketing countries, early first-class matches were mostly against touring teams from the UK. The first of these was the R.S.Lucas team in 1895 when three first-class matches were played at Sabina Park. All first-class matches were played here until 1909 when Melbourne Park became a venue. These two grounds continued to be the only ones used for first-class cricket until 1965 when a match was played at Montego Bay. In 1991 a match was played at Innswood.

A total of 299 cricketers have represented Jamaica including Garry Sobers, Wesley Hall and Conrad Hunte who played for a Jamaica Invitation XI against Worcestershire in 1966.

Obtaining biographical details of the cricketers has not been easy and these would no doubt have been more complete if several people well known in Jamaican cricket had followed up promises of assistance. For all that, details of some sort have been found for all but a handful of the players.

A good many Jamaican cricketers have left their native island. In the UK will be found J.H.Cameron, M.C.Frederick, S.R.Goodridge, C.Headlam, R.G.A.Headley, I.Iffla, Reg Scarlett and Cec Wright. D.Aitchison, D.T.Dewdney and J.M.Groves are in Canada but most have headed for the USA where there will be found A.P.Binns, N.L.Bonitto, L.G.Fidee, E.D.S.A.McMorris, D.Miller, R.C.Miller, C.Minott, H.Parris, A.J.Powe, Robert Scarlett, A.H.P.Scott, A.L.Valentine and K.H.Weekes.

Of the cricketers themselves who have kindly assisted we would like to thank Alfred Binns, the late Arthur Bonitto, John Cameron, Stanley Goodridge, Irving Iffla, Esmond Kentish, Aston Powe, the late Ken Rickards, Reg Scarlett, Alfred Scott and Cec Wright along with the relatives of deceased cricketers.

From the ACS we appreciate the help of Don Ambrose, Brian Austin, Lionel King, Howard Milton, Mike Spurrier and Peter Wynne-Thomas. Particular thanks go to Ray Goble for completing the career records.

Philip Bailey
Bill Lane
Philip Thorn
February 1996

CRICKETERS WHO HAVE PLAYED FIRST-CLASS CRICKET FOR JAMAICA BETWEEN 1894/95 AND 1994/95

ABRAHAMS, Sidney McWhinnie. b 3.8.1915 Chapelton, Clarendon. d 27.7.1983 Kingston. rhb, lbg.

ACTON, Edward Vincent Joseph. b 28.2.1871 Wolverton Hall, Pershore, Worcestershire, England. d 31.10.1912 Trinidad. Trinidad.

ADAMS, James Clive. b 9.1.1968 Port Maria, St. Mary. lhb, sla, wkt. Tours (5). Rest of World to England. Young West Indies to Zimbabwe. West Indies (22). Nottinghamshire.

AITCHESON, Donald. b 1916. rhb, wkt.

ALEXANDER, Franz Copeland Murray. b 2.11.1928 Kingston. rhb., wkt. Tours (3). West Indies (25). Cambridge University.

ALLEN, Samuel Forbes. b 28.5.1943. rhb, ob.

ALLISON, Owen. b 24.8.1949 Spanish Town, St. Catherine. rhb, ob.

ANDREWS, Anthony James. b 11.3.1967 Westmoreland. rhb, rfm.

AUSTIN, Richard Arkwright. b 5.9.1954 Kingston. rhb, rm. West Indian XI to South Africa. West Indies (2).

BAILEY, Cleveland William. b 15.3.1918 Mount Industry, St. Catherine. rhb, rm.

BAINES, G. M.

BANTON, Clive. b 20.1.1969. rhb, rfm.

BARCLAY, Kanute. b 1936. d June 1994 Kingston. rhb.

BARNETT, Kenneth. rhb, rfm.

BARRETT, Arthur George. b 4.4.1944 Kingston. rhb, lbg. Tour (1). Jamaica to England. West Indies (6).

BARROW, Ivanhoe Mordred. b 16.1.1911 Beef Pen, St. Thomas. d 2.4.1979 Kingston. rhb, wkt. Tours (3). West Indies (11).

BAUGH, Carlton. b 12.11.1953. rhb.

BECKFORD, Donald Percival Stanford. b 7.6.1907 Port Maria, St. Mary. rhb.

BECKFORD, Wilfred George. b 1909. d July 1959 Kingston. lhb.

BENNETT, Herman Archibald Augustus. b 22.12.1939 St. Catherine. rhb, sla.

BICKNELL, Henry Fremlin. b 4.2.1903 Kingston. d 7.7.1978 Kingston. rhb.

BINNS, Alfred Philip. b 24.7.1929 Kingston. rhb, wkt. Tour (1). West Indies (5). Son of M.J.Binns.

BINNS, Michael Joseph. b 24.1.1902 Kingston. d October 1987, Half Way Tree, Kingston. rhb, ob. Father of A.P.Binns.

BLOOMFIELD, Cyprian Alexander. b 16.3.1900 Cave Valley, St. Ann. d 1988 Half Way Tree, Kingston.

BLOOMFIELD, Colin Owen. b 1918. d 24.11.1984, Half Way Tree, Kingston. rhb.

BONITTO, Arthur Rudolph. b 20.2.1914 Kingston. d 5.10.1990 Kingston. rhb, lb. Brother of N.L.Bonitto, cousin of C.G.Bonitto.

BONITTO, Colin George. b circa 1920. d circa 1985 Kingston. rhb. Cousin of A.R.Bonitto and N.L.Bonitto.

BONITTO, Neville Leopold. b 15.8.1924 Kingston. rhb. Brother of A.R.Bonitto, cousin of C.G.Bonitto.

BOY, Carl Richard Claus. b 2.7.1899 Cross Roads, Kingston.

BRONSTORPH, Frank Longden. b 26.4.1898 Kingston. d 1987 Constant Spring, St. Andrew.

BROWN, Errol Earl. b 16.6.1952 St. Catherine. rhb, ob. Tour (1).

BUCHANAN, Paul Lennox. b 28.1.1949 Jones Town, Kingston. rhb.

BURKE, Edward Estcourt. b 28.4.1870 Kingston.

BURTON, Charles H. b circa 1875. d circa 1948. rhb.

BYNG, Arthur Maitland. b 26.10.1872 Southsea, Hampshire, England. d 14.9.1914 Vailly, France. rhb. Brother of J.A.Byng (Transvaal), grandson of W.F.Maitland (Oxford University), nephew of F.Stephens (MCC). Hampshire.

CALNICK, Edwin. b 22.11.1937 Kingston. rhb, rfm.

CAMERON, Francis James. b 22.6.1923 Kingston. d 10.6.1994 Kingston. rhb, ob. Tour (1). Canada to England. West Indies (5). Son of J.J.Cameron, brother of J.H.Cameron, nephew of E.G.Hull. Canada.

CAMERON, John Hemsley. b 8.4.1914 Kingston. rhb, ob, lbg. Tour (1). Oxford and Cambridge University to Jamaica. West Indies (2). Son of J.J.Cameron, brother of F.J.Cameron, nephew of E.G.Hull. Somerset, Cambridge University.

CAMERON, John Joseph. b 18.5.1882 Kingston. d 12.12.1954 Kingston. rhb, lb. Tour (1). Father of F.J.Cameron and J.H.Cameron, brother-in-law of E.G.Hull. Gentlemen of England.

CAMPBELL, Clive. b 21.1.1951 Kingston. rhb, ob.

CAMPBELL, Euly Anthony. b 25.9.1950 Kingston. rhb, wkt. Jamica to England.

CAMPBELL, Herbert Sydney. b 15.3.1889 Kingston. d 11.3.1974 Kingston. Brother-in-law of C.H.L.Valencia.

CARTER, Carlton de Lisle. b 19.11.1972. rhb, sla.

CASTLE, Harold Duncan Boycott. b 11.12.1861 Futtehpoore, India. d 4.2.1934 Malvern, St. Elizabeth. wkt.

CAWLEY, Clifton Lynden Oscar. b 26.11.1906 Highgate, St. Mary. d 1986 Kingston. rhb.

CHAMBERS, Leonard. b 31.12.1941. rhb, ob.

CHANDLER, Charles Reginald Watson. b 23.11.1870 Guys Hill, St. Mary. d circa 1940 Guys Hill, St. Mary.

CHANG, Herbert Samuel. b 2.7.1952 Kingston. lhb, rm. Tour (1). West Indian XI to South Africa (did not play in first-class matches). West Indies (1).

CHISHOLM, S. C. b 1899 Kingston. rhb.

COHEN, Rudolph Alexander. b 4.8.1942 Kingston. rhb, rfm. Tour (1).

COLLINS, Charles Glen. b 19.4.1880 Partick, Lanarkshire, Scotland.

CORKE, Terrence Anthony. b 27.12.1955 Ewarton, St. Catherine. rhb, rm.

COX, George Sergeant. b 1.11.1877. d 25.10.1945 Kingston.

CRUICKSHANK, O'Neill Washington. b 1.1.1968. rhb, rm.

CRUTCHLEY, L. J. wkt.

CUNNINGHAM, Frank Alexander. b 19.9.1962 Montego Bay, St. James. rhb, lbg. Brother of L.O.Cunningham.

CUNNINGHAM, Lawrence Oliver. b 23.10.1963 Montego Bay, St. James. rhb, lbg. Brother of F.A.Cunningham.

CUNNINGHAM, Oswald J. b 1920 Kingston. rhb.

DA COSTA, Oscar Constantine. b 11.9.1907 Kingston. d 1.10.1936 Kingston. rhb, rm. Tour (1). West Indies (5).

DALEY, Aaron George. b 2.5.1956 Kitson Town, St. Catherine. rhb, rfm.

DALEY, Courtenay Eddison. b 6.11.1950 Kingston. lhb, sla.

DAVIDSON, Cleveland Anthony. b 14.7.1960 Little London, Westmoreland. rhb, ob.

DAVIS, Winston. b 1.7.1940.

DE CORDOVA, Cecil. b 8.2.1876 Kingston. d circa 1948 Kingston. wkt.

DELGADO, C. H. b 1890.

DENNIS, Kenrick Alexander. b 7.11.1966. rhb, rfm.

DEWDNEY, David Thomas. b 23.10.1933 Kingston. rhb, rf. Tours (3). Commonwealth XI to England. West Indies (9).

DIXON, Deron Cecil. b 18.1.1967 Kingston. rhb, rfm.

DOWE, Uton George. b 29.3.1949 St. Mary. rhb, rf. West Indies (4).

DRURY, Byron Henry. b 3.10.1870 Lucknow, India. d 12.11.1897 Trafalgar Point, St. Andrew.

DUFF, Arthur Vivian. b 29.3.1883 St. Ann's Bay, St. Ann.

DUJON, Leroy Vitalis St.Just. b 22.11.1918 Lyndhurst Town, Kingston. d 10.1.1967 St. Andrew. rhb. Father of P.J.L.Dujon.

DUJON, Peter Jeffrey Leroy. b 28.5.1956 Kingston. rhb, wkt. Tours (11). Young West Indies to Zimbabwe. Rest of World to England. West Indies (81). Son of L.V.St.J.Dujon.

DUNCKER, Henry Cecil. b 4.3.1885 Kingston.

DYER, L.

EBANKS, Kirk Francois. b 23.7.1968. lhb, sla.

FARQUHARSON, Charles Henry Campbell. b circa 1875 Santa Cruz, St. Elizabeth. d circa 1948 May Pen, Clarendon.

FARQUHARSON, William George Robertson. b 9.8.1864 Santa Cruz, St. Elizabeth. d 3.8.1928 Croydon, Surrey, England. Brother of W.H.K.Farquharson.

FARQUHARSON, Walter Henry King. b 26.6.1859 Brampton Bryan, Santa Cruz, St. Elizabeth. d 21.1.1930 Retreat, St. Mary. Brother of W.G.R.Farquharson.

FIDEE, Lawrence G. b 6.8.1922 Kingston. rhb.

FLETCHER, Colin Worrell. b 22.2.1953 Rae Town, Kingston. rhb, rm.

FOLKES, Castell. b 29.7.1944 Kingston. rhb, rfm. Jamaica to England.

FOLKES, Clifton Ricardon. b 16.9.1970 St. Elizabeth. rhb, rfm.

FORD, Shane George Bancroft. b 8.9.1969. rhb, wkt.

FOSTER, Frederick Adolphus. b 23.3.1882 Clarendon. d circa 1955 Windward Road, Kingston.

FOSTER, Gerald Claude Eugene. b 30.11.1885. d 1966 Kingston.

FOSTER, Maurice Linton Churchill. b 9.5.1943 Retreat, St. Mary. rhb, ob. Tours (2). Jamaica to England. West Indies (14).

FOSTER, Robert Charles Benjamin. b 23.10.1880 Cross Roads, Kingston. d 13.5.1946 Cross Roads, Kingston.

FRANCIS, Prince Audley. b 15.7.1957 Ocho Rios, St. Ann. lhb, wkt.

FRANCIS, Samuel Adolphus. b 8.2.1958 St. Vincent. rhb, lbg.

FRAY, Victor. b 18.8.1944. rhb.

FREDERICK, Michael Campbell. b 6.5.1927 Mile and a Quarter, St. Peter, Barbados. rhb. rm. West Indies (1). Cousin of M.R.Bynoe (Barbados). Barbados, Derbyshire.

FULLER, Hugh Alexander (known as Hugo). b 27.4.1912 Kingston. d March 1965 Havendale, Kingston. rhb, rfm. Cousin of R.L.Fuller.

FULLER, Richard Livingston. b 30.1.1913 St. Ann's Bay, St. Ann. d 3.5.1987 Kingston. rhb, rfm. West Indies (1). Cousin of H.A.Fuller.

GAYLE, Patrick Augustus. b 26.10.1965. rhb, wkt.

GIBB, J.M. b 1871. d 14.1.1907 Kingston.

GILCHRIST, Roy. b 28.6.1934 Seaforth, St.Thomas. rhb, rf. Tours (2). West Indies (13). Hyderabad.

GIVANCE, Alford. b 24.3.1974. rhb, ob.

GLADSTONE, George. Please see entry under G.G.Morais.

GOODEN, Locksley G. b 1920 Montego Bay, St. James. rhb, rmf.

GOODRIDGE, Stanley Roy. b 28.10.1928 Kingston. rhb, rfm.

GORDON, Carlton Christopher (1978/79). b 26.6.1950 Keith, St. Ann. rhb, rfm.

GORDON, Colin Cowdrey (1982/83). b 8.7.1960. rhb, lbg.

GORDON, Hylton George. b 5.10.1954 Kingston. lhb, sla.

GORDON, John Anthony. b 8.8.1956 Kingston. rhb, lbg.

GORDON, Steve Constantine. b 22.11.1967. rhb, rm.

GORDON, Steve Winston. b 18.1.1970. rhb, lfm.

GRANT, Joseph Benjamin. b 17.12.1968 Montego Bay, St. James. rhb, rfm.

GRIFFITH, Edward Hallam Cosmo. b 18.3.1936 Brittons Cross Road, St. Michael, Barbados. lhb, rm. Son of H.C.Griffith (Barbados), brother of H.L.V.Griffith (Barbados) and G.H.C.Griffith (Cambridge University). Barbados.

GROVES, John Miller. b 21.7.1914 Kingston. rhb, wkt.

GUNTER, Sir Geoffrey Campbell. b 30.4.1876 Kingston. d 17.9.1961 Kingston. wkt.

HAMILTON, John

HARDY, V.

HARRISON, Richard. b 26.11.1877.

HARVEY, Ferdinand. b 16.12.1926 Kingston. rhb, ob.

HAWKINS, Neville. b 5.9.1936. rhb, ob.

HAYE, William. b 15.9.1948 St. Catherine. rhb, rfm. Jamaica to England.

HAYNES, Robert Christopher. b 2.11.1964 Kingston. lhb, lbg. Tours (2).

HEADLAM, Clinton. b 16.11.1929 Stony Hill, St. Andrew. rhb, wkt.

HEADLEY, George Alphonso. b 30.5.1909 Colon, Panama. d 30.11.1983 Meadowbridge, Kingston. rhb, lbg. Tours (4). Commonwealth XI to England. West Indies (22). Father of R.G.A.Headley (Worcestershire), grandfather of D.W.Headley (Middlesex and Kent).

HEADLEY, Ronald George Alphonso. b 29.6.1939. Mountain View, Kingston. lhb, lbg. Tour (1). Worcestershire World Tour. Worcestershire to Jamaica. Commonwealth to Pakistan. Cavaliers to West Indies. West Indies (2). Son of G.A.Headley, father of D.W.Headley (Middlesex and Kent). Worcestershire.

HEALING, Robert Kingsbury. b 31.10.1873 Tewkesbury, Gloucestershire, England. d 23.5.1950 Camberley, Surrey, England.

HEMMING, Sir Augustus William Lawson. b 2.9.1841 Westminster, London, England. d 27.3.1907 Cairo, Egypt. rhb, rf. MCC.

HENDRICKS, John Leslie. b 21.12.1933 St. Andrew. rhb, sra, wkt. Tours (6). Jamaica to England (did not play in first-class matches). West Indies (20).

HENRY, Trevor. b 7.5.1947. rhb, rm.

HERBERT, Robert Kentish. b 9.3.1863 Clerkenwell, London, England. d 23.10.1920 Ash, Canterbury, Kent, England.

HERON, George Anthony. b 28.4.1962 May Pen, Clarendon. rhb, ob.

HOBSON, Edward Schell Cripps. b 14.7.1869. d 22.8.1923 Bridge End, Warwickshire, England.

HOLDING, Michael Anthony. b 16.2.1954 Half Way Tree, Kingston. rhb, rf. Tours (11). International XI to Pakistan. West Indies (60). Lancashire, Tasmania, Derbyshire, Canterbury.

HOLT, Joseph Kenneth. b 10.1.1885 Trelawny. d 7.8.1968 Vineyard Town, Kingston. rhb, rm. Tour (1). Father of J.K.C.Holt.

HOLT, John Kenneth Constantine. b 12.8.1923 Kingston. rhb, ob. Tour (1). Commonwealth to India, Pakistan and Ceylon. West Indies (17). Son of J.K.Holt.

HONIBALL, Robert Dunscombe. b 28.12.1874 Amity Hall, St. Thomas. d 14.1.1907 Kingston.

HOSANG, Neil Cornell. b 10.10.1946 Montego Bay, St. James. lhb, sla.

HULL, Edward George. b 1880 Kingston. d 1951 Staten Island, New York, USA. Uncle of F.J.Cameron and J.H.Cameron, brother-in-law of J.J.Cameron.

HURDITCH, Charles Percy. b 1.2.1869 Hampstead, London, England. d 24.1.1917 Kilpool, Madras, India. Europeans (India).

HUTTON, Joseph W. rhb, rfm.

HUTTON, Robert.

HYLTON, Leslie George. b 29.3.1905 Kingston. d 17.5.1955 Spanish Town, St. Catherine. rhb, rf. Tour (1). West Indies (6).

IFFLA, Irving. b 20.1.1924 Kingston. rhb, ob.

JOHNSON, Hophnie Hobah Hines. b 13.7.1910 Kingston. d 24.6.1987 Miami, Florida, USA. rhb, rf. Tour (1). West Indies (3).

JOSEPHS, Milton A. b 24.9.1931. rhb, rm.

KENNEDY, Henry Alexander. b 16.2.1882 Kingston.

KENNEDY, Nigel. b 27.8.1964. lhb.

KENTISH, Esmond Seymour Maurice. b 21.11.1916 Cornwall Mountain, Westmoreland. rhb, rfm. West Indies (2). Oxford University.

KERR, Henry Farquharson. b 18.7.1874 Keynsham, Manchester. d 19.8.1933 Mundesley, Norfolk, England.

KERR, Malcolm McLeod. b 28.8.1877, Spanish Town, St. Catherine. wkt. Tour (1 - not first-class).

KING, Lester Anthony. b 27.2.1939 St. Catherine. rhb, rf. Tours (3). West Indian XI to England. West Indies (2). Bengal.

LAWRENCE, Ambrose.

LAWSON, Cecil Ernest. b 19.4.1944. rhb, lfm.

LEVY, Leonard Nathaniel. b 8.5.1939 Kingston. rhb, ob.

LEWIS, Desmond Michael. b 21.2.1946 Kingston. rhb, wkt. Jamaica to England. West Indies (3).
LEWIS, Frank R. b 19.1.1933 Kingston. rhb, ob.
LEWIS, Wayne Walton. b 17.8.1962 Kingston. rhb, ob.
LINTON, George Constantine. b 27.7.1873 Williamsfield, Manchester. d 20.1.1960 Kingston.
LIVINGSTON, Gilbert Vivian. b 22.11.1877. Tour (1 - not first-class).
LUMSDEN, Vincent Roy. b 19.7.1930 Buff Bay, Portland. rhb, ob. Cambridge University.
LYNCH, Francis George Mackinnon. b 1857 Kingston. d circa 1945 Kingston. wkt.

McCATTY, Roy.
McCORMACK, Vincent Constantine. b 4.7.1892 Sandwell, Kingston. d 2.4.1966 Kingston.
McCUTCHIN, Sidney Cameron. b circa 1870. d 1946 Kingston.
McKENZIE, Arthur E. b 1914 Kingston. d circa 1955 Kingston.
McKENZIE, Brenton James. b 10.12.1955 Bath, St. Thomas. rhb, rfm.
McKOY, Neville Joseph. b 4.8.1946. d 11.2.1988 Spanish Town, St. Catherine. lhb, ob.
McLEOD, Kenneth Walcott. b 18.3.1964 Fyffes Pen, St. Elizabeth. rhb, lfm. Lancashire.
McLEOD, V. O. John. b 1931 Kingston. rhb, lb.
MacMAHON, N. rhb, lb.
McMORRIS, Easton Dudley St.John Ashley. b 4.4.1935 Kingston. rhb, ob. Tours (2). Jamaica to England. West Indies (13).
MALCOLM, Donovan O'Connor. b 12.1.1959. lhb, sla.
MARAGH, Robert. b 25.12.1934 Kingston. d 10.4.1985 Gregory Park, St. Catherine. lhb, sla.
MARLEY, Robert Cecil. b 20.6.1909 Half Way Tree, Kingston. d 13.5.1995 Clearwater, Florida, USA. rhb.
MARTIN, Frank Reginald. b 12.10.1893 Kingston. d 23.11.1967 Kingston. lhb, sla. Tours (3). West Indies (9).
MATTHEWS, Lawson Rudolph. b 18.3.1943 Kingston. rhb.
MATTIS, Everton Hugh. b 11.4.1957 Kingston. rhb, ob. Young West Indies to Zimbabwe. West Indian XI to South Africa (2). West Indies (4).
MEIKLE, Hiram Ivanhoe. b 28.7.1897 Port Maria, St. Mary. d 25.6.1989 Kingston. rhb, sra.
MERCIER, Thomas Clarke. b 8.1.1890 St. Mary.
MESSADO, Leonard. b circa 1915. d circa 1980 New Zealand.
MESSIAS, Fitzherbert Sterling. d 23.12.1945 Linstead, St. Catherine.
MILES, Othniel. b 23.9.1939 Clarendon. d February 1982 Kingston. rhb, ob. Jamaica to England.
MILLER, Donald. b 1934 Kingston.
MILLER, Roy C. b 24.12.1924 Kingston. rhb rfm. West Indies (1).
MINOTT, Calbert. b 1932 St. Thomas. rhb, rm.
MITCHELL, Owen. b 24.10.1940.
MORAIS, George Gladstone. b 14.1.1901. d 19.5.1978 Kingston. lhb, sla. West Indies (1). He played under the name of George Gladstone.
MORALES, Charles McLarty. b 4.4.1895 Lucea, Hanover. d 18.3.1987. wkt.
MORGAN, Alexander Anthony. b 30.1.1959 Kingston. lhb, ob.
MORGAN, Delroy Simeon. b 4.3.1967 Rollington Town, Kingston. rhb, ob. Young West Indies to Zimbabwe.
MORGAN, Lloyd Hamilton. b 15.4.1945 Kingston. rhb, sla.
MORGAN, Samuel Augustus. b 7.8.1950 Half Way Tree, Kingston. rhb. Jamaica to England.
MORRISON, Charles Stuart. b 27.5.1883 Kingston. d 25.11.1948 Kingston. rhb, smrab. Tour (1).
MOTTA, Alfred Evelyn. b 20.12.1882 Kingston. d 23.3.1932 New York, USA. rhb.
MOYSTON, M. M.
MUDIE, George Horatio. b 26.11.1915. Spanish Town, St. Catherine. rhb, sla. West Indies (1).
MULLINGS, Joseph Adolphus. b 1.4.1874 Mount Joyle, St. Elizabeth. rf.
MULLINGS, Leonard C. b 21.3.1929. rhb, rf.
MURPHY, Brian Samuel. b 7.4.1973. rhb, lbg.

NEITA, Mark Churchill. b 8.11.1960 Kingston. rhb, rm, wkt. Young West Indies to Zimbabwe (did not play in first-class matches).
NELSON, Wallwood Leopold. b 12.1.1884 Springfield, St. Elizabeth. wkt.

NETHERSOLE, Noel Newton. b 17.11.1903 Kingston. d 17.3.1959 Kingston. lhb.

NICHOLSON, Thomas Brinsley. b 15.3.1876 Madras, India. d 3.10.1939 Cambridge, England. rhb. London County.

NUNES, Robert Karl. b 7.6.1894 Kingston. d 22.7.1958 Paddington, London, England. lhb, wkt. Tours (2). West Indies (4).

O'CONNOR, Courtney St.George. b 12.8.1960 Kingston. rhb, rm.

OWEN, Sydney Lloyd. b 27.2.1872 Southsea, Hampshire, England. d 24.2.1925 Newport, Isle of Wight, England.

PALMER, Dixeth Washington. b 26.1.1968 St. Elizabeth. rhb.

PARRIS, Hume. b circa 1935 St. Ann's Bay, St. Ann. rhb, wkt.

PASSAILAGUE, Charles Clarence. b 4.8.1901 Kingston. d 7.1.1972 Montego Bay, St. James. rhb. West Indies (1).

PATTERSON, Balfour Patrick. b 15.9.1961 Happy Grove, Portland. rhb, rf. Tours (8). West Indies (28). Lancashire, Tasmania.

PAUL, Roy Anthony. b 11.11.1943 Kingston. rhb, lb.

PEARCE, Frank Leopold. b 31.3.1869 Kingston. d 2.1.1933 Montreal, Canada. Brother of G.E.R.Pearce.

PEARCE, George E. R. b 1864 Kingston. Brother of F.L.Pearce.

PENNANT, Orville George. b 16.3.1971 Manchester. lhb, wkt.

PERRY, Nehemiah Odolphus. b 16.6.1968. rhb, ob. Young West Indies to Zimbabwe.

PETERS, Ordelmo Wilberforce. b 20.12.1958 St. Catherine. rhb. Young West Indies to Zimbabwe.

PHILLIPS, E. Louis. b 3.7.1883.

PHILLIPS, Raymond L. b circa 1900. d circa 1970. rhb, sra. Tour (1).

PINNOCK, Renford Augustus. b 26.9.1937 Spanish Town, St. Catherine. rhb, wkt. Jamaica to England.

PLUMMER, Wilfred. b 17.11.1957 Trelawny. lhb, sla.

POOLE, C. F. b 1876. Brother of E.D.Poole.

POOLE, Ernest Duncan. b 8.8.1874 Cheapside, Manchester. Brother of C.F.Poole.

POWE, Aston Joseph. b 25.7.1919 Kingston. rhb, lbg.

POWELL, George. b 23.12.1955 Mandeville, Manchester. lhb.

POWELL, Tony Orlando. b 22.12.1972 St. Catherine. lhb, rm.

PRESCOD, John Enos. b 12.12.1923 Milton, Manchester. rhb, sra.

PRYCE, Harold. b 1931 Port Maria, St. Mary. rhb, rfm.

RAE, Allan Fitzroy. b 30.9.1922 Rollington Town, Kingston. lhb. Tours (3). West Indies (15). Son of E.A.Rae.

RAE, Ernest Allan. b 8.11.1897 Cross Roads, Kingston. d 28.6.1969 Mona, Kingston. rhb, lb. Tour (1). Father of A.F.Rae.

RATTIGAN, Errol Clive. b 17.6.1956.

REDWOOD, Frederick Ralph. b 6.10.1964 Clarendon. rhb, rm.

REID, Horace. b 8.5.1935 Kingston. lhb.

RICHMOND, Sir Robert Daniel. b 29.10.1879 Enson Pen, St. Catherine. d 1.5.1948 Efford Mill, Everton, Hampshire, England. Europeans (India).

RICKARDS, Kenneth Roy. b 22.8.1923 Rollington Town, Kingston. d 21.8.1995 Kingston. rhb, lb. Tours (2). Commonwealth XI to England. West Indies (2). Essex.

RILEY, Rueben S. rhb, lbg.

ROBINSON, Gladstone Adolph. b 24.1.1943 Rollington Town, Kingston. rhb.

ROSE, Franklyn Albert. b 1.2.1972 St. Ann's Bay, St. Ann. rhb, rf.

ROWE, Lawrence George. b 8.1.1949 Whitfield Town, Kingston. rhb, lfm. Tours (5). Cavaliers to England. Jamaica to England. West Indian XI to South Africa (2). West Indies (30). Derbyshire.

ROWE, Seymour Fisher. b 31.5.1876 Westminster, London, England. d 27.2.1916, Mundesley, Norfolk, England.

ROYES, Ralph McIntyre. b 17.5.1908 Cross Roads, Kingston. d 13.12.1972 Hope, Kingston.

SAMUELS, Robert George. b 13.3.1971. lhb.
SAMUELS, Trevor Roy. b 15.12.1967 Negril, Westmoreland. rhb, rmf.
SAREL, Andrew Innes Molyneux. b 15.12.1875 Dover, Kent, England. d 2.8.1903 St. John's, Newfoundland, Canada. Twin brother of W.G.M.Sarel (Surrey, Trinidad, Kent and Sussex).
SASSO, Vernon Glendon. b 10.2.1897 Kingston.
SAUNDERS, Luther Egbert. b 26.8.1906 Port Maria, St. Mary. rhb, ob.
SAVARIAU, Ronald Saulonge. b 7.12.1946 Vineyard Town, Kingston. rhb, ob.
SCARLETT, Robert Lucian. b 23.5.1943 Port Maria, St. Mary. rhb. Brother of R.O.Scarlett.
SCARLETT, Reginald Osmond. b 15.8.1934 Port Maria, St. Mary. rhb, ob. West Indies (3). Brother of R.L.Scarlett.
SCOTT, Alfred Homer Patrick. b 29.7.1934 Spanish Town, St. Catherine. rhb, lb. West Indies (1). Son of O.C.Scott.
SCOTT, Oscar Charles. b 14.8.1892 Franklyn Town, Kingston. d 15.6.1961 Matilda's Corner, St. Andrew. rhb, lb. Tours (2). West Indies (8). Father of A.H.P.Scott.
SEWELL, Henry Gordon. b 21.8.1935 St. Ann's Bay, St. Ann. rhb, rfm.
SHANNON, H.
SIDGWICK, Robert. b 7.8.1851 Embsay Kirk, Yorkshire, England. d 1934 Kingston. Yorkshire.
SILVERA, Allan Lyndon Marchallack. b 24.11.1895 Kingston.
SMITH, Frank. rhb, lbg.
SMITH, George. b 8.10.1934 St. Andrew. rhb.
SMITH, O'Neil Gordon. b 5.5.1933 Denham Town, Kingston. d 9.9.1959 Stoke-on-Trent, Staffordshire, England. rhb, ob. Tours (3). Commonwealth XI to England. West Indies (26). Half-brother of L.N.G.Wright.
SNOW, Samuel C. d 8.9.1931 Venezuela. rf. British Guiana.
STAPLE, Richard Wayne. b 25.11.1969 Kingston. rhb, rm. (Tour 1 - 1 match in emergency).
STAPLETON-COTTON, Richard Greville Arthur Wellington. b 7.11.1873 Westminster, London, England. d 5.1.1953 Bryntiron, Corwen, Merioneth, Wales.
STEPHENSON, Osmond Constantine. b 8.1.1910 Cross Roads, Kingston. rhb.
STODDART, A. L.

TARILTON, Arthur Foderingham. b 21.8.1878 Ragged Point Lighthouse, St. Philip, Barbados. rhb. Brother of P.H.Tarilton (Barbados).
TARVER, William Knapp. b 2.11.1872 Filgrave, Newport Pagnell, Buckinghamshire, England. d 8.4.1952 Bayham Grange, Folkestone, Kent, England.
TAYLOR, Rohan Arspie. b 8.1.1965 Clarendon. lhb, lfm.
THOMPSON, Clement Unita. b 6.4.1956 Bath, St. Thomas. rhb, rfm.
THORBOURNE, Dennis Oliver. b 1927 St. Ann. d 9.3.1967 Mona, Kingston. rhb, rm.
TOMLINSON, Percival Uriah. b 12.10.1959 rhb, rfm.
TOONE, John William. b 2.7.1872 Alfreton, Derbyshire, England. d 1.9.1927, New York, USA. rhb, rf.
TUCKER, Marlon Alexander. b 29.11.1960 Trench Town, Kingston. rhb, ob. Young West Indies to Zimbabwe.
TULLOCH, Horace Aloysius. b 10.10.1930 Vineyard Town, Kingston. rhb, lbg.

UTER, Samuel. b circa 1885 Port Antonio, Portland.

VALENCIA, Charles Harold Lushington. b 1.1.1880. d 17.1.1959 Half Way Tree, Kingston. rhb, rm. Brother-in-law of H.S.Campbell.
VALENTINE, Alfred Louis. b 28.4.1930 Kingston. rhb, sla. Tours (6). West Indies (36).
VALENTINE, Vincent Adolphus. b 4.4.1908 Buff Bay, Portland. d 6.7.1972 Hope, Kingston. rhb, rfm. Tour (1). West Indies (2).
VENTURA, Mario Dimitri. b 21.4.1974 Kingston. lhb.
VERLEY, Bertie Louis. b 28.12.1873 Kingston. d 14.1.1907 Kingston.

WALSH, Courtney Andrew. b 30.10.1962 Kingston. rhb, rf. Tours (11). Young West Indies to Zimbabwe. Rest of World to England. West Indies (80). Gloucestershire.
WATSON, Chester Donald. b 1.7.1938 Negril, Westmoreland. rhb, rf. Tour (1). Cavaliers to South Africa. Commonwealth to Pakistan. West Indies (7). Delhi.
WEEKES, Kenneth Hunnell. b 24.1.1912 Boston, Mass., USA. lhb, lab, wkt. Tour (1). West Indies (2). Cousin of E.de C.Weekes (Barbados).
WELLINGTON, Altemont Beresford. b 12.7.1934 Kingston. lhb, sla.
WELLINGTON, Livern. b 5.1.1950 Kingston. rhb, rfm. Jamaica to England.
WHITTINGHAM, Everett. b 25.2.1954 Kingston. rhb, rm.
WILLIAMS, Alvadon Basil. b 21.11.1949 Caymanas Estate, St. Catherine. rhb. Tour (1). West Indies (7).
WILLIAMS, Junior Alfred. b 1.6.1950 Trelawny. rhb, rfm. International XI to Pakistan. Wellington.
WILLIAMS, Lloyd. b 15.5.1939 Savanna-La-Mar, Westmoreland.
WILLIAMS, Laurie Rohan. b 12.12.1968. rhb, rm.
WILLIAMS, Medroy Wycliffe. b 17.5.1953 Boscobel, St. Mary. rhb.
WILLIAMS, Walford. rhb, ob.
WILSON, Errol Lloyd. b 18.11.1959 Braes River, St. Elizabeth. rhb, ob.
WILSON, Francis Stuart. b 18.1.1883 Campden Hill, London, England. d 24.5.1915 Helles, Gallipoli, Turkey.
WITHERS, G. H.
WOOLLASTON, Gerald. b 17.9.1936 Kingston.
WORRELL, Sir Frank Mortimer Maglinne. b 1.8.1924 Bank Hall, Bridgetown, Barbados. d 13.3.1967 Mona, Kingston. rhb, lm, sla. Tours (5). Commonwealth to India, Pakistan and Ceylon. Commonwealth to India and Ceylon (2). West Indian XI to England. West Indies (51). Cousin of L.R.Worrell (Hampshire). Barbados.
WRIGHT, Edwin Fortescue. b 11.3.1858 Coburg, Chudleigh, Devon, England. d 23.11.1904 Kingston. rhb, rf. Father of A.E.H.Wright (Royal Navy). Gloucestershire, British Guiana.
WRIGHT, Lyndel Norman George. b 18.4.1950 Kingston. rhb, lb. Jamaica to England. Half-brother of O.G.Smith.
WRIGHT, Samuel Cecil. b 6.12.1933 Santa Cruz, St. Elizabeth. rhb, rf.
WYNTER, Ray Ricardo. b 27.11.1955 Kingston. rhb, rfm. West Indian XI to South Africa.

YOUNG, Hubert Bancroft. b 28.5.1911 Kingston.
YOUNG, Samuel Constantine. b 10.10.1902 Pear Tree Grove, St. Catherine.

The following Barbados players appeared only for the Combined Jamaica XI in 1964/65 or the Jamaica Invitation XI in 1965/66:

HALL, Wesley Winfield. b 12.9.1937 Glebe Land, St. Michael, Barbados. Tours (7). Commonwealth to Rhodesia. Rest of the World to England (2). Barbados to England. West Indies (48). Barbados, Trinidad, Queensland.
HUNTE, Conrad Cleophas. b 9.5.1932 Greenland Plantation, St. Andrew, Barbados. Tours (5). Prime Minister's XI to India. Rest of World to England (2). West Indies (44). Barbados.
SOBERS, Sir Garfield St.Aubrun. b 28.7.1936 Chelsea Road, Bay Land, Bridgetown, Barbados. lhb, lfm, sla. Tours (13). West Indian XI to England. Rest of World to England (4). Swanton to India. Cavaliers to India. West Indies (93). Barbados, South Australia, Nottinghamshire.

Notes:
1) *The date of birth or death is represented by b or d.*
2) *Official West Indies tours are shown as Tours (number), all playing first-class matches except the 1900 tour to England.*
3) *English counties (or overseas equivalents) are shown if the player appeared in a first-class match.*
4) *Tests are shown as West Indies (number).*

JAMAICA CAREER RECORDS

	First	Last	M	I	NO	Runs	HS	Avg	100	50	Runs	Wkts	Avg	Best	5i	10m	ct	st
Abrahams SM	1938/39	1951/52	5	8	0	229	110	28.62	1	0	49	0					1	
Acton EVJ	1894/95	1896/97	3	5	0	56	18	11.20	0	0							0	
	1894/95	1904/05	10	18	0	240	48	13.33	0	0	7	0					2	
Adams JC	1984/85	1993/94	36	62	8	2345	133	43.42	6	12	313	9	34.77	2-26	0	0	38	
	1984/85	1995	106	175	32	6200	174*	43.35	14	30	1902	50	38.04	4-43	0	0	101	
Aitcheson D	1945/46		2	3	0	11	8	3.66	0	0							4	1
Alexander FCM	1956/57	1959/60	7	13	2	297	70	27.00	0	2							16	3
	1952	1960/61	92	141	30	3238	108	29.17	1	21	7	0					217	39
Allen SF	1975/76		2	2	0	54	36	27.00	0	0	21	0					1	
Allison O	1972/73		3	5	0	106	57	21.20	0	1	6	0					2	
Andrews AJ	1992/93	1993/94	3	5	2	12	9	4.00	0	0	220	3	73.33	1-44	0	0	4	
Austin RA	1974/75	1981/82	32	54	1	1896	141	35.77	4	13	2096	73	28.71	8-71	3	2	23	
	1974/75	1982/83	38	63	1	2097	141	33.82	4	14	2279	73	31.21	8-71	3	2	27	
Bailey CW	1945/46	1947/48	5	6	0	22	13	3.66	0	0	446	12	37.16	3-52	0	0	2	
Baines GM	1901/02		2	4	0	37	14	9.25	0	0	46	1	46.00	1-46	0	0	2	
Banton C	1988/89	1989/90	2	2	1	0	0*	0.00	0	0	209	5	41.80	3-64	0	0	1	
Barclay K	1954/55	1961/62	3	5	0	109	31	21.80	0	0							3	
Barnett K	1965/66		4	6	1	37	25	7.40	0	0	398	9	44.22	5-51	1	0	0	
Barrett AG	1966/67	1980/81	42	57	10	857	102*	18.23	1	0	3912	134	29.19	7-90	9	2	50	
	1966/67	1980/81	57	75	13	1086	102*	17.51	1	0	5276	169	31.21	7-90	9	2	54	
Barrow IM	1928/29	1945/46	15	24	2	920	169	41.81	2	5	20	0					15	9
	1928/29	1945/46	68	113	6	2551	169	23.84	3	10	34	0					73	27
Baugh C	1980/81	1982/83	4	7	0	125	32	17.85	0	0	9	1	9.00	1-9	0	0	0	
Beckford DPS	1931/32	1946/47	12	19	6	310	114	23.84	1	0	1400	49	28.57	5-90	1	0	11	
Beckford WG	1926/27	1935/36	8	13	1	292	74	24.33	0	3	48	0					4	
	1926/27	1935/36	9	15	1	339	74	24.21	0	3	48	0					5	
Bennett HAA	1964/65	1969/70	11	18	2	369	64	23.06	0	2	49	1	49.00	1-27	0	0	4	
Bicknell HF	1926/27		2	2	1	32	30*	32.00	0	0							2	
Binns AP	1949/50	1956/57	17	30	3	1265	157	46.85	4	4							29	12
	1949/50	1956/57	25	43	4	1446	157	37.07	4	4							48	17
Binns MJ	1926/27		1	2	1	19	14*	19.00	0	0	31	1	31.00	1-31	0	0	1	
Bloomfield CA	1925/26		1	1	0	5	5	5.00	0	0	81	0					0	
Bloomfield CO	1946/47	1947/48	2	4	0	82	42	20.50	0	0							0	
Bonitto AR	1945/46	1951/52	9	12	2	86	22	8.60	0	0	835	24	34.79	6-105	1	0	3	
Bonitto CG	1945/46	1952/53	7	14	0	373	100	26.64	1	2							0	
Bonitto NL	1947/48	1956/57	17	30	6	1413	207*	58.52	4	6	15	0					11	
Boy CRC	1931/32	1935/36	2	3	0	173	139	57.66	1	0	8	0					1	
Bronstorph FL	1925/26		1	2	0	19	15	9.50	0	0	14	0					0	
Brown EE	1977/78	1984/85	11	16	4	131	27	10.91	0	0	944	26	36.30	6-62	1	0	3	
	1977/78	1984/85	19	26	9	290	41*	17.05	0	0	1402	34	41.23	6-62	1	0	3	
Buchanan PL	1966/67		1	1	0	26	26	26.00	0	0							0	
Burke EE	1894/95		2	4	0	11	4	2.75	0	0							0	
Burton CH	1894/95	1905/06	13	25	3	349	63*	15.86	0	1							7	

	First	Last	M	I	NO	Runs	HS	Avg	100	50	Runs	Wkts	Avg	Best	5i	10m	ct	st
Byng AM	1896/97		5	10	0	212	70	21.20	0	1	152	7	21.71	3-53	0	0	8	
	1896/97	1905	8	15	0	252	70	16.80	0	1	168	7	24.00	3-53	0	0	8	
Calnick E	1958/59		2	2	1	31	18*	31.00	0	0	113	2	56.50	1-20	0	0	0	
Cameron FJ	1945/46	1959/60	3	4	0	94	50	23.50	0	1	222	9	24.66	3-56	0	0	0	
	1945/46	1959/60	21	27	5	551	75*	25.04	0	3	1411	29	48.65	4-52	0	0	9	
Cameron JH	1945/46		1	1	0	9	9	9.00	0	0	44	4	11.00	3-32	0	0	0	
	1932	1947	105	164	12	2772	113	18.23	4	4	5662	184	30.77	7-73	7	0	64	
Cameron JJ	1908/09	1927/28	6	9	0	220	52	24.44	0	1	112	5	22.40	2-36	0	0	3	
	1906	1927/28	13	21	2	272	52	14.31	0	1	213	10	21.30	5-83	1	0	7	
Campbell C	1971/72		4	5	2	28	11*	9.33	0	0	328	14	23.42	4-14	0	0	3	
	1971/72		5	6	2	28	11*	7.00	0	0	385	14	27.50	4-14	0	0	3	
Campbell EA	1969/70	1979/80	22	35	3	509	48*	15.90	0	0							49	9
Campbell HS	1925/26	1926/27	3	4	1	91	37*	30.33	0	0	80	1	80.00	1-39	0	0	3	
Carter CD	1988/89	1989/90	2	2	1	47	35*	47.00	0	0	267	2	133.50	2-129	0	0	0	
Castle HDB	1894/95	1896/97	5	9	1	56	12*	7.00	0	0							2	1
Cawley CLO	1938/39		1	1	0	2	2	2.00	0	0	3	2	1.50	2-3	0	0	0	
Chambers L	1965/66	1974/75	8	11	2	185	52	20.55	0	1	279	11	25.36	3-22	0	0	2	
Chandler CRW	1894/95	1896/97	8	15	5	80	20*	8.00	0	0	492	29	16.96	7-77	2	1	3	
Chang HS	1972/73	1982/83	48	79	5	2847	155	38.47	5	18	16	0					27	
	1972/73	1982/83	58	98	5	3273	155	35.19	5	21	32	0					31	
Chisholm SC	1925/26	1926/27	5	5	0	77	29	15.40	0	0	6	0					1	
Cohen RA	1963/64	1966/67	17	23	10	73	13*	5.61	0	0	1538	39 +1	39.43	4-41	0	0	5	
	1963/64	1966/67	37	42	20	160	32*	7.27	0	0	2576	81 +1	31.80	6-71	1	0	15	
Collins CG	1901/02		1	2	0	3	3	1.50	0	0	31	0					1	
Corke TA	1983/84	1984/85	5	10	0	208	62	20.80	0	1	95	1	95.00	1-37	0	0	4	
Cox GS	1905/06		1	2	0	31	18	15.50	0	0	48	3	16.00	2-24	0	0	0	
Cruickshank OW	1990/91		1	2	0	16	16	8.00	0	0	17	0					0	
Crutchley LJ	1901/02		1	2	1	19	12*	19.00	0	0							0	1
Cunningham FA	1985/86	1987/88	9	17	3	268	47	19.14	0	0	3	0					7	
Cunningham LO	1985/86	1987/88	2	4	0	90	46	22.50	0	0							0	
Cunningham OJ	1938/39	1950/51	9	17	2	604	145	40.26	1	4							5	
Da Costa OC	1928/29	1934/35	9	14	4	349	84*	34.90	0	2	555	9	61.66	2-20	0	0	9	
	1928/29	1934/35	39	64	11	1563	105*	29.49	1	9	1766	44	40.13	4-31	0	0	30	
Daley AG	1982/83	1990/91	23	37	3	569	79	16.73	0	2	2234	77	29.01	6-103	2	0	12	
	1982/83	1990/91	24	38	3	569	79	16.25	0	2	2306	77	29.94	6-103	2	0	12	
Daley CE	1971/72	1975/76	5	4	2	13	7*	6.50	0	0	255	6	42.50	2-17	0	0	2	
Davidson CA	1982/83	1993/94	46	77	11	2260	200*	34.24	1	15	200	4	50.00	1-18	0	0	35	
	1982/83	1993/94	47	77	11	2260	200*	34.24	1	15	200	4	50.00	1-18	0	0	35	
Davis W	1963/64	1971/72	6	12	0	145	33	12.08	0	0							7	
De Cordova C	1896/97		3	6	0	53	21	8.83	0	0							4	2
Delgado CH	1910/11		2	4	1	29	18	9.66	0	0	17	1	17.00	1-11	0	0	1	
Dennis KA	1986/87		1	1	1	0	0*		0	0	63	2	31.50	2-56	0	0	0	

	First	Last	M	I	NO	Runs	HS	Avg	100	50	Runs	Wkts	Avg	Best	5i	10m	ct	st
Dewdney DT	1954/55	1957/58	6	7	1	37	13*	6.16	0	0	572	18	31.77	7-55	1	0	4	
	1954/55	1961	40	49	19	171	37*	5.70	0	0	2828	92	30.73	7-55	4	0	6	
Dixon DC	1984/85	1987/88	5	9	0	145	75	16.11	0	1	419	7	59.85	3-80	0	0	2	
Dowe UG	1969/70	1976/77	23	24	7	120	25*	7.05	0	0	2169	85	25.51	7-19	3	0	6	
	1969/70	1976/77	27	27	9	128	25*	7.11	0	0	2703	97	27.86	7-19	3	0	9	
Drury BH	1896/97		3	6	0	84	65	14.00	0	1	16	0					3	
Duff AV	1905/06		1	2	0	8	8	4.00	0	0	29	0					0	
Dujon LVS	1946/47		1	2	0	35	18	17.50	0	0							0	
Dujon PJL	1974/75	1992/93	70	114	18	3927	163*	40.90	8	23	1	0					107	13
	1974/75	1992/93	200	298	48	9763	163*	39.05	21	50	45	1	45.00	1-43	0	0	447	22
Duncker HC	1905/06	1910/11	4	8	1	183	55	26.14	0	1	151	3	50.33	2-61	0	0	4	
Dyer L	1965/66		1	1	0	4	4	4.00	0	0							1	
Ebanks KF	1991/92	1992/93	4	5	1	4	3	1.00	0	0	86	8	10.75	3-10	0	0	0	
Farquharson CHC	1901/02		1	2	0	17	9	8.50	0	0	25	2	12.50	2-25	0	0	2	
Farquharson WGR	1894/95	1896/97	5	10	1	115	43	12.77	0	0	33	1	33.00	1-15	0	0	2	
Farquharson WHK	1894/95		2	4	0	18	16	4.50	0	0	73	2	36.50	2-33	0	0	0	
Fidee LG	1947/48		1	1	0	8	8	8.00	0	0							1	
Fletcher CW	1978/79	1982/83	14	25	2	844	122	36.69	1	3	237	4	59.25	2-84	0	0	8	
Folkes C	1967/68	1970/71	13	9	1	36	9	4.50	0	0	745	25	29.80	5-22	2	0	1	
Folkes CR	1990/91	1992/93	3	4	0	23	18	5.75	0	0	211	6	35.16	2-18	0	0	0	
Ford SGB	1993/94	1994/95	6	9	3	158	50	26.33	0	1							13	6
Foster FA	1901/02	1924/25	8	16	1	269	56	17.93	0	1	430	19	22.63	6-128	2	0	2	
Foster GCE	1908/09	1925/26	9	16	4	321	61	26.75	0	1	296	8	37.00	3-43	0	0	4	
Foster MLC	1963/64	1977/78	68	109	9	4845	234	48.45	15	23	2835	101	28.06	5-65	2	0	27	
	1963/64	1977/78	112	175	26	6731	234	45.17	17	35	4056	132	30.72	5-65	2	0	37	
Foster RCB	1910/11		1	2	0	4	4	2.00	0	0							1	1
Francis PA	1982/83	1987/88	15	25	4	212	36	10.95	0	0							24	4
Francis SA	1977/78		5	6	1	40	37	8.00	0	0	408	13	31.38	6-108	1	0	6	
Fray V	1965/66	1969/70	11	19	3	486	67	30.37	0	5	19	0					9	
Frederick MC	1953/54		2	4	0	158	60	39.50	0	2							2	
	1944/45	1953/54	6	10	0	294	84	29.40	0	3							3	
Fuller HA	1949/50		1	2	0	8	7	4.00	0	0	50	0					0	
Fuller RL	1934/35	1946/47	7	12	3	279	113*	31.00	1	0	512	12	42.66	4-69	0	0	5	
	1934/35	1946/47	8	13	3	280	113*	28.00	1	0	524	12	43.66	4-69	0	0	5	
Gayle PA	1988/89	1993/94	10	15	4	153	33*	13.90	0	0							18	2
Gibb JM	1894/95	1901/02	4	8	1	28	10*	4.00	0	0							0	
Gilchrist R	1956/57	1961/62	5	8	1	60	16	8.57	0	0	774	16	48.37	5-110	1	0	1	
	1956/57	1962/63	42	43	10	258	43*	7.81	0	0	4342	167	26.00	6-16	7	1	10	
Givance A	1992/93		2	2	0	35	22	17.50	0	0	155	3	51.66	3-97	0	0	0	
Gooden LG	1946/47	1947/48	3	4	0	40	18	10.00	0	0	349	12	29.08	4-44	0	0	0	
Goodridge SR	1949/50	1953/54	9	13	1	137	33	11.41	0	0	872	26	33.53	6-28	3	0	7	
Gordon CC	1978/79		1	1	0	46	46	46.00	0	0	61	1	61.00	1-61	0	0	0	

	First	Last	M	I	NO	Runs	HS	Avg	100	50	Runs	Wkts	Avg	Best	5i	10m	ct	st
Gordon CC	1982/83		4	6	1	78	21	15.60	0	0	416	13	32.00	4-40	0	0	2	
Gordon HG	1973/74	1979/80	20	30	5	669	78*	26.76	0	4	860	28	30.71	4-43	0	0	18	
Gordon JA	1976/77	1983/84	16	24	2	257	49	11.68	0	0	1199	27	44.40	7-55	2	0	2	
Gordon SC	1987/88	1993/94	2	3	0	42	27	14.00	0	0							3	
Gordon SW	1988/89		1	1	0	12	12	12.00	0	0	129	4	32.25	2-26	0	0	1	
Grant JB	1990/91	1994/95	10	14	7	78	36*	11.14	0	0	586	15	39.06	3-43	0	0	2	
Griffith EHC	1959/60	1966/67	21	41	1	1511	150	37.77	3	7	1011	22 +1	45.95	3-64	0	0	11	
	1953/54	1966/67	25	48	1	1690	150	35.95	3	7	1159	24 +1	48.29	3-64	0	0	11	
Groves JM	1934/35	1949/50	5	8	0	126	38	15.75	0	0	91	0					3	2
Gunter GC	1905/06		2	2	1	17	10*	17.00	0	0							0	2
Hamilton J	1965/66		1	1	1	8	8*		0	0	114	6	19.00	3-53	0	0	0	
Hardy V	1927/28		1	1	0	11	11	11.00	0	0	55	0					1	
	1927/28		4	4	1	20	11	6.66	0	0	300	4	75.00	2-89	0	0	1	
Harrison R	1901/02		1	2	0	16	15	8.00	0	0	85	1	85.00	1-85	0	0	1	
Harvey F	1959/60	1966/67	9	14	0	362	69	25.85	0	3	114	1	114.00	1-15	0	0	7	
Hawkins N	1963/64	1966/67	7	13	2	116	44	10.54	0	0	672	13	51.69	6-66	1	0	3	
Haye W	1970	1971/72	7	8	0	198	60	24.75	0	1	287	6	47.83	1-8	0	0	1	
Haynes RC	1981/82	1994/95	59	94	3	1966	98	21.60	0	10	5668	197	28.77	6-53	9	1	53	
	1981/82	1994/95	65	104	4	2166	98	21.66	0	10	6327	221	28.62	6-53	10	1	55	
Headlam C	1957/58	1958/59	4	7	1	193	127*	32.16	1	0							4	
Headley GA	1927/28	1953/54	27	39	9	2848	344*	94.93	9	15	767	23	33.34	5-33	1	0	30	
	1927/28	1954	103	164	22	9921	344*	69.86	33	44	1842	51	36.11	5-33	1	0	76	
Headley RGA	1965/66	1973/74	9	13	0	489	86	37.61	0	4	10	0					7	
	1958	1974	423	758	61	21695	187	31.12	32	117	588	12	49.00	4-40	0	0	356	
Healing RK	1896/97		6	12	2	55	20	5.50	0	0	282	11	25.63	4-30	0	0	2	
Hemming AWL	1901/02		1	2	1	9	9	9.00	0	0							0	
	1866	1901/02	6	9	1	56	16	7.00	0	0	127	6	21.16	5-69	1	0	3	
Hendricks JL	1953/54	1966/67	22	35	5	492	73*	16.40	0	2							36	19
	1953/54	1969	83	113	23	1568	82	17.42	0	9	61	0					140	50
Henry T	1976/77		1	2	0	4	4	2.00	0	0							1	
Herbert RK	1896/97		3	6	0	99	39	16.50	0	0							2	
Heron GA	1985/86	1987/88	4	7	1	52	12*	8.66	0	0	36	0					4	
Hobson ESC	1905/06		2	3	1	5	4	2.50	0	0	194	4	48.50	3-57	0	0	1	
Holding MA	1972/73	1988/89	34	47	5	454	34	10.80	0	0	2323	90	25.81	5-96	1	0	29	
	1972/73	1989	222	283	43	3600	80	15.00	0	14	18233	778	23.43	8-92	39	5	125	
Holt JK	1905/06	1929/30	23	39	2	1123	142	30.35	3	5	955	24	39.79	3-34	0	0	19	1
	1905/06	1929/30	36	60	2	1600	142	27.58	4	8	1054	26	40.53	3-34	0	0	25	1
Holt JKC	1945/46	1961/62	26	45	4	1736	172	42.34	4	9	153	4	38.25	1-2	0	0	18	1
	1945/46	1961/62	71	115	12	4258	172	41.33	9	22	177	5	35.40	1-2	0	0	30	1
Honiball RD	1894/95	1896/97	4	8	0	124	69	15.50	0	1							0	
Hosang NC	1974/75		2	2	0	11	10	5.50	0	0	84	1	84.00	1-19	0	0	0	
Hull EG	1901/02	1910/11	9	17	0	201	34	11.82	0	0	42	1	42.00	1-10	0	0	8	
Hurditch CP	1894/95		2	3	0	15	15	5.00	0	0							3	
	1894/95	1916/17	3	5	1	45	30	11.25	0	0							4	

	First	Last	M	I	NO	Runs	HS	Avg	100	50	Runs	Wkts	Avg	Best	5i	10m	ct	st
Hutton JW	1901/02		3	6	3	18	9*	6.00	0	0	231	8	28.87	4-86	0	0	0	
Hutton R	1904/05	1908/09	9	17	1	204	54	12.75	0	1	273	8	34.12	2-30	0	0	5	
Hylton LG	1926/27	1938/39	18	25	4	552	80	26.28	0	4	1591	61	26.08	5-24	2	0	19	
	1926/27	1939	40	54	9	843	80	18.73	0	5	3075	120	25.62	5-24	3	0	31	
Iffla I	1947/48	1949/50	4	4	0	37	23	9.25	0	0	390	10	39.00	5-90	1	0	2	
Johnson HHH	1934/35	1950/51	10	13	8	124	39*	24.80	0	0	539	24	22.45	5-33	2	0	8	
	1934/35	1950/51	28	30	12	316	39*	17.55	0	0	1589	68	23.36	5-33	5	1	13	
Josephs MA	1959/60	1961/62	3	5	0	93	46	18.60	0	0							2	
Kennedy HA	1905/06	1910/11	4	8	0	80	42	10.00	0	0	280	18	15.55	6-47	1	0	3	
Kennedy N	1987/88	1988/89	2	3	1	52	27*	26.00	0	0							3	
Kentish ESM	1947/48	1956/57	11	14	10	90	15*	22.50	0	0	772	26	29.69	5-36	1	0	2	
	1947/48	1956/57	27	29	21	109	15*	13.62	0	0	2084	78	26.71	5-36	4	0	6	
Kerr HF	1905/06		2	4	0	46	18	11.50	0	0							2	
Kerr MM	1901/02	1908/09	10	20	1	223	44	11.73	0	0	182	9	20.22	6-30	1	0	3	4
King LA	1961/62	1967/68	16	23	3	551	89	27.55	0	6	1426	35	40.74	3-31	0	0	14	
	1961/62	1968/69	62	87	19	1404	89	20.64	0	6	4463	142	31.42	5-46	3	0	38	
Lawrence A	1924/25		1	1	0	6	6	6.00	0	0	11	0					0	
Lawson CE	1971/72	1977/78	16	19	2	88	22	5.17	0	0	985	29	33.96	5-47	1	0	5	
	1971/72	1977/78	17	20	2	92	22	5.11	0	0	1099	29	37.89	5-47	1	0	5	
Levy LN	1961/62	1973/74	15	22	6	124	21	7.75	0	0	1442	40	36.05	3-13	0	0	5	
Lewis DM	1970	1975/76	33	51	3	1364	96	28.41	0	9							59	11
	1970	1975/76	36	56	5	1623	96	31.82	0	12							67	11
Lewis FR	1956/57	1958/59	4	6	0	57	30	9.50	0	0	148	5	29.60	1-14	0	0	2	
Lewis WW	1984/85	1994/95	31	54	2	1523	132	29.28	4	5							18	
	1984/85	1994/95	32	56	3	1599	132	30.16	4	5							18	
Linton GC	1896/97	1901/02	6	12	0	138	60	11.50	0	1							6	
Livingston GV	1896/97	1904/05	4	8	2	30	11	5.00	0	0	184	17	10.82	7-49	1	0	1	
Lumsden VR	1949/50	1959/60	8	15	1	490	91	35.00	0	4	164	7	23.42	4-20	0	0	5	
	1949/50	1959/60	57	102	5	2699	107	27.82	1	14	355	11	32.27	4-20	0	0	36	
Lynch FGM	1894/95		1	2	0	6	6	3.00	0	0							0	2
McCatty R	1968/69	1969/70	7	6	3	31	15*	10.33	0	0	360	14	25.71	4.40	0	0	6	
McCormack VC	1925/26		1	2	0	25	21	12.50	0	0							0	
McCutchin SC	1894/95		1	1	0	1	1	1.00	0	0							0	
McKenzie AE	1946/47	1947/48	4	5	0	115	51	23.00	0	1							7	
McKenzie BJ	1984/85		1	2	1	9	6*	9.00	0	0	76	2	38.00	2-67	0	0	0	
McKoy NJ	1970/71	1972/73	5	8	0	166	60	20.75	0	2	38	1	38.00	1-31	0	0	3	
McLeod KW	1983/84	1987/88	7	11	1	36	13	3.60	0	0	488	11	44.36	3-10	0	0	3	
	1983/84	1987/88	13	17	1	128	31	8.00	0	0	897	28	32.03	5-8	2	0	4	
McLeod VOJ	1951/52	1952/53	3	6	0	105	79	17.50	0	1							1	

	First	Last	M	I	NO	Runs	HS	Avg	100	50	Runs	Wkts	Avg	Best	5i	10m	ct	st
MacMahon N	1927/28		1	2	0	8	4	4.00	0	0	62	3	20.66	3-35	0	0	1	
McMorris EDSA	1956/57	1971/72	50	86	10	3800	218	50.00	13	14	37	0					21	
	1956/57	1971/72	95	158	18	5906	218	42.18	18	22	107	0					36	
Malcolm DO	1980/81	1981/82	8	12	0	100	26	8.33	0	0	584	15	38.93	3-53	0	0	6	
Maragh R	1956/57	1958/59	4	5	2	50	37	16.66	0	0	427	13	32.84	4-67	0	0	1	
Marley RC	1928/29	1945/46	7	12	0	191	40	15.91	0	0							7	
Martin FR	1924/25	1929/30	15	25	7	1262	204*	70.11	4	5	845	17	49.70	4-67	0	0	7	
	1924/25	1933	65	108	13	3589	204*	37.77	6	16	3149	74	42.55	5-90	1	0	19	
Matthews LR	1964/65	1965/66	3	4	1	18	8*	6.00	0	0	203	4	50.75	2-70	0	0	1	
Mattis EH	1976/77	1981/82	23	40	3	1490	132	40.27	2	9	70	8	8.75	4-22	0	0	14	
	1976/77	1983/84	38	65	3	2064	132	33.29	3	11	89	9	9.88	4-22	0	0	25	
Meikle HI	1938/39		1	1	0	4	4	4.00	0	0	62	1	62.00	1-62	0	0	0	
Mercier TC	1924/25	1925/26	3	4	0	37	32	9.25	0	0	126	1	126.00	1-43	0	0	0	
Messado L	1938/39		2	4	0	68	60	17.00	0	1							3	1
Messias FS	1894/95		1	2	0	1	1	0.50	0	0	46	0					0	
Miles O	1967/68	1975/76	21	22	6	214	43*	13.37	0	0	1588	58	27.37	7-71	2	0	15	
Miller D	1961/62		1	2	0	30	23	15.00	0	0	33	0					1	
Miller RC	1950/51	1953/54	7	10	2	208	86	25.66	0	1	607	14	43.35	3-65	0	0	2	
	1950/51	1953/54	8	11	2	231	86	25.66	0	1	635	14	45.35	3-65	0	0	2	
Minott C	1954/55		1	1	0	14	14	14.00	0	0	102	3	34.00	2-49	0	0	0	
Mitchell O	1961/62	1964/65	5	9	0	108	60	12.00	0	1							2	
Morais GG	1929/30		1	1	1	14	14*		0	0	252	9	28.00	6-142	1	0	1	
	1929/30		2	2	2	26	14*		0	0	441	10	44.10	6-142	1	0	1	
Morales CM	1924/25	1928/29	12	18	1	610	143	35.88	1	3							4	1
Morgan AA	1983/84		2	3	0	71	57	23.66	0	1							0	
Morgan DS	1986/87	1994/95	41	73	3	2073	122	29.61	3	9	137	5	27.40	4-31	0	0	42	
	1986/87	1994/95	45	79	3	2209	122	29.06	3	9	139	5	27.80	4-31	0	0	44	
Morgan LH	1968/69	1972/73	4	4	0	35	15	8.75	0	0	132	6	22.00	2-31	0	0	4	
Morgan SA	1969/70	1973/74	21	34	3	966	126	31.16	1	7	57	0					10	
	1969/70	1973/74	22	35	3	998	126	31.18	1	7	82	1	82.00	1-16	0	0	10	
Morrison CS	1904/05	1925/26	14	24	3	284	54	13.52	0	1	846	45	18.80	7-44	2	1	7	
	1904/05	1925/26	25	44	10	396	54	11.64	0	1	1236	60	20.60	7-44	2	1	13	
Motta AE	1904/05	1908/09	8	16	2	226	45	16.14	0	0							5	
Moyston MM	1904/05	1908/09	6	12	2	113	30	11.30	0	0	484	20	24.20	5-49	2	0	4	
Mudie GH	1931/32	1951/52	17	28	5	565	94	24.56	0	4	1366	36	37.94	5-32	2	0	11	
	1931/32	1951/52	19	31	5	578	94	22.23	0	4	1489	42	35.45	5-32	2	0	11	
Mullings JA	1894/95	1896/97	6	11	3	36	8	4.50	0	0	201	10	20.10	4-51	0	0	3	
Mullings LC	1954/55	1959/60	5	7	2	58	33	11.60	0	0	611	11	55.54	4-66	0	0	6	
Murphy BS	1993/94	1994/95	4	7	1	37	18*	6.16	0	0	184	3	61.33	3-65	0	0	2	
Neita MC	1978/79	1991/92	45	75	6	2253	133	32.65	2	15	318	8	39.75	2-29	0	0	28	1
Nelson WL	1904/05	1908/09	6	11	1	73	22	7.30	0	0	35	2	17.50	2-18	0	0	3	8
Nethersole NN	1926/27	1938/39	13	17	3	348	71	24.85	0	1	553	7	79.00	1-7	0	0	4	
	1926/27	1938/39	16	22	3	429	71	22.57	0	1	692	9	76.88	1-7	0	0	6	

	First	Last	M	I	NO	Runs	HS	Avg	100	50	Runs	Wkts	Avg	Best	5i	10m	ct	st
Nicholson TB	1908/09	1910/11	6	11	0	217	70	19.72	0	2							5	
	1904	1910/11	12	22	2	470	73*	23.50	0	3							10	
Nunes RK	1924/25	1931/32	18	28	3	1263	200*	50.52	5	3	83	3	27.66	2-49	0	0	15	8
	1923	1931/32	61	94	8	2695	200*	31.33	6	11	83	3	27.66	2-49	0	0	31	8
O'Connor CS	1986/87	1987/88	3	6	1	90	37	18.00	0	0							1	
Owen SL	1896/97		3	6	1	24	10	4.80	0	0							1	
Palmer DW	1990/91	1991/92	5	10	0	100	27	10.00	0	0							2	
Parris H	1961/62		1	1	1	15	15*		0	0							1	
	1961/62	1963/64	3	5	1	44	15*	11.00	0	0							5	2
Passailague CC	1929/30	1938/39	10	14	2	733	261*	61.08	2	2	56	1	56.00	1-22	0	0	8	
	1929/30	1938/39	12	18	3	788	261*	52.53	2	2	56	1	56.00	1-22	0	0	11	
Patterson BP	1982/83	1991/92	23	33	10	106	19	4.60	0	0	1836	83	22.12	7-24	5	0	7	
	1982/83	1992/93	161	164	58	618	29	5.83	0	0	13563	493	27.51	7-24	25	2	32	
Paul RA	1971/72		2	3	1	10	8	5.00	0	0							2	
Pearce FL	1894/95	1908/09	12	23	1	253	50	11.50	0	1	301	12	25.08	4-27	0	0	6	
Pearce GER	1894/95		1	1	0	1	1	1.00	0	0							0	
Pennant OG	1993/94	1994/95	3	4	0	56	38	14.00	0	0							0	
Perry NO	1986/87	1994/95	38	56	8	1040	160	21.66	1	4	2757	122	22.59	8-45	6	1	23	
	1986/87	1994/95	49	70	9	1216	160	19.93	1	5	3704	151	24.52	8-45	7	1	28	
Peters OW	1982/83	1989/90	20	36	0	902	89	25.05	0	5							23	
	1982/83	1989/90	21	38	0	946	89	24.89	0	5							24	
Phillips EL	1905/06	1908/09	4	8	2	97	69*	16.16	0	1	119	1	119.00	1-14	0	0	1	
Phillips RL	1925/26	1927/28	6	5	1	69	38	17.25	0	0	601	24	25.04	5-68	1	0	3	
	1923	1927/28	7	5	1	69	38	17.25	0	0	622	24	25.91	5-68	1	0	3	
Pinnock RA	1963/64	1974/75	44	71	5	2662	176	40.33	6	16	52	1	52.00	1-25	0	0	26	5
Plummer W	1978/79		1	1	0	14	14	14.00	0	0	62	0					0	
Poole CF	1896/97		5	10	0	68	41	6.80	0	0							1	
Poole ED	1896/97		3	6	1	40	21	8.00	0	0							4	
Powe AJ	1947/48		1	1	0	0	0	0.00	0	0	133	5	26.60	4-80	0	0	1	
Powell G	1981/82	1987/88	19	34	0	944	110	27.76	1	4							10	
	1981/82	1987/88	20	35	0	960	110	27.42	1	4	8	0					11	
Powell TO	1991/92	1993/94	8	15	0	206	49	13.73	0	0							13	
Prescod JE	1947/48	1952/53	7	13	0	255	45	19.62	0	0	27	3	9.00	3-27	0	0	9	1
Pryce H	1954/55		1	2	0	0	0	0.00	0	0	78	0					1	
Rae AF	1946/47	1959/60	21	38	2	1464	142	40.66	5	6	8	0					14	
	1946/47	1959/60	80	128	7	4798	179	39.65	17	15	26	0					42	
Rae EA	1924/25	1935/36	18	27	6	822	121	39.14	1	4	345	10	34.50	4-50	0	0	20	
	1924/25	1935/36	29	43	6	1118	121	30.21	1	6	368	10	36.80	4-50	0	0	27	
Rattigan EC	1973/74		1	1	0	0	0	0.00	0	0	75	1	75.00	1-75	0	0	0	
Redwood FR	1991/92	1994/95	12	19	2	433	62*	25.47	0	3	504	11	45.81	3-36	0	0	3	
Reid H	1961/62	1963/64	4	8	1	252	101*	36.00	1	1							3	

	First	Last	M	I	NO	Runs	HS	Avg	100	50	Runs	Wkts	Avg	Best	5i	10m	ct	st
Richmond RD	1896/97		2	4	0	74	60	18.50	0	1	24	1	24.00	1-12	0	0	2	
	1896/97	1927/28	7	13	2	381	74	34.63	0	4	518	23	22.52	5-73	1	0	2	
Rickards KR	1945/46	1958/59	17	31	5	1265	195	48.65	2	9	113	1	113.00	1-66	0	0	2	
	1945/46	1958/59	37	60	7	2065	195	38.96	2	15	128	1	128.00	1-66	0	0	10	
Riley RS	1925/26	1935/36	5	8	2	59	15*	9.83	0	0	371	5	74.20	3-77	0	0	5	
Robinson GA	1963/64	1964/65	3	6	0	75	53	12.50	0	1							2	
Rose FA	1992/93	1994/95	15	22	7	292	47*	19.46	0	0	1346	45	29.91	5-65	1	0	4	
	1992/93	1994/95	16	24	7	295	47*	17.35	0	0	1451	47	30.87	5-65	1	0	4	
Rowe LG	1968/69	1981/82	53	89	6	3487	227	42.01	9	17	74	1	74.00	1-19	0	0	57	
	1968/69	1983/84	149	245	12	8755	302	37.57	18	38	224	2	112.00	1-19	0	0	118	
Rowe SF	1901/02		1	2	0	51	35	25.50	0	0	18	0					0	
Royes RM	1931/32		1	1	1	0	0*		0	0	36	1	36.00	1-18	0	0	0	
Samuels RG	1988/89	1994/95	29	54	3	1764	159	34.58	2	9							13	
	1988/89	1994/95	36	67	4	2176	159	34.53	2	12							13	
Samuels TR	1987/88		1	1	0	5	5	5.00	0	0	69	0					0	
Sarel AIM	1901/02		1	2	1	5	3	5.00	0	0							0	
Sasso VG	1929/30		1	2	1	25	18*	25.00	0	0	144	1	144.00	1-87	0	0	2	
Saunders LE	1950/51	1951/52	2	3	0	32	29	10.66	0	0	93	2	46.50	2-49	0	0	1	
Savariau RS	1976/77		2	3	0	15	11	5.00	0	0	158	4	39.50	3-87	0	0	0	
Scarlett RL	1963/64		4	8	2	44	24	7.33	0	0	439	9	48.77	5-95	1	0	0	
Scarlett RO	1951/52	1959/60	14	23	6	423	72*	24.88	0	2	1429	46	31.06	5-69	2	0	4	
	1951/52	1959/60	17	27	7	477	72*	23.85	0	2	1638	48	34.12	5-69	2	0	6	
Scott AHP	1952/53	1953/54	4	4	2	33	17*	16.50	0	0	454	18	25.22	4-46	0	0	3	
	1952/53	1953/54	5	5	2	38	17*	12.66	0	0	594	18	33.00	4-46	0	0	3	
Scott OC	1910/11	1934/35	19	25	3	715	94	32.50	0	6	2781	105	26.48	8-67	10	5	10	
	1910/11	1934/35	45	66	12	1317	94	24.38	0	9	5556	182	30.52	8-67	14	5	14	
Sewell HG	1957/58	1959/60	3	3	2	26	16*	26.00	0	0	187	1	187.00	1-25	0	0	0	
Shannon H	1904/05	1908/09	8	14	4	17	13	1.70	0	0	483	27	17.88	6-59	1	0	1	
Sidgwick R	1894/95		1	2	0	8	8	4.00	0	0							0	
	1882	1894/95	10	15	0	72	17	4.80	0	0							7	
Silvera ALM	1924/25		3	4	1	14	8*	4.66	0	0							1	
Smith F	1938/39		3	3	0	17	9	5.66	0	0	214	9	23.77	3-48	0	0	1	
Smith G	1956/57		3	6	2	90	26*	22.50	0	0							1	
Smith OG	1954/55	1957/58	8	14	1	873	169	67.15	4	3	859	26	33.03	4-71	0	0	7	
	1954/55	1958/59	70	112	12	4031	169	40.31	10	20	3754	121	31.02	5-63	2	0	39	
Snow SC	1901/02	1910/11	6	12	2	209	54	20.90	0	1	163	3	54.33	1-17	0	0	2	
	1901/02	1910/11	13	24	2	401	54	18.22	0	2	439	19	23.10	5-51	1	0	10	
Staple RW	1989/90	1994/95	19	34	1	556	79	16.84	0	2	34	0					9	
	1989/90	1994/95	20	36	1	652	79	18.62	0	3	90	0					11	
Stapleton-Cotton RGAW	1901/02		1	2	0	3	3	1.50	0	0							1	
Stephenson OC	1927/28	1938/39	10	15	0	355	76	23.66	0	3	276	3	92.00	2-93	0	0	10	
Stoddart AL	1904/05		2	4	1	38	30*	12.66	0	0	63	2	31.50	2-45	0	0	0	
Tarilton AF	1904/05		1	2	0	9	7	4.50	0	0							1	

	First	Last	M	I	NO	Runs	HS	Avg	100	50	Runs	Wkts	Avg	Best	5i	10m	ct	st
Tarver WK	1901/02		3	6	0	46	15	7.66	0	0							1	
Taylor RA	1990/91	1991/92	5	6	2	7	3	1.75	0	0	388	12	32.33	3-86	0	0	2	
Thompson CU	1976/77	1984/85	20	29	12	238	28*	14.00	0	0	1619	50	32.38	6-74	4	0	5	
Thorbourne DO	1949/50	1958/59	10	19	0	511	95	26.89	0	4	194	8	24.25	3-26	0	0	2	
Tomlinson PU	1980/81		1	1	0	7	7	7.00	0	0	105	2	52.50	2-60	0	0	1	
Toone JW	1894/95		1	1	0	0	0	0.00	0	0	80	13	6.15	7-29	2	1	1	
Tucker MA	1979/80	1989/90	26	43	8	657	61	18.77	0	3	1553	54	28.75	6-38	2	1	6	
	1979/80	1989/90	29	48	9	740	61	18.97	0	3	1741	61	28.54	6-38	3	1	7	
Tulloch HA	1951/52	1961/62	4	7	0	29	12	4.14	0	0	322	5	64.40	2-9	0	0	2	
Uter S	1910/11		3	6	0	74	21	12.33	0	0	66	3	22.00	2-4	0	0	1	
Valencia CHL	1901/02		3	6	0	29	16	4.83	0	0	138	3	46.00	2-39	0	0	1	
Valentine AL	1949/50	1964/65	26	36	6	223	24	7.43	0	0	3078	89	34.58	8-78	7	1	11	
	1949/50	1964/65	125	142	48	470	24*	5.00	0	0	12451	475	26.21	8-26	32	6	45	
Valentine VA	1931/32	1938/39	4	4	0	104	36	26.00	0	0	372	12	31.00	4-119	0	0	0	
	1931/32	1938/39	24	33	5	500	59*	17.85	0	1	1980	49	40.40	4-83	0	0	11	
Ventura MD	1992/93	1994/95	5	8	1	123	45	17.57	0	0							2	
Verley BL	1894/95	1896/97	5	10	2	62	28	7.75	0	0	103	9	11.44	3-34	0	0	5	
Walsh CA	1981/82	1993/94	45	69	15	559	34*	10.35	0	0	4213	208	20.25	8-92	13	1	21	
	1981/82	1995	320	400	90	3837	66	12.37	0	8	29200	1305	22.37	9-72	75	15	82	
Watson CD	1958/59	1961/62	7	7	1	25	9	4.16	0	0	667	22	30.31	6-33	1	0	4	
	1958/59	1963/64	32	34	8	197	50	7.57	0	1	2726	85	32.07	6-33	1	0	15	
Weekes KH	1938/39	1947/48	11	19	3	928	106	58.00	2	7	464	12	38.66	3-84	0	0	15	1
	1938/39	1947/48	30	47	4	1731	146	40.25	4	12	464	12	38.66	3-84	0	0	21	1
Wellington AB	1965/66	1968/69	8	11	3	31	13	3.75	0	0	850	26	32.69	6-23	1	0	2	
Wellington L	1969/70	1970/71	11	14	6	208	49	26.00	0	0	483	12	40.25	3-29	0	0	7	
Whittingham E	1984/85		1	2	0	67	54	33.50	0	1	72	2	36.00	2-72	0	0	0	
Williams AB	1969/70	1984/85	33	56	1	1790	123	32.54	2	11	49	0					10	
	1969/70	1984/85	46	77	2	2702	126*	36.02	5	15	49	0					19	
Williams JA	1974/75	1982/83	17	23	7	192	33	12.00	0	0	1172	26	45.07	3-59	0	0	2	
	1974/75	1982/83	26	36	9	281	33	10.40	0	0	1890	52	36.34	4-26	0	0	4	
Williams L	1957/58		1	1	0	0	0	0.00	0	0	113	2	56.50	2-77	0	0	0	
Williams LR	1989/90	1994/95	10	17	3	328	65	23.42	0	3	728	27	26.96	5-41	1	0	4	
Williams MW	1984/85		1	2	0	3	3	1.50	0	0							0	
Williams W	1979/80		1	2	0	1	1	0.50	0	0	26	0					2	
Wilson EL	1982/83	1990/91	11	17	8	84	17*	9.33	0	0	1087	30	36.23	5-63	1	0	2	
Wilson FS	1904/05	1905/06	5	10	0	197	63	19.70	0	2	23	0					2	
Withers GH	1901/02		3	6	0	59	30	9.83	0	0	200	7	28.57	5-77	1	0	0	
Woollaston G	1959/60	1967/68	2	3	0	5	5	1.66	0	0							0	
Worrell FMM	1947/48	1963/64	13	19	4	698	106*	46.53	2	4	650	20	32.50	5-87	1	0	6	
	1941/42	1964	208	326	49	15025	308*	54.24	39	78	10115	349	28.98	7-70	13	0	139	
Wright EF	1901/02		3	6	0	48	15	8.00	0	0	93	3	31.00	2-40	0	0	1	
	1878	1901/02	18	32	0	759	123	23.71	1	3	602	47	12.80	7-15	3	2	11	

	First	Last	M	I	NO	Runs	HS	Avg	100	50	Runs	Wkts	Avg	Best	5i	10m	ct	st
Wright LNG	1968/69	1978/79	24	30	11	316	33	16.83	0	0	1073	40	26.82	5-36	2	0	23	
Wright SC	1958/59		1	2	1	1	1*	1.00	0	0	41	0					0	
Wynter RR	1975/76	1981/82	17	20	8	61	13	5.08	0	0	1180	31	38.06	5-48	1	0	9	
	1975/76	1982/83	18	22	9	70	13	5.38	0	0	1239	33	37.54	5-48	1	0	10	
Young HB	1931/32		2	1	0	32	32	32.00	0	0	182	3	60.66	2-76	0	0	0	
Young SC	1924/25	1927/28	6	7	3	44	27*	11.00	0	0	232	2	116.00	1-19	0	0	4	1

The following Barbados players appeared only for the Combined Jamaica XI in 1964/65 or the Jamaica Invitation XI in 1965/66:

	First	Last	M	I	NO	Runs	HS	Avg	100	50	Runs	Wkts	Avg	Best	5i	10m	ct	st
Hall WW	1964/65		1	2	1	26	16	26.00	0	0	87	5	17.40	4-46	0	0	1	
	1955/56	1970/71	170	215	38	2673	102*	15.10	1	6	14273	546	26.14	7-51	19	2	58	
Hunte CC	1964/65		1	2	0	90	78	45.00	0	1							0	
	1950/51	1966/67	132	222	19	8916	263	43.92	16	57	644	17	37.88	3-5	0	0	68	1
Sobers GS	1964/65	1965/66	2	3	0	267	129	89.00	2	0	205	7	29.28	3-41	0	0	2	
	1952/53	1974	383	609	93	28315	365*	54.87	86	118	28941	1043	27.74	9-49	36	1	407	

Where two line are shown, the first is for Jamaica matches only and the second for all first-class matches.

The following matches have been included in the Jamaica figures: Jamaica Born v Lucas' XI 1894/95, Jamaica and United Services v Bennett's XI 1901/02, Jamaica Born v Bennett's XI 1901/02, Combined Jamaica XI v Cavaliers 1964/65, Jamaica Invitation XI v Worcestershire 1965/66, Jamaica Tour of England 1970 (4 matches). The 1964/65 and 1965/66 games are considered similar to Tasmania Combined XI matches played in Australia, as only W.W.Hall, C.C.Hunte and G.S.Sobers in 1964/65, and Sobers in 1965/66 were not Jamaican players.

There are no bowling analyses for the second innings of the match v Cavaliers 1964/65 - these wickets are shown as +1 (although details for A.L.Valentine have been discovered).

Figures complete to the end of the 1995 English season.

ESSEX CRICKETERS 1876-1986

Compiled and Published by
The Association of Cricket Statisticians
Haughton Mill, Retford, Notts

Price: £2.25 (issued free to members of the Association in 1987)

Printed by Peartree Printers, Noel Street, Derby

CAMBRIDGESHIRE
SUFFOLK
HERTFORDSHIRE
KENT
GREATER LONDON
ELMDON
WENDEN LOFTS
SAFFRON WALDEN
WIMBISH
BIRDBROOK
PEBMARSH
BOXTED
MANNINGTREE
MISTLEY
NEWPORT
RICKLING
BERDEN
FINCHINGFIELD
HALSTEAD
WHITE COLNE
EARLS COLNE
COLCHESTER
TENDRING
GREAT BENTLEY
FARNHAM
STANSTED MOUNTFITCHET
STEBBING
BRAINTREE
GREAT DUNMOW
FELSTED
BIRCH
LAYER-DE-LA-HAYE
BRIGHTLINGSEA
FRINTON-ON-SEA
CLACTON-ON-SEA
HARTFORD END
GREAT LEIGHS
HATFIELD BROAD OAK
FORD END
TERLING
WITHAM
TIPTREE
PLESHEY
GREAT WALTHAM
LITTLE WALTHAM
GREAT BRAXTED
WEST MERSEA
WICKHAM BISHOPS
GREAT TOTHAM
MATCHING GREEN
CHIGNALL ST JAMES
HATFIELD PEVEREL
BOREHAM
HARLOW
MALDON
CHELMSFORD
WRITTLE
DANBURY
GREAT BADDOW
CHIPPING ONGAR
HIGH ONGAR
FRYERNING
LOWER MAYLAND
DENGIE
WALTHAM ABBEY
EPPING
STONDON MASSEY
INGATESTONE
HIGH BEACH
NAVESTOCK
BURNHAM-ON-CROUCH
LOUGHTON
HUTTON
BILLERICAY
SOUTH WEALD
CHIGWELL
BRENTWOOD
WARLEY
ROCHFORD
BASILDON
HADLEIGH
BULPHAN
LEIGH-ON-SEA
WESTCLIFF-ON-SEA
SOUTHEND-ON-SEA
THORPE BAY
CORRINGHAM
ORSETT
GRAYS THURROCK
PURFLEET
CHADWELL ST MARY
GREATER LONDON
1. Harold Hill
2. Havering-Atte-Bower
3. Romford
4. Gidea Park
5. Hornchurch
6. Upminster
7. Chadwell Heath
8. Goodmayes
9. Barking
10. Dagenham
11. Seven Kings
12. Redbridge
13. Ilford
14. Manor Park
15. Upton Park
16. West Ham
17. Plaistow
18. Beckton
19. Forest Gate
20. Stratford
21. Walthamstow
22. Eton Manor
23. Leyton
24. Leytonstone
25. Wanstead
26. Whipps Cross
27. Snaresbrook
28. Chingford
29. Woodford Wells
30. Woodford Green
31. Buckhurst Hill (Essex)
32. Clayhall
33. Hainault
34. Bancrofts School
35. Woodford
36. Forest School
37. East Ham
38. Fairlop

INTRODUCTION

This booklet on Essex Cricketers is the 22nd in the Association's "County and State Cricketers" Series and the 14th concerning a first class county. As such it attempts to conform to the established pattern of the series, although in certain respects this acts as a constraint on originality. The writer would have wished to have seen the inclusion of overs, and possibly maidens, in the bowling figures, particularly now that the value of runs per over for comparative purposes is becoming recognised. Similarly, many capable batsmen compile a surprising number of fifties but few magic centuries and most modern statistical tables recognise this.

On the subject of schools a difficult choice had to be made. The inclusion of only those loosely defined "public schools"—often they are not—beloved of certain venerable publications seemed an extremely outmoded piece of snobbery in 1986 and where the information is available details of all categories of educational establishment have been included. It is also felt that associations with other counties, Minor as well as first class, is of value, and details of relationships to other cricketers similarly so. The practice of the Australian and Irish booklets in the series of giving details of clubs has much to commend it and its absence is regretted. On the other hand no attempt has been made to give details of nicknames or of prowess in other sports—this topic has received some attention in a number of excellent articles in recent numbers of "The Cricket Statistician".

Where the correct Christian names of a player do not conform with what has been incorrectly shown in earlier publications, no attempt has been made stubbornly to perpetuate inaccuracies, although this will doubtless attract criticism from those who make a virtue of avoiding change. Fortunately in the Essex lists the examples of this are few.

Having dealt with contention it is pleasant to turn to the non-controversial. The present Essex County Cricket Club was formed at a public meeting held at the Shire Hall, Chelmsford, on the 14th January 1876. First class status was achieved in 1894 and the county entered the championship competition in 1895.

It follows that few difficulties arise as to the classification of Essex matches and the figures are based on the Association's "Guide to First Class Cricket Matches Played in the British Isles", first published in 1976. The following three-day matches have consequently been disregarded:

Essex v. Hampshire at Leyton and at Southampton, 1894
Essex v. Dublin University at Dublin, 1905
Essex v. Sir Julien Cahn's XI at West Bridgford, 1930
Essex v. Wilfred Issacs's XI at Basildon, 1969
Essex v. Scotland at Perth, 1973.

The Association's Guides to First Class Cricket in Australia, New Zealand, India, South Africa and West Indies have also been followed for full career figures.

A list is also included giving biographical details of cricketers who appeared for the county between 1876 and 1893. No attempt has been made to list players who played for county sides at the end of the eighteenth/early nineteenth century or for the county club which existed for some years in the 1860s, although there is obviously some overlap with the players who appeared in the sides fielded in the first years of the present county club.

The maps which appear show most of the places associated with Essex players. Where no county is given in the lists it is implied that the town or village is in Essex. In this respect, re-organisations of local government and its boundaries pose some problems, particularly the formation of the London County Council in 1888 and the Greater London Council in 1965. The term "Essex" is used in the cricketing sense, i.e. the county is regarded as continuing to include the London Boroughs of Barking & Dagenham, Havering, Newham, Redbridge and Waltham Forest. In other areas the counties given are those in which the town or village was located at the time of the birth or death.

There are only a few players in the first class list where details are almost entirely lacking. The writer would welcome anything further about W. Cooper, W. Davis, J. Harris, W. Naylor and G. Sutton. Apart from Davis all played for the Beckton Club. Information about pre-1894 players would also be appreciated.

Finally there is the intriguing mystery of A. Brown (v. Gloucestershire and Middlesex, July 1921) who is shown in contemporary scoresheets and the Essex scorebook but whose figures are then without explanation merged with those of F. J. Cooper. My research in national and local newspapers has, to date, produced no valid reason for doubting the existence of "A. Brown" and the late Mr. Ernest K. Gross in correspondence in May 1971 was of the opinion that he was an Arthur Brown against whom he had played in club cricket in the Epping/Walthamstow area in the 1920s. Until convincing evidence is produced to refute this contention I shall continue to list him separately.

Essex are extremely fortunate in having an almost complete run of scorebooks dating back to 1879. With the exception of 1922, which is missing, the Essex statistics have been compiled directly from these and I am deeply indebted to the County Club and successive secretaries, Major C. A. Brown, Ronnie Cox and Peter Edwards and their deputies David Collier and Malcolm Stammers, for the opportunities they have so readily afforded for this research.

For the remainder of the statistical material it has been a great comfort to exchange information with Philip Bailey and I have also been helped by Geoffrey Saulez, Tony Webb and the late Arthur Wagg with difficult queries, particularly on overseas matches.

Philip Thorn has been a source of much information on biographical matters and again there has been a regular mutual exchange process. Robert Brooke, the late Gordon Tratalos, Jim Coldham, R. L. Arrowsmith, Frank Peach, the late Denys Heesom and other members of the Association have from time to time provided details or clues as to where information could be obtained and to these must be added the many cricketers and their relatives, schoolmasters, bursars and school secretaries who have answered queries. Newspaper editors and staff have afforded facilities for examination of copies of early newspapers, particularly the "Essex Chronicle" and "Walthamstow Guardian".

Wisden's Cricketers Almanack, The Cricketer Quarterly and all of the overseas Annuals have been invaluable sources of information. Most of all, I am indebted to those unsung heroes, the Essex scorers from 1879 through to the late C. V. Jenkinson, the late Jack Bartlam and Clem Driver, without whose efforts it would not be possible to compile reliable statistics.

Leslie Newnham
Maldon, Essex, November 1986.

CRICKETERS WHO HAVE APPEARED FOR ESSEX IN A FIRST CLASS MATCH

Acfield, David Laurence, b. Chelmsford 24.7.1947. RHB ROB, ed. Brentwood Sch. CU(2) MCC(1) MCC Schools to SA(not fc)

Appleyard, Francis, b. Clifton, Yorks 26.9.1905, d. Stevenage, Herts. 11.10.1971. RHB RFM. Hertfordshire. Father of J. D. & P. R. (Herts)

Arkwright, Harold Arthur, b. Oswestry, Shropshire 10.11.1872, d. Virginia Water, Surrey 10.12.1942. RHB RM, ed. Eton. OU(1) Mitchell to N. America. Cambridgeshire

Ashton, Claude Thesiger, b. Calcutta, India 19.2.1901, d. Carmarthen 31.10.1942. RHB RFM, ed. Winchester. CU(3) Brother of H. & P. (Essex) and G. (Worcestershire)

Ashton, Sir Hubert, b. Calcutta, India 13.2.1898, d. South Weald 17.6.1979. RHB, ed. Winchester. CU(3) President of MCC 1960. Europeans, India, Burma, Rangoon Gymkhana. Brother of C. T. & P. (Essex) and G. (Worcestershire)

Ashton, Percy, b. Calcutta, India 27.2.1895, d. Bigbury-on-Sea, Devon 18.9.1934. RFM, ed. Winchester. Brother of C. T. & H. (Essex) and G. (Worcestershire)

Avery, Alfred Victor, b. New Beckton 19.12.1914. RHB SLA, ed. Winsor Intermediate Sch., Beckton

Ayres, George White, b. Thames Ditton, Surrey 5.7.1871, d. Felpham, Sussex 28.8.1934. RHB. Read to South Africa (no fc matches) Surrey, Buckinghamshire

Bailey, Jack Arthur, b. Brixton, London 22.6.1930. RHB RFM, ed. Christ's Hospital. OU(3) MCC(4—none fc) Secretary of MCC & ICC since 1974

Bailey, Trevor Edward, b. Westcliff-on-Sea 3.12.1923. RHB RFM, ed. Dulwich, CU(2) Eng(61), MCC(5), Cavaliers to West Indies(2), Defence Fund Match in India(1). Father of J.T.(Essex II)

Baker, Richard Kenneth, b. Gidea Park 28.4.1952. RHB WK, ed. Brentwood Sch. CU(2)

Banfield, Arthur Ernest, b. Hackney, London 28.1.1897, d. Raynes Park, Surrey 3.1.1972

Barber, Arthur Norman, b. West Ham 23.11.1898

Barker, Gordon, b. Bramley, Leeds, Yorks 6.7.1931. RHB RM/ROB

Barnfather, James David, b. Leicester 22.7.1896, d. Grays Thurrock 21.8.1957. RHB RFM ed. Southampton GS & Palmer's Sch., Grays Thurrock

Barrow, Patrick Lindsay, b. Bromley, Kent 22.1.1893, d. Adstock, Bucks 7.5.1974. LHB ed. Wellington. Dorset

Bawtree, John Francis, b. Witham 26.11.1873, d. Great Totham 25.3.1938. SLA, ed. Haileybury

Bear, Michael John, b. Brentwood 23.2.1934. LHB RLB, ed. Brentwood SM Sch. MCC(2—one not fc, one co-opted in non fc match) Canterbury (not fc)

Belle, Brian Henry, b. Woodford Green 7.4.1914. RHB RM, ed. Forest Sch. OU(1) Oxford & Cambridge to Jamaica. Suffolk

Benham, Charles Edward, b. East Ham 24.6.1881, d. Bangour Hospital, West Lothian 13.12. 1961. RHB RF, ed. Beckton GS. Scotland. Father of F. C. (Scotland)

Berkley, Rev. Maurice, b. Navestock 6.9.1872, d. Bangor, Caernarvonshire 9.8.1947. RHB RS, ed. Fettes. OU(not fc)

Billham, Frank Denis, b. Georgetown, British Guiana 27.9.1896, d. Sudbury, Suffolk 16.11.1980. RHB SLA, ed. Framlingham

Bonner, John Wardell, b. Mile End, Middlesex 3.4.1869, d. Bournemouth, Hants 26.11.1936. RHB, ed. Forest Sch.

Border, Allan Robert, b. Cremorne, Sydney, Australia 27.7.1955. LHB SLA, ed. North Sydney BHS. Australia(81) Australian Tours(11 + 4 not fc) New South Wales, Queensland, Gloucestershire.

Borradaile, Oswell Robert, b. Westminster 9.5.1859, d. Bexhill, Sussex 11.5.1935. RHB RM, ed. Westminster Sch.

Borrett, Norman Francis, b. Wanstead 1.10.1917, RHB SLA, ed. Framlingham, CU(not fc) Devon

Boswell, Cecil Stanley Reginald, b. Edmonton, Middlesex 19.1.1910, d. Brundall, Norfolk 15.8.1985. RHB RLBG, Norfolk

Boyce, Keith David, b. Ashton Hall, St. Peter, Barbados 11.10.1943. RHB RFM, ed. Coleridge Parry Sec. Sch., St Peter, Barbados. WI(21) WI Tours(3), Commonwealth to Pakistan, World XI to Pakistan, Kent to WI (not fc) Barbados, Kent (not fc)

Boyers, Michael John Herbert, b. Plaistow 16.4.1948. RHB RFM, ed. Sir George Monoux GS, Walthamstow & Loughborough College.

Bradfield, Arthur, b. Box, Wilts 5.1.1892, d. Mochdre, Clwyd, Wales 25.12.1978. RHB WK

Bray, Charlie (known as Charles), b. Brighton, Sussex 6.4.1898. RHB RM, ed. Luton Modern

Bristowe, Orme Chesshyre, b. Great Baddow 12.4.1895, d. Freiston Shore, Lincs. 27.12.1938. RHB RLBG, ed. Eton OU(1) Cheshire

Brooks, Victor Charles George, b. East Ham 29.6.1948. LHB occ. WK, ed. East Ham GS, Manchester University. London Schs. to India & Ceylon

Brown, Arthur

Brown, George Rainy Reynolds, b. Maldon 8.12.1905. RHB SLA, ed. Felsted CU(no Blue) Europeans (India)

Brunwin, Herbert Jack, b. Layer-de-la-Haye 28.4.1912. RHB RMF, ed. Colchester RGS. London University

Buckenham, Claude Percival, b. Herne Hill, Surrey 16.1.1876, d. Dundee, Angus, Scotland 23.2.1937. RHB RF, ed. Alleyn's Sch., Dulwich. Eng(4) (MCC(1)

Bull, Frederick George, b. Hackney, Middlesex 2.4.1875, d. St. Annes-on-Sea, Lancs 16.9.1910. RHB ROB, ed, Audley House Sch., Lee. Warner to USA. Scotland

Burns, James, b. Liverpool, Lancs 20.6.1865, d. Hampstead, London 11.9.57. RHB SLA Lancashire (not fc)

Burns, Neil David, b. Chelmsford 19.9.1965. LHB WK, ed. Moulsham HS., Chelmsford. England YC to WI (not fc) Western Province "B". Brother of Ian (Essex II)

Burrell, Rev. Herbert John Edwin, b. Kirtling, Cambs 15.11.1866, d. Cambridge 22.5.1949. RHB RM, ed. Charterhouse, OU(no Blue) Hertfordshire, Norfolk. Brother of R.J.

Burrell, Reginald John, b. Kirtling, Cambs 26.8.1870, d. Risby, Suffolk 16.3.1948. ed. Charterhouse. Suffolk. Brother of H.J.E.

Calnan, Clement Noel, b. Mile End, London 25.12.1888, d. Southend 30.1.1974

Campbell, Percival, b. West Ham 26.12.1887, d. Woodford 18.3.1960 ed. Eastbourne

Capel-Cure, George Nigel, b. London 28.9.1908. LHB, ed. Eton. CU(not fc) Nephew of A. & F.

Carbutt, Noel John Obelin, b. Gingindhlovu, Zululand, S. Africa 25.12.1895, d. Durban, S. Africa 31.10.1964. RHB RLBG, ed. Pietermaritzburg College, S. Africa. Europeans, Karachi, Northern India, Army

Carpenter, Herbert Arthur, b. Cambridge 12.7.1869, d. Whipps Cross 12.12.1933. RHB ROB Cambridgeshire, uncle of J. O'Connor (Essex). Son of R. P. (Cambs), nephew of G. (Cambridge Town)

Carr, Ronald Bernard, b. Johannesburg, S. Africa 12.1.1938. RHB RLBG, ed. Marist Bros. College, Johannesburg, S. Africa. Transvaal

Carter, George, b. Stoke Newington, London 10.5.1901. RHB RM, ed. Grocers' Co. Sch., Hackney Downs

Cass, George Rodney, b. Overton, Yorks 23.4.1940. LHB WK, ed. Dewsbury Tech. College. Worcestershire, Tasmania, Shropshire

Castor, Brian Kenneth, b. Mahaica, British Guiana 21.10.1889, d. Maida Hill, London, 2.10.1979. RHB

Chapman, Ivan b. Pudsey, Yorks 12.10.1906, d. Hamilton, New Zealand .2.1976. RHB RFM, ed. Littlemor Sch., Pudsey, Yorks

Childs, John Henry, b. Plymouth, Devon 15.8.1951. LHB SLA, ed. Audley Park SMS, Torquay, Devon. Devon, Gloucestershire

Clark, Horace George, b. West Ham 23.1.1889. d. Epping 28.2.1967

Clark, Leonard Stanley, b. Manor Park 6.3.1914. RHB RM, ed. Leigh Hall College, Leigh-on-Sea

Clark, Ronald Disston, b. Romford 22.2.1895, d. East Wittering, West Sussex 20.2.1983. RHB WK, ed. Christ's Hospital

Clarke, Dr. Carlos Bertram, b. Bridgetown, Barbados 7.4.1918. RHB RLBG, ed. Harrison College, Barbados & Guy's Hospital, London. WI(3) WI Tours(1) Barbados, Northamptonshire

Cock, David Frederick, b. Great Dunmow 22.10.1914. RHB ed. Bishops Stortford Coll. Hertfordshire, Cambridgeshire

Coleman, Edward Charles, b. Southend 5.9.1891, d. Salonika, Greece 2.4.1917. LHB WK, ed. Dulwich CU(not fc)

Connor, Edward James, b. Hackney, Middlesex 1872, d. Enfield, Middlesex 11.1.1947. RM

Cooke, Robert Michael Oliver, b. Adlington, Cheshire 3.9.1943. LHB RLBG, ed. Rossall. Cheshire

Cooper, Albert Vincent, b. Stoke Newington, London 3.12.1893, d. Stoke Newington, London, 3.5.1977. RHB ROB/RLB, ed. Bancroft's Sch.

Cooper, Frederick Joseph, b. Wetherby, Yorks 1888, d. York 27.6.1958. RM. Shropshire
Cooper, Walter LHB SLA
Cottam, Francis, b. Redhill, Surrey 6.6.1900. RHB SLA, ed. St. John's Sch., Redhill
Cousens, Peter, b. Durban, South Africa 15.5.1932. RHB SLA, ed. Loughton Sch.
Crabtree, Harry Pollard, b. Barnoldswick, Yorks 30.4.1906, d. Great Baddow 28.5.1982. RHB RM, ed. Ermysted's GS, Skipton, Yorks., Int. College of PE, Silkeborg, Denmark
Crawley, Charles Lambart, b. Brandon, Suffolk 1.5.1908, d. Sunderland, Durham 24.7.1935. ed. Harrow. Brother of L. G.
Crawley, Leonard George, b. Nacton, Suffolk 26.7.1903, d. Worlington, Suffolk 9.7.1981. RHB RM, ed. Harrow CU(3) MCC(1) Worcestershire, Durham. Brother of C. L.
Cray, Stanley James, b. Stratford 29.5.1921. RHB Services XI in India. Devon
Cutmore, James Albert, b. Walthamstow 28.12.1898, d. Brentwood 30.11.1985, RHB RM, ed. Clark's College, Ilford

Daer, Arthur George, b. Bishopsgate, London 22.11.1906, d. Torquay, Devon 16.7.1980. RHB RFM, ed. Latymer Sch. Brother of H. B.
Daer, Harry Bruce, b. Hammersmith, London 10.12.1918, d. Plymouth, Devon 19.12.1980. RHB RM, ed. Royal Liberty Sch., Romford, Brother of A. G.
Davies, Geoffrey Boisselier, b. Poplar, London 26.10.1892, d. Hulluch, France 26.9.1915. RHB RSM, ed. Rossall CU(2)
Davis, W
Denness, Michael Henry, b. Bellshill, Lanarkshire, Scotland 1.12.1940. RHB RM/ROB, ed. Ayr Academy, Scotland. Eng(28) MCC(3 + 1 not fc) International Team to Sierra Leone, East Africa, Pakistan, India, Ceylon, Singapore, Malaysia, Thailand & Hong Hong; Duke of Norfolk to WI; International Wanderers to SA; Robins to Malaysia, Singapore, Hong Kong & Sri Lanka. Scotland, Kent
Dennis, John Newman, b. Leytonstone 4.1.1913, RHB ed. Forest Sch.; Law Society's Sch. of Law
De Zoete, Herman Walter, b. Bromley, Kent 13.2.1877, d. Ipswich, Suffolk 26.3.1957 RHB LM/SLA, ed. Eton. CU(2)
Dines, William James, b. Colchester 14.9.1916. RHB RM/ROB, ed. Victoria Sch., Chelmsford
Dinsdale, Stephen Charles, b. Buckhurst Hill 30.12.1948. LHB LM, ed. Sir George Monoux GS, Walthamstow, Rhodesia, Transvaal "B"
Dixon, Joseph Gilbert, b. Chelmsford 3.9.1895, d. Great Baddow 19.11.1954. RHB RFM, ed. Felsted
Dodds, Thomas Carter, b. Bedford 19.5.1919. RHB RM/RLB, ed. Warwick Sch., Wellingborough Sch. Services XI in India
Douglas, Cecil Herbert, b. Clapton, Middlesex 28.6.1886, d. Frinton-on-Sea 30.9.1954. RHB RS, ed. Felsted. Brother of J. W. H. T.
Douglas, John William Henry Tyler, b. Clapton, Middlesex 3.9.1882, d. near Laeso, The Cattegat, Denmark 19.12.1930. RHB RFM, ed. Moulton GS, Lincs. & Felsted. Eng(23) MCC(6) Incogniti to Malta (not fc), London County. Brother of C. H.
Dow, William David Fraser, b. Glasgow, Scotland 27.11.1933. RHB RFM, ed. St. Aloysius College, Glasgow. Scotland, Cumberland
Durley, Anthony William, b. Ilford 30.9.1933. RHB WK, ed. SW Essex Tech. Sch. Bedfordshire

East, David Edward, b. Clapton, London 27.7.1959. RHB WK, ed. Hackney Downs Sch., Univ. of E. Anglia
East, Raymond Eric, b. Manningtree 20.6.1947. RHB SLA, ed. East Bergholt SMS, Suffolk Robins to SA, Overseas XI to India, English Counties to WI (not fc), Warwickshire to Zambia (not fc), Warwickshire (not fc)
Eastman, George Frederick, b. Leyton 7.4.1903. RHB WK, ed. Ruckholt Road Sch., Leyton & Leyton Tech. Institute. Brother of L. C.
Eastman, Lawrence Charles, b. Enfield Wash, Middlesex 3.6.1897, d. Harefield, Middlesex 17.4.1941. RHB RM/RLB, ed. Ruckholt Road Sch., Leyton. Brinckman to South America. Otago. Brother of G. F. Father of M. L. (Essex II)
Edmeades, Brian Ernest Arthur, b. Matlock, Derbyshire 17.9.1941. RHB RM, ed. Mark House Sch., Walthamstow
Edwards, Guy Janion, b. Kensington 11.5.1881, d. Upper Slaughter, Gloucs. 30.9.1962. RHB ed. Eton

Elliott, Herbert Denis Edleston, b. Newport, Shropshire 30.3.1887, d Bognor Regis, Sussex 26.4.1973. ed. Newport, Shropshire. CU (not fc)

Evans, Ronald Ernest, b. East Ham 22.7.1922. RHB. ed. Highfield College, Leigh-on-Sea

Evans, Victor James, b. Woodford 4.3.1912, d. Barking 28.3.1975. RHB RM/ROB

Eve, Stanley Charles, b. Stepney, London 18.12.1925. RHB RM, ed. Gaynes Sec. Sch., Upminster

Fane, Frederick Luther, b. 27.4.1875 Curragh Camp, Ireland, d. Brentwood 27.11.1960. RHB ed. Charterhouse OU(2) Eng(14), MCC(3), Bennett to WI, Hawke to USA, NZ & Australia, Leveson-Gower to Rhodesia. London County. Son of F. J.

Faragher, Harold Alker, b. Reddish, Lancs 20.7.1917. RHB RM/RLBG, ed. Ilford CHS. Father of J. L. (Essex II)

Farnes, Kenneth, b. Leytonstone 8.7.1911, d. Chipping Warden, Northants 20.10.1941. RHB RF, ed. Royal Liberty Sch., Romford CU(3) Eng(15), MCC(3)

Farnfield, Geoffrey George, b. West Ham 13.7.1897, d. Leamington Spa, Warwickshire 22.3.1974. RHB

Faviell, William Frederick Oliver, b. Loughton 5.6.1882, d. Nairobi, Kenya 14.2.1950. RHB RM, ed. Forest Sch. Europeans

Fletcher, Keith William Robert, b. Worcester 20.5.1944. RHB RLB, ed. Comberton Village College, Cambs. Eng(59), MCC(7), Eng. Tours(1), MCC Under 25(1), Cavaliers to WI, International Team to Sierra Leone, East Africa, Pakistan, India, Ceylon, Singapore, Malaysia, Thailand & Hong Kong

Fosh, Matthew Kailey, b. Epping 26.9.1957. LHB RM, ed. Harrow CU(2) Young England to WI (not fc)

Foster, Neil Alan, b. Colchester 6.5.1962. RHB RFM, ed. Philip Morant Sec. Comp. Sch., Colchester. Eng(14), Eng. Tours(3 + 1 not fc) England Young Cricketers to WI (not fc)

Francis, Bruce Colin, b. Sydney, Australia 18.2.1948. RHB RM, ed. Vaucluse HS, Sydney University. Australia(3) Australian Tours(1), International Wanderers to Rhodesia, Robins to SA(2). New South Wales

Franklin, Henry William Fernehough, b. Ford End 30.6.1901, d. Worthing, West Sussex 25.8.1985. RHB RLB, ed. Christ's Hospital OU(1) Martineau to Egypt (not fc). Free Foresters to Holland (not fc). Surrey. Brother of R. C.

Franklin, Ronald Christian, b. Ford End 9.9.1904, d. Prestwood, Bucks 28.9.1982. RHB RM, ed. Christ's Hospital. Brother of H. W. F.

Freeman, Alfred James, b. Edmonton, Middlesex 2.4.1892, d. Chelmsford 28.4.1972. LM Cousin of E. J. & J. R. (Essex) and A. P. (Kent)

Freeman, Edward Charles, b. Lewisham, Kent 7.12.1860, d. Sherborne, Dorset 16.10.1939. RHB. Father of E. J. (Essex), Grandfather of D. P. (Kent) & E. J. Junr. (Dorset), Uncle of J. R. (Essex) & A. P. (Kent)

Freeman, Edward John, b. Ladywell, Kent 16.10.1880, d. Sherborne, Dorset 22.2.1964. Dorset. Son of E. C., Father of D. P. (Kent) & E. J. Junr. (Dorset), Cousin of A. J. & J. R. (Essex) & A. P. (Kent)

Freeman, John Robert, b. Ladywell, Kent 3.9.1883, d. Napsbury, Herts 8.8.1958. RHB RM WK. Brother of A. P. (Kent), Nephew of E. C., Cousin of A. J. & E. J.

Garrett, William Thomas, b. Camberwell, Surrey 9.1.1876, d. Buckhurst Hill 16.2.1953. RHB

Gentry, Jack Sydney Bates, b. Wanstead 4.10.1899, d. Loxwood West Sussex 16.4.1978. RHB SLA, ed. Christ's Hospital. Surrey, Hampshire

Gibb, Paul Antony, b. Brandsby, Yorks 11.7.1913, d. Guildford, Surrey 7.12.1977. RHB WK, ed. St. Edward's Sch., Oxford CU(4) Eng(8) MCC(2) Cahn to North America (not fc), Yorkshire to Jamaica, Tennyson to India, Commonwealth to India. Scotland, Yorkshire

Gibson, Archibald Lesley, b. Kingsclere, Hants 4.9.1877, d. Nakuru, Kenya 29.7.1943. RHB RSM, ed. Winchester. Ceylon to Madras (not fc), Ceylon to India (not fc), Ceylon, Up-County XI

Gibson. Sir Kenneth Lloyd, b. London 11.5.1888, d. Marylebone, London 14.5.1967. RHB WK. ed. Eton. (MCC(1 not fc)

Gilligan, Frank William, b. Denmark Hill, London 20.9.1893, d. Wanganui, New Zealand 4.5.1960. RHB WK, ed. Dulwich OU(2). Brother of A. E. R. & A. H. H. (Sussex)

Gillingham, Rev. Canon Frank Hay, b. Tokyo, Japan 6.9.1875, d. Monaco 1.4.1953. RHB WK, ed. Dulwich, Durham University. MCC(2)—not fc), Tennyson to Jamaica

Gladwin, Christopher, b. East Ham 10.5.1962. LHB RM, ed. Langdon Comp. Sch., East Ham. England Young Cricketers to WI(not fc)

Golding, Andrew Kenneth, b. Colchester 5.10.1963. RHB SLA, ed. Colchester RGS. CU(1) English Schools to Zimbabwe (not fc)

Gooch, Graham Alan, b. Leytonstone 23.7.1953. RHB RM occ.WK, ed. Norlington Jun. HS, Leytonstone, Eng (59) Eng Tours(5) SAB English XI to SA, England Young Cricketers to WI (not fc) Western Province. Second cousin of G. J. Saville

Gosling, Cecil Henry, b. Dunmow 22.2.1910, d. Hatfield Broad Oak 19.5.1974. RHB ed. Eton OU(no Blue) Nephew of R. C.

Gosling, Robert Cunliffe, b. Farnham, Essex 15.6.1868, d. Farnham, Essex 8.4.1922. RHB RS, ed. Eton CU(3) Brother of G.B. Uncle of C. H.

Graham, Leonard, b. Leyton 20.8.1901, d. Kensington, London 21.12.1962

Gray, David Anthony Athelstan, b. London 19.6.1922. RHB SLA, ed. Winchester. CU(no Blue)

Gray, William Johns, b. Chelmsford 26.11.1864, d. Chelmsford 18.12.1898. ed. Mill Hill

Green, Michael Arthur, b. Bristol 3.10.1891, d. Kensington, London 28.12.1971. RHB MCC(2 as manager) Gloucestershire, Europeans.

Greensmith, William Thomas, b. Middlesbrough, Yorks 16.8.1930. RHB RLBG. Brother of R. H. (Essex II)

Griffiths, Colin, b. Upminster 9.12.1930. RHB RM, ed. Brentwood Sch., Brother of P. A. (Essex II)

Grimwood, Alfred Stanley, b. West Ham 8.9.1905. LHB. ed. Walthamstow Jun. Tech. Sch.

Grinter, Trayton Golding, b. Leytonstone 12.12.1885, d. Frinton-on-Sea 21.4.1966. RHB RFM, ed. Newport GS

Gunary, William Charles, b. Dagenham 5.8.1895, d. Upminster 26.1.1969. RHB LFM, ed. George Green GS, East Ham

Hadden, Sidney, b. Hastings, Sussex 26.8.1877, d. West Ham 1934. WK

Hailey, Henry, b. Bow, Middlesex 1851, d. Southend 24.9.1932. RHB

Hardie, Brian Ross, b. Stenhousemuir, Stirlingshire, Scotland 14.1.1950. RHB RM, ed. Larbert HS Scotland. Son of J. M. (Scotland), Brother of K. M. (Scotland)

Hare, Steriker Norman, b. Tottenham, Middlesex 31.3.1900, d. Meadle, Bucks. 30.9.1977. RHB. ed. Chigwell

Harris, J. WK

Harrold, James George William, b. 1892, d. Epsom, Surrey 7.10.1950. RHB ROB

Harvey, Ronald Charles, b. Ingatestone 7.5.1934. LHB RFM, ed. Rainsford Sec. Sch., Chelmsford

Hawker, Sir Frank Cyril, b. Epping 21.7.1900. ed. City of London Sch., President of MCC 1970-71. Grandson of J. Bastow. Brother-in-law of T. N. Pearce

Hayzelden, Allan Frederick George, b. Leytonstone 10.1.1904, d. Harefield, Middlesex 10.4.1955. RHB RF, ed. Merchant Taylors Sch.

Hazelton, Edward Wyndham, b. Buckingham 1894, d. Dunmow 13.3.1958. RHB RM/RLBG, ed. Wellingborough Sch. Buckinghamshire

Heatley, Arthur Edward, b. Brighton, Sussex 1866, d. Brentwood 1.7.1941

Heaven, Raymond Maurice, b. Shoreham-by-Sea, Sussex 8.10.1918. RHB RLB, ed. Leigh Hall College, Leigh-on-Sea

Hector, Patrick Anthony, b. Islington, London 29.7.1958. RHB RM, ed. Warren Comp. Sch., Chadwell Heath

Herbert, Reuben, b. Cape Town, South Africa 1.12.1957. RHB ROB, ed. Barstable Comp Sch., Basildon. Suffolk

Herringshaw, John Percy, b. Derby 22.5.1892, d. Yapton, West Sussex 13.11.1974. LHB SLA, ed. Blandford Sch., Dorset

Higgins, George Frederick, b. Hackney, Middlesex 1868, d. Woodford Green 16.8.1951. RHB

Hills. Harry Mountford, b. Mayland 28.9.1886. RHB RLB

Hilton, Colin, b. Atherton, Lancs 26.9.1937. RHB RF Lancashire

Hipkin, Augustus Bernard, b. Brancaster, Norfolk, 8.8.1900, d. Carluke, Lanarkshire, Scotland 11.2.1957. LHB SLA. Scotland

Hobbs, Robin Nicholas Stuart, b. Chippenham, Wilts 8.5.1942. RHB RLBG, ed. Raines Foundation Sch., Stepney. Eng(7) MCC(4), MCC Under 25(1), Cavaliers to Jamaica, Duke of Norfolk to WI, Commonwealth to Pakistan & Kuwait, Robins to SA; World Team to Pakistan. Glamorgan, Suffolk

Hockey, George William, b. Ipswich, Suffolk 1.1.1905. RHB RM, ed. Ipswich Sch., Suffolk

Horrex, Graham Wade, b. Goodmayes 27.12.1932. RHB. ed. Brentwood Sch.

Horsfall, Richard, b. Todmorden, Yorks 26.6.1920, d. Halifax, Yorks 25.8.1981. RHB. Glamorgan

Hubble, William George, b. Leyton 20.6.1898, d. Bishops Waltham, Hants 1978. LHB SLA, ed. Kirkdale Road Sch., Leytonstone

Hughes, Mervyn Gregory, b. Euroa, Victoria, Australia 23.11.1961. RHB RFM, ed. Werribee HS. Australia(1). Victoria

Hugonin, Francis Edgar, b. London 16.8.1897, d. Stainton-in-Cleveland, Yorks 5.3.1967. RHB WK, ed. Eastbourne College. Berkshire.

Hurd, Alan, b. Ilford 7.9.1937. LHB ROB, ed. Chigwell CU(3)

Hurst, Geoffrey Charles, b. Ashton-under-Lyne, Lancs 8.12.1941. RHB WK, ed. Rainsford Sec. Mod. Sch., Chelmsford

Hyndson, Robert Wilberforce James Gerard, b. Cape Town, South Africa 1894, d. Bradford, Yorks 27.9.1943. Brother of J. G. W. (Surrey)

Inns, John Herbert, b. Writtle 30.3.1876, d. Writtle 14.6.1905. WK

Insole, Douglas John, b. Clapton, London 18.4.1926. RHB RM occ.WK, ed. Sir George Monoux GS, Walthamstow CU(3), Eng(9), MCC(1), Eng. Tours(2 as manager) Chairman of TCCB 1975-78

Irvine, Brian Lee, b. Durban, South Africa 9.3.1944. LHB RM WK, ed. Durban HS. SA(4) Isaacs to UK, Demark & Holland (not fc), Natal, Transvaal

Jarvis, Victor Edmund, b. Hampstead, London 30.9.1898, d. Stokenchurch, Bucks 30.4.1975. RHB SLA, ed. Hampstead C. of E. Sch.

Jenkinson, Cecil Victor, b. Ilford 15.5.1891, d. Pembury, Kent 6.11.1980. RHB WK

Jerman, Lindsey Crawford Stapleton, b. Old Fletton, Peterborough 23.4.1915. RHB RFM, ed. Rhyl GS. Cambridgeshire

Johnston, Arthur Sannox, b. Hornsey, Middlesex 16.3.1863, d. Eltham, London 8.8.1929. RHB RM, ed. Mill Hill. Middlesex

Jorden, Anthony Mervyn, b. Radlett, Herts 28.1.1947. RHB RFM, ed. Monmouth Sch. CU(3) MCC Schools to SA(not fc) Bedfordshire

Joy, Ronald Cecil Graham, b. Colchester 30.7.1898, d. Ditchingham, Norfolk 12.12.1974. RHB RFM, ed. Winchester. Europeans, Hyderabad, Egypt(not fc). Son-in-law of F. Penn (Kent)

Keigwin, Henry David, b. Colchester 14.5.1881, d. Thiepval, France 20.9.1916. RHB LM, ed. St. Paul's CU(not fc). Scotland. Brother of R. P. (Essex) & H. S. (London County & Rhodesia)

Keigwin, Richard Prescott, b. Colchester 8.4.1883, d. Polstead, Suffolk 26.11.1972. RHB RS, ed. Clifton CU(4) MCC(3 not fc) Free Foresters to Holland(2 not fc) Gloucestershire. Brother of H. D. (Essex) & H. S. (London County & Rhodesia)

Kenny, Charles John Michael, b. Wallington, Surrey 19.5.1929. RHB RFM, ed. Ampleforth CU(1) MCC(1 not fc) Ireland

Kent, Terence, b. Battersea, London 21.10.1939. RHB SLA, ed. Battersea County Sec. Sch.

King, Ian Metcalf, b. Leeds, Yorks 10.11.1931. LHB SLA, ed. Hanley Castle GS, Worcester. Warwickshire. Cousin of A. M. (Yorkshire)

King, Robert Jasper Stuart, b. Leigh-on-Sea 10.5.1909. RHB RLB, ed. Felsted

Knight, Barry Rolfe, b. Chesterfield, Derbyshire 18.2.1938. RHB RFM, ed. East Ham GS. Eng(29) MCC(4) Commonwealth to India, Cavaliers to WI. Leicestershire

Kortright, Charles Jesse, b. Fryerning 9.1.1871. d. South Weald 12.12.1952. RHB RF, ed. Brentwood Sch. & Tonbridge

Laker, James Charles, b. Frizinghall, Bradford, Yorks. 9.2.1922, d. Putney, London 23.4.1986. RHB ROB, ed. Salts HS, Saltaire, Yorks. Eng(46) MCC(4) Commonwealth to India, Cavaliers to WI(2) Surrey, Auckland

Lapham, Arthur William Edwards, b. 1879, d. Portsmouth, Hants. 9.2.1964. Wiltshire

Lashbrooke, Albert Edward, b. West Ham 30.11.1883, d. Oldham, Lancs. 1963.

Lavers, Alan Braden, b. Melbourne, Australia 6.9.1912. RHB RM/ROB, ed. Chigwell

Lawrence, Terence Patrick, b. Waltham Abbey 26.4.1910. RHB RLB, ed. Uppingham CU(not fc) Hertfordshire, Berkshire

Leiper, John Morton, b. Woodford Green 17.2.1921. LHB RFM occ.WK, ed. Chigwell. Father of R. J.

Leiper, Robert James, b. Woodford Green 30.8.1961. LHB RM, ed. Chigwell. English Schools to India (not fc), England Young Cricketers to WI (not fc). Son of J. M.

Lever, John Kenneth, b. Stepney, London 24.2.1949. RHB LFM, ed. Dane Sec. Mod. Sch., Ilford. Eng(21) MCC(1) Eng. Tours(4), Robins to SA(2), to Malaysia, Singapore, Hong Kong & Sri Lanka(1), SAB English XI to SA, English Counties to WI (not fc), Overseas XI to India. Natal

Levick, Deryck Cyril, b. Acton, Middlesex 27.5.1929. RHB RM/ROB, ed. Acton CHS.

Lilley, Alan William, b. Ilford 8.5.1959. RHB RM occ. WK, ed. Caterham Sec. HS, Clayhall, Ilford

Lindsey, Peter John, b. Matlock, Derbyshire 29.5.1944. RHB ROB

Littlehales, Rev. Charles Gough, b. Bulphan 20.5.1871, d. Wickham Bishops 28.8.1945. RHB WK, ed. Forest Sch. OU(not fc)

Littlewood, Jesse, b. Yorkshire 8.4.1878, d. Kidderminster, Worcs. 27.10.1942

Locks, George Melbourne, b. Leytonstone 1898, d. Redbridge 17.9.1965

Louden, George Marshall, b. Forest Gate 6.9.1885, d. Amersham, Bucks. 28.12.1972 RHB RFM

Loveday, Francis Alfred, b. Hackney, London 14.9.1892, d. North Walsham, Norfolk 18.10.1954. LHB ed. City of London Sch. Cambridgeshire

Lucas, Alfred Perry, b. Westminster 20.2.1857, d. Great Waltham 12.10.1923, RHB RM/ROB, ed. Uppingham CU(4) Eng(5) Harris to Australia. Surrey, Middlesex. Cousin of C. J., F. M. & M. P. (Sussex) & A. G. (MCC)

Luckin, Roger Alfred Geoffrey, b. Pleshey 25.11.1939. LHB ed. Felsted. Cambridgeshire

Lynch, Ronald Victor, b. Stratford 22.5.1923. RHB SLA, ed. St. Paul's

Lywood, Lewis William, b. Walthamstow 23.12.1906, d. Caterham, Surrey 31.10.1971. RHB RFM, Surrey

McEvoy, Michael Stephen Anthony, b. Jorhat, India 25.1.1956. RHB RM, ed. Colchester RGS, Borough Rd. Coll. of Education. Minor Counties to East Africa (not fc). Worcestershire, Cambridgeshire, Suffolk

McEwan, Kenneth, Scott, b. Bedford, South Africa 16.7.1952. RHB ROB WK, ed. Queen's Coll. Queenstown, S. Africa. Eastern Province, Western Province, South Africa, Western Australia

McGahey, Charles Percy, b. Hackney, Middlesex 12.12.1871, d. Whipps Cross 10.1.1935. RHB RLB. Eng(2) MacLaren to Australia. London County

McIver, Colin Donald, b. Hong Kong 23.1.1881, d. Oxford 13.5.1954. RHB RS WK, ed. Forest Sch. OU(2)

Mackinnon, Malcolm, b. Toward Point, Argyll, Scotland 11.5.1891, d. Sunningdale, Berks 13.2.1975. RHB ROB, ed. in Switzerland. OU (not fc) Europeans

Malone, Steven John, b. Chelmsford 19.10.1953. RHB RFM, ed. King's Sch., Ely. Hampshire, Glamorgan, Durham

Marston, John William, b. Rosario, Argentina 25.10.1893, d. Lambeth, London 9.7.1938. RHB RLBG, ed. Haileybury

Martin, Arthur Dalby, b. Hackney, London 1888, d. Harrow, Middlesex 1958

Martin, Eric, Gordon, b. Rock Ferry, Cheshire 4.2.1907, d. Chelsea, London 27.1.1978. RHB RM/OB/LB, ed. Birkenhead Sch.

Martyn, Oswald, b. Wandsworth, Surrey 1887, d. Patcham, Sussex 14.9.1959

Mayes, William Henry James, b. Marylebone, Middlesex 17.7.1885, d. Esher, Surrey 5.2.1946. RHB RF

Mead, Harold, b. Walthamstow 13.6.1895, d. Epping .4.1921. RHB SLA: Son of Walter

Mead, Walter, b. Clapton, Middlesex 1.4.1868, d. Chipping Ongar 18.3.1954. RHB RM/OB/LB. Eng(1) London County. Father of Harold

Melluish, Gordon Christopher, b. Walthamstow 25.8.1906, d. Bushey, Herts. 14.4.1977. RHB SLA, ed. Haberdashers' Aske's, Hampstead

Mercer, Charles Frederick, b. Hackney, London 1896, d. Brentwood 1965. LHB

Meston, Alexander Hubert, b. Leytonstone 1.6.1898, d. Camborne, Cornwall 1980. RHB ed. Kirkdale Road Sch., Leytonstone. Brother of S. P.

Meston, Samuel Paul, b. Loughton 19.11.1882, d. Vancouver, Canada 9.1.1960. RHB RM, ed. St. John's Sch., Loughton & Salway College, Leyton. Gloucestershire, Manitoba (not fc). Brother of A. H.

Milner, Joseph, b. Johannesburg, South Africa 22.8.1937. RHB ed. Athlone HS, Johannesburg

Missen, Edward Sebley, b. Cambridge 1875, d. Colchester 17.11.1927. RM. Cambridgeshire

Mitchell, George Frederick, b. West Ham .3.1897. LHB

Moore, Kenneth Francis, b. Croydon, Surrey 4.1.1940. RHB LFM

Morris, Harold Marsh, b. Wanstead 16.4.1898, d. Brighton, East Sussex 30.11.1984. RHB RM, ed. Repton CU (no Blue). Tennyson to Jamaica

Morris, Philip Edward, b. Kennington, Surrey 26.11.1877, d. Hove, Sussex 6.7.1945. RLB, ed. Mill Hill & Bancroft's. CU (not fc)

Morris, William Bancroft, b. Kingston, Jamaica 28.5.1917. RHB ROB, ed. Montreal HS. Cambridgeshire

Mortlock, Harry Clive, b. Hackney, London 13.10.1892, d. Brentwood 29.3.1963. SLA, ed. Brentwood Sch. & Felsted

Moule, Alfred Samuel, b. West Ham 31.7.1894, d. Shoreham-by-Sea, Sussex 5.2.1973. RHB. Devon

Naylor, W. WK

Nicholas, Frederick William Herbert, b. Federated Malay States 25.7.1893, d. Kensington, London 20.10.1962. RHB WK, ed. Forest Sch. OU(not fc). Joel to SA, Cahn to Jamaica and to Argentina. Bedfordshire

Nichols, Morris Stanley, b. Stondon Massey 6.10.1900, d. Newark, Notts 26.1.1961. LHB RF. Eng(14) MCC(2) Cahn to Jamaica, Tennyson to Jamaica

Nolan, Geoffrey John, b. Colchester 6.10.1937. RHB ed. Endsleigh Sch. Colchester

Norman, George, b. London 23.8.1890, d. Virginia Water, Surrey 24.11.1964. ed. Bancroft's Sch

Norman, Dr. Ralph Oliver Geoffrey, b. Southend 30.7.1911, d. Thorpe Bay 26.7.1983. RHB LM, ed. Rugby CU (not fc)

O'Connor, Jack. b. Cambridge 6.11.1897, d. Buckhurst Hill 22.2.1977. RHB RLB/OB, Eng(4) MCC(1) Tennyson to Jamaica, Cahn to Jamaica. Buckinghamshire. Son of John (Derbyshire), nephew of H. A. Carpenter

Orman, Charles Edward Linton, b. Roorkee, Inda 6.9.1859, d. Epping 11.2.1927. ed. Felsted. Bedfordshire

Owen, Hugh Glendwr Palmer, b. Bath, Somerset 19.5.1859, d. Dengie 20.10.1912. RHB RM CU (no Blue)

Palmer, Eric John, b. Romford 16.6.1931. LHB RFM, ed. Hylands Sec. Mod. Sch., Hornchurch

Palmer, Harold James, b. Epping 30.8.1890, d. Battle, Sussex 12.2.1967. RHB RFMLB ed. Loughton Sch. & London University. Incogniti to Malta (not fc)

Parslow, Leonard Frederick, b. London 11.11.1909, d. Rochford 6.8.1963. RHB ed. Central Foundation Sch., Whitechapel

Pascoe, Charles Henry, b. Shoreditch, Middlesex 1877, d. Walthamstow 26.1.1957. SLA

Paterson, Robert Fraser Troutbeck, b. Stansted 8.9.1916, d. Edinburgh, Scotland 29.5.1980. RHB RM WK, ed. Brighton College

Pawle, John Hanbury, b. Widford, Herts 18.5.1915. RHB ed. Harrow CU(2) Hertfordshire. Brother-in-law of W. A. Anderson (Free Foresters)

Pearce, Thomas Neill, b. Stoke Newington, London 3.11.1905. RHB RM, ed. Christ's Hospital. MCC(1 as Manager) Martineau to Egypt (not fc). Brother-in-law of Sir Frank Hawker

Perrin, Percival Albert, b. Hackney, Middlesex 26.5.1876, d. Hickling, Norfolk 20.11.1945. RHB RS, ed. Margate College. London County

Phelan, Patrick John, b. Chingford 9.2.1938. LHB ROB, ed. Newport GS.

Phillip, Norbert, b. Bioche, Dominica 12.6.1948. RHB RFM, ed. Dominica GS, Roseau. WI(9) WI Tours(1) Windward Islands, Combined Islands, Dominica (not fc)

Phillips, Leslie Jack, b. Leyton 20.1.1899, d. Woodford Wells 22.4.1979. RHB SLA, ed. Westminster Abbey Sch.

Pickering, Harry Gordon, b. Hackney, London 18.1.1917, d. Seaford, East Sussex 4.3.1984. RHB RS, ed. Glendale County Sch., N. London. Leicestershire

Pickett, Henry, b. Stratford 26.3.1862, d. Aberavon, Glamorgan 3.10.1907. RHB RF

Plumb, Stephen George, b. Wimbish 17.1.1954. RHB RM/ROB, ed. Elmbridge Sch., Cranleigh & Saffron Walden CHS, Writtle Agricultural Coll. MCC(1 not fc) Norfolk

Pont, Ian Leslie, b. Brentwood 28.8.1961. RHB RMF, ed. Brentwood Sch. Nottinghamshire, Natal, Buckinghamshire. Brother of K. R. (Essex) & Kelvin (Essex II)

Pont, Keith Rupert, b. Wanstead 16.1.1953. RHB RM, ed. St. Martin's Sec. Sch., Hutton. Brother of I. L. (Essex) & Kelvin (Essex II)

Pope, Dudley Fairbridge, b. Barnes, Surrey 28.10.1906, d. Writtle 8.9.1934. RHB ed. Clark's College, Ealing. Gloucestershire

Powell, Adam Gordon, b. Boxted 17.8.1912, d. Sandwich, Kent 7.6.1982, RHB WK, ed. Charterhouse CU(1) MCC(1 + 2 not fc), Martineau to Egypt(3 not fc) Suffolk

Preece, Henry Charles, b. Weobley, Herefordshire 27.10.1867, d. Highgate, London 17.9.1937. ed. Hereford County College. Cheshire

Presland, Edward Robert, b. High Beach 27.3.1943. RHB RM/ROB, ed. Thomas Lethaby Sec. Mod. Sch., East Ham

Preston, Kenneth Charles, b. Goodmayes 22.8.1925. RHB RFM, ed. Romford Intermediate Sch.

Price, Eric James, b. Middleton, Lancs. 27.10.1918. LHB SLA, ed. St. Leonard's C.ofE. Sch., Middleton. Lancashire

Prichard, Paul John, b. Billericay 7.1.1965. RHB. ed. Brentwood CHS

Pringle, Derek Raymond, b. Nairobi, Kenya 18.9.1958. RHB RFM, ed. St. Mary's Sch., Nairobi & Felsted CU(3) Eng(14) Eng. Tours(1), "B" Tours(1), English Schs. to India (not fc), Eng. Tour (1 not fc). Son of D. J. (Kenya & East Africa)

Pritchard, Graham Charles, b. Farnborough, Hants. 14.1.1942. RHB RFM, ed. King's Sch., Canterbury. CU(1)

Proffitt, Stanley, b. Oldham, Lancs. 8.10.1910. LHB SLA

Puddefoot, Sydney Charles, b. Limehouse, London 17.10.1894, d. Rochford 2.10.1972 RHB LM, ed. Park Sch., West Ham

Pullinger, George Richard, b. Islington, London 14.3.1920, d. 4.8.1982. RHB RFM, ed. Chadwell St. Mary Sch.

Purves, James Hamilton, b. Hemel Hempstead, Herts 4.12.1937. LHB RM, ed. Uppingham

Quick, Arnold Bertram, b. Clacton-on-Sea 10.2.1915. RHB, ed. Bungay Sch. MCC(1 not fc). Suffolk

Quin, Stanley Edgar Vivian, b. Bishops Glen, Orange Free State, S. Africa 3.4.1896, d. Bishops Glen, Orange Free State, S. Africa 9.4.1970. RHB RM/ROB, Orange Free State

Raison, Max, b. Wanstead 7.11.1901. RHB RM, ed. Forest Sch. Son of C. (Essex II)

Ralph, Louis Henry Roy, b. East Ham 22.5.1920. RHB RM, ed. Clark's College, Ilford

Read, Arnold Holcombe, b. Snaresbrook 24.1.1880, d. Englefield Green, Surrey 20.5.1957. RHB RSM, ed. Winchester. Father of H. D. Nephew of J. J.

Read, Holcombe Douglas, b. Woodford Green 28.1.1910. RHB RF, ed, Winchester. Eng(1) MCC(1), Martineau to Egypt (not fc), Free Foresters to Holland (not fc), Surrey. Son of A. H.

Reese, Daniel, b. Christchurch, New Zealand 26.1.1879, d. Christchurch, New Zealand 12.6.1953. LHB LM/SLA, ed. Christchurch, NZ. NZ Tours(2), Canterbury, New Zealand, London County. Brother of T. W. (Canterbury). President of NZ Cricket Council 1929-31 & 1935-36

Reeves, William, b. Cambridge 22.6.1875, d. Hammersmith, London 22.3.1944. RHB RM/ROB, Son-in-law of E. C. Freeman

Richards, Robert John, b. Winchester, Hants. 5.6.1934. RHB WK, ed. Craylands Sch., Basildon

Richardson, Charles Stewart, b. Terling 23.3.1885, d. Great Totham 5.4.1948. LHB SLA, ed. King Edward VI Sch., Chelmsford

Richardson, James Vere, b. Heswall, Cheshire 16.12.1903. RHB RM, ed. Uppingham OU(1)

Richardson, Percy John, b. West Ham 2.4.1891, d. Reigate, Surrey 23.3.1964. ed. Clifton CU (no Blue)

Rickards, Kenneth Roy, b. Rollington Town, Kingston, Jamaica 22.8.1923. RHB RLB. WI(2), WI Tours(2), Jamaica

Riding, Henry Wadsworth, b. Epping 19.9.1899, d. Chingford 21.5.1923. ed. Bancroft's Sch.

Ridley, Gerald Vernon Newport, b. Felsted 23.10.1897, d. Chignall St. James 12.11.1953. RHB RM, ed. Marlborough

Rist, Frank Henry, b. Wandsworth, London 30.3.1914. RHB RM WK, ed. Farmer Rd. Sch., Leyton

Robinson, Douglas Charles, b. Bristol 20.4.1884, d. Charlton Kings, Gloucs. 30.7.1963. RHB WK, ed. Marlborough. MCC(1—did not play through illness), Tennyson to Jamaica (no fc matches) Gloucestershire. Son of A. (Gloucs.), Brother of V. J. (Gloucs.)

Robinson, Ralf Hubert, b. West Ham 1885, d. Westhoek Ridge, Ypres, Belgium 23.8.1917. WK

Round, Charles James, b. Kensington 3.9.1885, d. Birch 6.10.1945. ed. Eton & Winchester. Free Foresters to Holland (3—not fc). Son of James Round

Rowe, Francis Erskine, b. Hartford End 30.11.1864, d. Littlehampton, Sussex 17.5.1928. RHB WK ed. Marlborough CU (not fc). Berkshire. Son of A. W. (Cambridge University)

Rowley, Sir George William, b. Brabourne, Kent 10.5.1896, d. Newlyn, Cornwall 8.8.1953. RHB. ed. Repton & RMC Sandhurst. Central Provinces & Berar

Russell, Alfred Edward, b. Lewisham, Kent 9.1.1875, d. Whipps Cross 8.9.1940. LHB WK Brother of T. M. Uncle of C. A. G.

Russell, Charles Albert George, b. Leyton 7.10.1887, d. Whipps Cross 23.3.1961. RHB RSM, ed. National Sch., High Rd., Leyton. Eng(10) MCC(2) Joel to SA. Son of T. M. Nephew of A. E.

Russell, Thomas Marychurch, b. Lewisham, Kent 6.7.1868, d. Leyton 28.2.1927. RHB RF WK. Father of C. A. G. Brother of A. E.

Sadiq Mohammad, b. Junagadh, India 5.5.1945. LHB RLBG, ed. Marie Colaco HS, Karachi & S. M. College, Karachi. Pakistan(41) Pakistan Tours(7), PIA Eaglets to Great Britain, PIA to Aden & East Africa, Gloucestershire to Zambia (not fc) International XI to WI (not fc), Karachi, PIA, United Bank, Gloucestershire, Cornwell, Tasmania. Brother of Hanif, Mustaq and Wazir (Pakistan) & Raees (Karachi), Uncle of Shoaib (Pakistan) & Shahid and Asif (PIA)

Sainsbury, Gary Edward, b. Wanstead 17.1.1958. RHB LFM, ed. Beal HS., Ilford, Bath University. Gloucestershire

Saint, Norman Hunt, b. Tollington Park, Islington, London 22.4.1901. d. Whitechapel, London 15.8.1930. RHB LM, ed. Merchant Taylors Sch. RMA, Woolwich. MCC(1 not fc)

Savill, Leslie Austin, b. Brentwood 30.6.1935. RHB. ed. Norlington Rd. Sec. Mod. Sch., Leyton. Devon

Saville, Graham John, b. Leytonstone 5.2.1944. RHB RLBG, ed. Sir George Monoux GS, Walthamstow. Norfolk. Second cousin of G. A. Gooch

Sayers, Denis. b. St. Pancras, London 17.3.1934. RHB RM, ed. Haverstock Hill GS.

Scoulding, Frederick John, b. Bow, Middlesex 1887, d. Whitechapel, London, 25.8.1928. SLA. Monmouthshire

Searle, Cyril John, b. Battersea, London 12.5.1921. RHB WK

Sears, Leslie Daniel, b. Wokingham, Berks. 12.1.1901. LHB. Berkshire

Semmence, Derek John, b. Worthing, Sussex 20.4.1938. RHB RM, ed. Shoreham GS. Sussex, Devon Northumberland, Cambridgeshire

Sewell, Edward Humphrey Dalrymple, b. Lingsugur, India 30.9.1872, d. Paddington, London 20.9.1947. RHB RM, ed. Bedford GS. India, Madras including Madras to Ceylon (not fc), London County, Bedfordshire, Buckinghamshire

Sharp, Robert Henry, b. Doncaster, Yorks 11.6.1893, d. Bradford-on-Avon, Wilts. 15.3.1961. RHB RFM, ed. Retford Sch. & Wye College

Sheffield, James Roy, b. Barking 19.11.1906. RHB WK, ed. Coopers Co. Sch., Bow. Wellington

Sherman, Howard Richard, b. Seven Kings 15.6.1943. RHB ROB, ed. Chigwell

Shorter, Richard Nicholas, b. Loughton 26.7.1906, d. Drogheda, Co. Meath, Ireland 20.1.1984. LHB RM, ed. Repton

Skinner, Ivor John, b. Walthamstow 1.4.1928. RHB RFM, ed. William Morris Sch., Walthamstow. Cornwall

Smith, Geoffrey John, b. Braintree 2.4.1935. RHB ROB, ed. Braintree CHS. Hertfordshire

Smith, George William Oswald, b. Halstead 7.3.1906. RHB WK, ed. Bishops Stortford Coll. CU (not fc) Suffolk

Smith, Harry Thomas Oliver, b. Warley 5.3.1906. RHB RFM

Smith, Harry William, b. Mile End, London 6.9.1890. RHB RFM

Smith, Neil, b. Dewsbury, Yorks. 1.4.1949. RHB WK, ed. Ossett GS. Yorkshire

Smith, Raymond, b. Boreham 10.8.1914. RHB RFM/ROB, ed. King Edward VI Sch., Chelmsford. Commonwealth to India, Pakistan & Ceylon. Cousin of T. P. B.

Smith, Thomas Peter Bromley, b. Ipswich, Suffolk 30.10.1908, d. Hyeres, France 4.8.1967. RHB RLBG, ed. Highfield College, Leigh-on-Sea; King Edward VI Sch., Chelmsford. Eng(4) MCC(1), Tennyson to India, Cahn to NZ. Cousin of Raymond

Spencer, Walter Gordon, b. Chingford 2.8.1912, d. Chelmsford 20.7.1971. RHB SLA, ed. Bancroft's Sch. Suffolk

Spicer, Peter Alfred, b. Ilford 11.5.1939, d. Hainault 18.8.1969. LHB SLA, ed. Fairlop Sec. Sch., Ilford

Spinks, Edwin Frederick, b. 3.8.1902, d. Orsett 19.10.1982

Spurr, Harold, b. Leytonstone 17.6.1889, d. Dunmow 21.12.1962. RHB. ed. Merchant Taylors' Sch.

Stanley, Ernest Arthur William, b. Leyton 27.9.1926. RHB ROB.

Stanyard, Anthony Roy, b. Plaistow 5.4.1938. RHB RM

Stead, Barry, b. Leeds, Yorkshire 21.6.1939, d. Drighlington, Yorks. 15.4.1980. LHB LFM, ed. Greenlane Sec. Mod. Sch., Leeds. Yorkshire, Nottinghamshire, Northern Transvaal. (Selected for Essex for a match in 1962 but failed to appear)

Stephenson, John Patrick, b. Stebbing 14.3.1965. RHB RM, ed. Felsted & Durham University. English Schs. C.A. Under -19 to Zimbabwe (not fc). Brother of G. C. (Essex II)

Stephenson, John William Arthur, b. Hong Kong 1.8.1907, d. Pulborough, West Sessex 20.5.1982. RHB RFM, ed. Clayesmore Sch. & RMC, Sandhurst. Victory Tests(1). Europeans. Madras, Worcestershire, Buckinghamshire

Steward, Exley Anthony Whitefoord, b. Durban, South Africa 27.6.1941. RHB RLB occ. WK, ed. Stanger HS & Maritzburg College, S. Africa. Natal "B"

Street, Frank, b. London 31.5.1870, d. Ovilliers la Boiselle, France 7.7.1916. RHB RM, ed. Westminster Sch. OU (not fc)

Strutton, Benjamin Thomas, b. 1892, d. Southwark, London 9.2.1968. SLA

Sutton, George

Swann, Charles Frederick, b. West Ham 1883, d. Leytonstone 7.3.1960. RHB ed. Bedford GS.

Swyer, Basil James, b. West Ham 6.6.1898, d. Nottingham 7.7.1964. RM. ed. Bancroft's Sch.

Taylor, Alfred George, b. West Ham 29.12.1891

Taylor, Brian, b. West Ham 19.6.1932. LHB WK, ed. Central Park Sch., East Ham. MCC (2—1 not fc)

Taylor, John Frederick, b. West Ham 9.6.1937. RHB WK

Taylor, Reginald Minshall, b. Southend 30.11.1909, d. Johannesburg, S. Africa .1.1984. RHB SLC, ed. Southend HS

Tedder, Ernest Cranfield, b. Woodford Green 5.9.1915, d. Ispwich, Suffolk 9.9.1972. RHB. ed. Chigwell

Thompson, Eddie Clarke, b. Leyton 27.2.1907. d. Torquay, Devon 18.3.1982. LHB SLA

Thorn, Hubert Wethered, b. Tiptree 21.4.1909, d. Colchester 20.5.1982. RHB. ed. Chichester

Toone, Percy, b. Ealing, Middlesex 1883, d. Colchester 1955. RHB RF

Topley, Thomas Donald, b. Canterbury Kent 25.2.1964. RHB RFM, ed. Royal Hospital Sch., Holbrook, Suffolk. Surrey, Norfolk. Brother of P. A. (Kent)

Tosetti, Gilbert, b. Bromley, Kent 1.8.1879, d. Eldoret, Kenya 16.4.1923. RHB RM, ed. Bancroft's Sch. Brother of D. (Essex II)

Toulmin, Evelyn Murrough O'Brien, b. Hatfield Peverel 13.8.1877, d. Paris, France 7.1.1945. LHB RSM, ed. King's Sch., Canterbury OU (not fc) Argentina

Townsend, Arthur Fenton Miles, b. Clifton, Gloucs. 1.8.1885, d. Chelsea, London 1948. RHB ed. Blair Lodge Sch. Gloucestershire. Son of F. (Gloucs.), Brother of C. L. & F. N. (Gloucs.), Uncle of D. C. H. & P. N. (Oxford Un.), Great-uncle of J. R. A. (Oxford Un.)

Treglown, Claude Jesse Helby, b. Herne Bay, Kent 13.2.1893, d. Worthing, West Sussex 7.5.1980. RHB. ed. Norwich GS CU (not fc) Norfolk

Tremlin, Bert, b. Bristol, Gloucs. 18.9.1877, d. 12.4.1936. RHB RM

Trick, Stanley Arthur, b. Stoke Newington, Middlesex 13.6.1884, d. Worcester Park, Surrey 11.2.1958. RHB RM, ed. Merchant Taylors' Sch.

Turner, Arthur Jervois, b. Mussorie, India 10.7.1878, d. Graffham, Sussex, 8.9.1952. RHB RM WK. ed. Bedford Modern Sch. & RMA, Woolwich. Bedfordshire, Egypt (not fc) Brother of W. M. F.

Turner, Stuart, b. Chester 18.7.1943. RHB RFM, ed. St. John's C. of E. Sec. Mod. Sch., Epping. Robins to SA, Robins to WI (not fc). Natal

Turner, Walter Martin FitzHerbert, b. Meerut, India 4.4.1881, d. Harrow, Middlesex 1.2.1948. RHB RM, ed. Wellington. Europeans. Brother of A. J.

Turrall, Percy Wakeford, b. Billericay .6.1883, d. Chelmsford 17.5.1941

Unwin, Ernest James, b. Birdbrook 18.9.1912. RHB RFM, ed. Haileybury & RMC, Sandhurst. Suffolk. Brother of F. St. G.

Unwin, Frederick St. George, b. Halstead 23.4.1911. RHB RM, ed. Haileybury & Wye College. Cambridge University Vandals to N. America (not fc), Martineau to Egypt (not fc) Suffolk. Brother of E. J.

Valiant, James, b. West Derby, Liverpool, Lancs. 1884. d. Gaza, Palestine 28.10.1917

Van Straubenzee, Henry Hamilton, b. Johannesburg, South Africa 7.3.1914. RHB SLA, ed. Winchester

Vere Hodge, Dr. Nicholas, b. Woodford Green 31.10.1912. RHB WK, ed. Uppingham CU (not fc). Martineau to Egypt (not fc)

Vigar, Frank Henry, b. Bruton, Somerset 14.7.1917. RHB RLBG, ed. Clacton-on-Sea Sec. Sch.

Waddington, John Ernest Walter, b. Woodford Green 22.5.1910. RHB SLC, ed. Chigwell CU (not fc)

Wade, Thomas Henry, b. Maldon 24.11.1910. LHB ROB WK, ed. Maldon GS. MCC (1—co-opted)

Wagstaff, Hugh, b. Romford 15.10.1895, d. Hornchurch 2.3.1970. RM

Wallace, Kenneth William, b. Romford 27.8.1936. RHB RM, ed. St. Edward's C. of E. Sch., Romford

Ward, Brian, b. Chelmsford 28.2.1944. RHB RM, ed. Moulsham Sch. & Chelmsford Tech. HS. Argentina (not fc)

Ward, Geoffrey Hubert, b. Rainham, Kent 22.11.1926. RHB WK, ed. King's Sch., Rochester; Sutton Valence Sch. Kent

Warsop, Brian b. Willesden, Middlesex 12.1.1904. RHB LM/SLA. Grandson of B. Warsop (Notts.)

Waterman, Alfred George, b. Walthamstow 13.5.1911. RHB RFM, ed. Bancroft's Sch.

Watkins, David, b. St. Albans, Herts. 18.8.1928. RHB RM, ed. Westcliff HS.

Watson, Arthur Campbell, b. Reigate, Surrey 17.3.1884, d. Shermanbury, Sussex 16.1.1952. RHB RF, ed. Uppingham. Sussex, Norfolk

Watts, Charles John Manning, b. Northampton 30.9.1905. RHB WK, ed. Repton; RMC, Sandhurst. Suffolk

Waugh, Hubert Percy, b. West Ham 24.12.1898, d. Dollis Hill, Middlesex 13.12.1954. RHB RM, ed. Forest Sch. Suffolk

West, Gordon Harry Sinclair, b. Upton Park 7.8.1923. RHB. ed. Southend HS

West, Leslie Harold, b. Leytonstone 24.1.1905, d. 12.11.1982. RHB ROB, ed. East Ham Sec. Sch.

Whitcombe, Henry Maurice, b. Hardwick, Bucks. 15.8.1900, d. Ware, Herts. 2.4.1984. RHB LFM, ed. Haileybury; RMA, Woolwich. Brother of P. S. Uncle of P. A. (Middlesex)

Whitcombe, Philip Sidney, b. Windsor, Berks 3.10.1893. RHB RFM, ed. Winchester. Europeans, Berkshire. Brother of H. M. Father of P. A. (Middlesex)

Wilcox, Denys Robert, b. Westcliff 4.6.1910, d. Westcliff 6.2.1953. RHB ROB, ed. Dulwich CU (3) Martineau to Egypt (5 not fc). Father of J. W. T.

Wilcox, John Warren Theodore, b. Newton Abbot, Devon 16.8.1940. RHB ROB, ed. Malvern CU (no Blue). Son of D. R.

Williams, Charles Cuthbert Powell (created Life Peer taking title of Baron Williams of Elvel of Llansantffraed in Elvel in the County of Powys, 1985), b. Oxford 9.2.1933. RHB. ed. Westminster Sch. OU(3). Oxfordshire

Williams, Herbert Reginald Hewett, b. Hendon, Middlesex 7.6.1900, d. Demark Hill, London 17.7.1974. RHB WK, ed. Charterhouse. Brazil to Argentina & Uruguay (not fc)

Womersley, Aleck Dale, b. 27.7.1889, d. Brentwood 11.4.1959. ed. Marlborough OU (not fc). Son of Dale (Essex), Brother of L. D. (Essex II)

Wright, Albert Edward, b. Great Leighs 11.8.1902. RHB RM, ed. Earls Colne GS. Brother of C. N. (Essex II)

Wright, John Vaughan, b. Colchester 31.12.1935. RHB. ed. Colchester RGS

Wrightson, Roger Wilfred, b. Elsecar, Yorks. 29.10.1939. LHB WK, ed. Palmer's Sch., Grays Thurrock; Loughborough College. Cumberland

Wykes, Norman Gordon, b. West Ham 19.3.1906. LHB. ed. Oundle. CU(1) MCC (4 not fc)

Young, Harding Isaac, b. Leyton 5.2.1876, d. Rochford 12.12.1964. RHB LM Eng(2) MCC(1)

CRICKETERS WHO APPEARED IN COUNTY MATCHES (i.e. AGAINST OTHER COUNTIES, M.C.C. OR TOURING TEAMS) FOR ESSEX 1876 to 1893

Extent of Career in these matches is shewn in brackets after the player's name. Full details of players marked with an (*) are given in the First Class list.

Abdy, Anthony John (1876) b. 26.4.1856, d. La-Tour-de-Peilz, Switzerland 4.7.1924. RHB ed. Charterhouse. Hampshire.

Abdy, Neville James (1877) b. Great Baddow 16.10.1857, d. Great Baddow 20.4.1878. ed. Charterhouse

Allport, Robert Leete (1882) b. Lambeth, Surrey 1848, d. London 1931.

Almond, Frederick Clarence (1883-89) b. Great Bentley 7.10.1855, d. Enfield, Middlesex 3.5.1910. RHB RS

*Arkwright, Harold Arthur (1893-95)

Bagot, Harry Richard Reginald (1880-84) b. Ashby-de-la-Zouch, Leicestershire 15.8.1860, d. Tewkesbury, Gloucs. 17.7.1908. ed. Radley. Staffordshire

Bailey, H. B. (1881)

Baines, William Norman (1882) b. Oakham, Rutland 1859, d. Rochford 1919

Baker, A. (1876)

Ballard, John (1876-80) b. Burnham-on-Crouch 28.4.1840, d. Chelmsford 22.5.1898. RHB WK

Barnes, A. H. (1886)

Barnes, Ernest Pemberton (1878-82) b. Romford 12.2.1855, d. Battle, Sussex 29.9.1920. ed. Brighton College

Barnes, P. P. (1881) b. Havering 16.4.1858, ed. Brighton College

Barnes, William Herbert Pemberton (1876-83) b. 1852, d. Williton, Somerset 1.2.1916. ed. Brighton College

Bastard, Segar Richard (1881-85) b. 1853, d. Epsom, Surrey, 20.3.1921

Bastow, John (1886-89) b. Bromley-by-Bow, Middlesex 30.10.1850, d. Haverstock Hill, Middlesex 1.6.1927. RHB WK. Middlesex. Grandfather of Sir F. C. Hawker

Bedford, C. S. (1880-81)

Bevington, John Currey (1891-93) b. Sydenham, Kent 6.4.1872, d. Chelmsford 4.4.1933. RHB. ed. Harrow CU (not fc). Middlesex. Brother of T. A. D. (Middlesex)

Bird, Eustace Edgar Godfrey (1876) b. 10.11.1848, d. Barrie Sinico, Ontario, Canada 31.10.1938. ed. Marlborough

Bishop, Arthur Theodore (1885-88) b. West Ham 2.9.1863, d. St. John's Wood, London 8.9.1931. RHB. Middlesex. Brother of F. A.

Bishop, Francis Augustus (1885-91) b. Wanstead 11.6.1862, d. Hendon, Middlesex 1942. RHB RF. Brother of A. T.

Blows, John J. (1882)

Boardman, William (1876) b. 1843, d. Ingatestone 1929.

*Borradaile, Oswell Robert (1891-94)

Borrowes, Sir Kildare Dixon, 10th Bart. (1878) b. Exeter, Devon 21.9.1852, d. Wateringbury, Kent 19.10.1924. RHB WK, ed. Cheltenham. Middlesex

Boyton, Henry (1887-91) b. Hornsey, Middlesex 27.9.1860, d. Crouch End, Middlesex 11.9.1909. RHB. ed. Tollington Sch., Islington

Bray, James (1887) b. Limehouse, Middlesex 18.1.1853, d. St. Pancras, London 30.8.1898. RHB RM. Kent

Brewster, Charles Edward (1876) b. Halstead 21.7.1849, ed. Rugby

Bruen, Henry (1882) b. Ireland 26.7.1856, d. Oak Park, Co. Carlow, Ireland 26.12.1927. RHB RS, ed. Harrow; RMA, Woolwich, Sanders to North America. Son of Sir Henry Bruen (Ireland)

Bryan, William (1887-88) b. Kimberley, Notts 22.9.1856, d. Cambridge 22.5.1933. RHB RM Cambridgeshire

Bullock, W. H. (1876-79). WK

Burghes, Arthur (1876-80) b. London 8.9.1848, d. Poplar, London 1916. RHB RRM. Middlesex, Surrey

*Burns, James (1887-96)

*Burrell, Rev. Herbert John Edwin (1888-95)

Buxton, Cyril Digby (1883-91) b. Woodford 25.6.1865, d. Woodford 10.5.1892. RHB RM, ed. Harrow CU(4). Son of E. N. (Essex)

Calvert, H. (1880)

Candler, George Herbert (1878) b. Tendring 1850, d. Tottenham, Middlesex 24.5.1929.

Capel-Cure, Arthur (1879-83) b. 14.3.1856, d. Aberdeen, Scotland 13.10.1898. Brother of F. Uncle of G. N.

Capel-Cure, Francis (1878) b. London 3.12.1854, d. Wolverhampton, Staffs. 17.10.1933. RHB. ed. Bradfield. Brother of A. Uncle of G. N.

*Carpenter, Herbert Arthur (1888-1920)

Chute, Rev. Theophilus Dacre (1881) b. 10.6.1852, d. Great Moulton, Norfolk 15.6.1926. ed. Eton. OU (not fc)

Cole, A. (1880) Middlesex

Collin, Spencer Compton (1881) b. Saffron Walden 1.8.1852, d. Brighton, Sussex 25.11.1923. ed. Winchester. CU (not fc)

Copland, Edmund (1880-82) b. Chelmsford 1860, d. West Mersea 12.9.1918. RHB ed. Felsted

Cornell, K. (1878)

Cotton, Rev. Edward Bathurst (1879-83) b. 1858, d. Crondall, Hants. 14.7.1919. ed. Chatham House Sch., Ramsgate; CU (not fc)

Curtis, Benjamin Collup (1883-84) b. 1859, d. Bexley Heath, Kent. 31.12.1898

Cutts, Thomas (1889-93) b. Hyson Green, Notts. 14.1.1865. RHB LM

Davey, Darnton Charles (1879) b. Mansfield, Notts. 7.7.1856, d. Durban, South Africa 7.10.1911. ed. Colchester. SA to Great Britain (not fc), Natal

Davies, R. O. (1886)

Despard, Rev. Arthur Vandeleur (1887) b. Hampstead, Middlesex 11.12.1861, d. Oyama, British Columbia, Canada 22.8.1947. ed. Merchant Taylors, Sch.

Dixon, John (1878) b. Danbury 1858. ed. Felsted

Dowsett, L. (1877) b. 1839, d. 1908

Druce, G. (1888-92)

Du Cane, Sir John Phillip (1882) b. 5.5.1865, d. London 5.4.1947. RHB ed. Wellington: Bombay

Earle, Rev. Charles (1877) b. Brentwood 1856, d. Littlehampton, Sussex 15.12.1919

Earle, Joseph Herbert (1876-81) b. Brentwood 8.3.1854, d. Baroda, India 14.8.1882.

Earps, Thomas (1877-80) b. Fenny Drayton Leicestershire 3.5.1854, d. Bournemouth, Hants. 29.4.1881

Earps, William Edward (1878-79) b. Fenny Drayton, Leicestershire 2.10.1859, d. Liverpool, Lancs. 11.5.1917

East, A. J. (1887-89) WK

Emson, Frederick (1881) b. 1850, d. Billericay 1916

Escott, Charles Hay Sweet (1876-80) b. London 27.5.1846, d. Brentwood 11.8.1920

Everett, W. (1881)

Fane, Frederick John (1876-79) b. 30.1.1840, d. Brentwood 4.6.1923. Ireland, Father of F. L.

Forbes, Eustace MacLeod (1890) b. Basildon 21.11.1862, d. Matabeleland, South Africa 11.2.1894. ed. Repton CU (not fc) Oxfordshire

Fortescue, Rev. Arthur Trosse (1882) b. Totnes, Devon 7.4.1848, d. Marylebone, London 21.11.1899, RHB WK, ed. Marlborough OU(3). Sanders to North America. Devon, Warwickshire (not fc). Lincolnshire

Fowler, Gerald (1884-89) b. Leytonstone 27.7.1866, d. Trull, Somerset 24.5.1916. RHB RFM ed. Clifton OU(1). Somerset. Brother of H. & W. H.

Fowler, Howard (1879-89) b. Tottenham, Middlesex 20.10.1857, d. Burnham-on-Sea, Somerset 6.5.1934. RHB WK, ed. Clifton. OU(3) Somerset. Brother of G. & W. H.

Fowler, William Herbert (1877) b. Tottenham, Middlesex 28.5.1856, d. Chelsea, London 13.4.1941. RHB RF WK, ed. Rottingdean & Grove House, Tottenham. Somerset. Brother of G. & H.

Francis, Francis Philip (1883-92) b. Upminster 15.9.1852, d. Claygate, Surrey 18.1.1926. WK. Middlesex

Francis, H. H. (1885)

Francis, Dr. William (1881-92) b. Little Waltham 21.3.1856, d. Forest Gate 28.4.1917. RHB. Sussex

*Freeman, Edward Charles (1887-96)

Gardiner, W. S. (1877)

George, Joseph (1878-81) b. Northants. 1853, d. Sudbury, Suffolk 7.12.1901. WK
Gepp, Hubert Majendie (1881) b. 1859, d. Sweden 13.12.1892. ed. Felsted
Giller, William John (1881) b. Stepney, Middlesex 1851, d. London 27.3.1906
Gillespie, W. (1881)
Godden, Vivian (1883) b. 1852, d. Cheltenham, Gloucs 26.9.1908
Gosling, George Bennett (1891) b. Farnham, Essex 26.8.1872, d. Central Africa 13.6.1906. RHB WK, ed. Eton; RMC, Sandhurst. Peshawar & District. Brother of R. C. Uncle of C. H.
*Gosling, Robert Cunliffe (1888-96)
Gouldstone, William (1879-82) b. 1843, d. West Ham 1924
Gray, F. (1876-77)
Green, Charles Ernest (1882-91) b. Walthamstow 26.8.1846, d. Epping 4.12.1916. RHB RRF, ed. Uppingham CU(4) Middlesex, Sussex, Herefordshire. President of MCC 1905. Great-uncle of R. M. N. (Essex II)
Grey, Robert Elton (1881) b. 17.3.1848, d. Weymouth, Dorset 22.7.1914
Grimston, Walter Edward (1876-82) b. Pebmarsh 16.5.1844, d. Earls Colne 28.7.1932. RHB WK, ed. Harrow. Southgate, Suffolk, Hertfordshire. Son of Hon. E. H. (OU), Nephew of 2nd Earl of Verulam (Gentlemen), Hon. F. S. (CU) & Hon. Robert (Middlesex)
Grout, Herbert (1876) b. 1856, d. Dunmow 25.9.1896
Growse, Edward Frederic (1880-81) b. Brentwood 8.7.1860, d. Red Sea 10.11.1905. ed. Charterhouse
Growse, Robert (1876-80) b. Brentwood 1853, d. Hereford 1.6.1908

*Hailey, Henry (1891-95)
Handley, Thomas (1882) b. Stratford 2.1.1834, d. West Ham 10.8.1887. RHB WK
Hayhurst-France, George Henry Hayhurst (1883) b. 1856, d. Llanfyllin, Montgomeryshire, Wales 2.3.1897. ed. Haileybury. Shropshire
Henry, R. B. (1879)
Hills, Henry Francis (1881-82) b. Braintree 1839, d. White Colne 24.3.1930
Hitchcock, Charles (1882) b. Bussage, Gloucs. 4.12.1860, d. San Rafael, California, USA 18.4.1933. RHB WK, ed. Marlborough
Hossack, Anthony Henry (1891) b. Walsall, Staffs. 2.5.1867, d. Torquay, Devon 24.1.1925. ed. Chigwell CU (no blue)
Howard, W. (1876-81)

Ind, Arthur Edward Burrell (1878-81) b. Cambridge 1855, d.

Jackson, A. H. (1889)
*Johnston, Arthur Sannox (1889-96)
Jones, John (1884-89) b. Birmingham 18.9.1858, d, Chalfont St. Giles, Bucks. 18.9.1937 RHB RM
Judd, Francis Savile Henry (1881) b. London 6.9.1855, d. Drayton Green, Middlesex 12.5.1933. ed. Eton

Kelley, W. (1892)
Kirkman, Henry (1883-84) b. Prescot, Lancs. 1862, d. Romford 23.1.1921
*Kortright, Charles Jesse (1889-1907 fc; one non-fc 1911)

Lacey, Charles John (1881) b. Chipping Ongar 1854, d. Chipping Ongar 1912
Lang, Godfrey George (1892) b. 24.4.1867, d. Reigate, Surrey 29.7.1923. ed. Clifton. All India XI, Oudh
Law, A. (1884-90)
Leaf, Henry Meredith (1887-88) b. Scarborough, Yorks. 18.10.1862, d. Westminster, London 23.4.1931. RHB ROB, ed. Clifton & Marlborough CU (not fc). Wiltshire
Littlewood, George William (1887-92) b. Holmfirth, Yorks 10.5.1857, d. Oldham, Lancs. 5.3.1928. RHB WK. Lancashire. Father of G. H. (Lancs.)
Lowe, (1880)
*Lucas, Alfred Perry (1889-1907)

McEwen, George (1884-87) b. 1852, d. Rochford 1926. WK
*McGahey, Charles Percy (1893-1921)
Mack, Rev. Edgar, Shepheard Paston (1883) b. Tunstead, Norfolk 8.1861, d. Swanmore, Hants 15.3.1944. RHB RF, ed. Bradfield. Norfolk, Suffolk.

Marten, William George (1876-78) b. Tunbridge Wells, Kent 5.9.1845, d. Stoke Newington, London 25.11.1907. RHB RRF. Kent, Surrey

Masterman, C. E. (1882)

*Mead, Walter (1890-1913)

Meares, George Brooke (1876-77) b. Glandovey Castle, Cardiganshire, Wales 26.10.1841, d. Hounslow, Middlesex 21.8.1894. RHB. ed. Bedford GS. Hampshire (not fc)

Merewether, Charles George (1876-82) b. 28.10.1849, d. Ingatestone 28.1.1902. ed. Rugby.

Morgan, T. (1880)

Moseley, James R. (1888) b. 1863, d. Colchester 1949

Myers, T. (1886) WK

Nicholas, A. (1876). Brother of T. O.

Nicholas, Thomas Offin (1876-79) b. Billericay 1844, d. Billericay 22.6.1892. Brother of A.

*Owen, Hugh Glendwr Palmer (1880-1902)

Palmer, Edward Charles (1882) b. Old Ford, Middlesex 29.2.1860, d. Woodford Green 21.8.1931. RHB RS, ed. Chigwell

Pearce, Sir William (1877-81) b. Poplar, Middlesex 18.3.1853, d. Walmer, Kent 24.8.1932. RHB RM. Kent

Perkins, Thomas Tosswill Norwood (1889) b. Strood, Kent 19.12.1870, d. Tonbridge, Kent 26.7.1946. RHB RF, ed. St. John's, Leatherhead CU(2). Kent, Hertfordshire, Wiltshire

Phillips, Francis Ashley (1892) b. Crumlin, Monmouthshire 11.4.1873, d. Holmer, Herefordshire 5.3.1955. RHB RM, ed. Rossall OU(3). Mitchell to North America. Somerset, Monmouthshire, Brecon

*Pickett, Henry (1881-97)

Pryor, Roderick (1877-80) b. Wandsworth, Surrey 1.3.1855, d. Weston, Herts 26.7.1930. WK

Rammell, Arthur William (1893) b. Blean, Kent 21.9.1868, d. Eastbourne, Sussex 10.3.1956

Rankin, Edgar Napier (1892) b. Rochford 26.4.1868, d. S. Africa 1962. ed. Unviersity College Sch.

Read, Ernest Arnold (1882-85) b. London 12.5.1854, d. Amersham, Bucks. 15.9.1936

Read, John Jervis (1882-91) b. Walthamstow 22.6.1858, d. Windsor, Berks. 3.4.1931. RHB. ed. Malvern. Uncle of A. H. Great-uncle of H. D

Regan, Charles (1884) b. Barnsley, Yorks. 11.5.1842, d. Southend 17.5.1921. RHB WK, ed. Hammersmith College. Derbyshire

Reid, Cecil Frederick (1876-80) b. 3.3.1842, d. Honiton, Devon 23.8.1898. ed. Harrow. Hampshire, Hertfordshire

Ridley, Charles Ernest (1876-82) b. Chelmsford 23.4.1847, d. Chelmsford 12.9.1936. WK, ed. Uppingham. Northumberland

Roberts, C. J. (1877-84)

Rodwell, William Hunter (1878-83) b. London 18.4.1850, d. Amersham, Bucks. 3.8.1929. ed. Harrow. Suffolk

Round, F. R. (1876)

Round, Rt. Hon. James (1876-80) b. Colchester 6.4.1842, d. Birch 24.12.1916. RHB RSLobs WK, ed. Eton OU (no Blue). Father of C. J. Father-in-law of C. E. Higginbotham (Army)

Rowan, Henry Bailey (1878-79) b. Omagh, Co. Tyrone, N. Ireland 2.8.1845, d. Malvern, Worcs. 25.2.1892. Tasmania

Rowe, Ernest Fentiman (1892) b. Felsted 27.1.1866, d. Hyde Park, London 14.4.1918. ed. Felsted. Berkshire, Bedfordshire

*Rowe, Francis Erskine (1886-95)

Ruggles-Brise, Sir Harold Goodeve (1883-88) b. Finchingfield 17.3.1864, d. Marylebone, London 24.6.1927. RHB RM, ed. Winchester OU(1)

*Russell, Thomas Marychurch (1888-1905)

Seabrook, Walter (1882) b. Bishops Stortford, Herts. 1849, d. Berden 4.7.1940. WK

Sewell, C. (1876-80) d. 1926

Sewell, Robert Page (1885-91) b. Maldon 3.9.1866, d. Surbiton, Surrey 7.2.1901. RHB RM, ed. Blackheath Proprietary Sch. Lucas to WI. Kent

Sewell, Rev. William Henry (1877) b. Eye, Suffolk 27.10.1836, d. Yaxley, Suffolk 14.11.1896. ed. Winchester. Rutland, Suffolk

Shaw, Rt. Rev. Edward Domett (1881) b. Passage West, Co. Cork, Ireland 5.10.1860, d. Bisham, Berks 5.11.1937. RHB RFM, ed. Forest Sch. OU(1) Middlesex Hertfordshire, Buckinghamshire. Father of E. A. (Oxford Un.) & R. J. (Royal Navy)

Silcock, Frank (1876-87) b. Sawbridgeworth, Herts. 2.10.1838, d. High Ongar 26.5.1897. RHB RRFM. Hertfordshire. Cousin of Joseph

Silcock, Joseph (1876-82) b. Matching Green 24.6.1832, d. Bishops Stortford, Herts. 21.3.1916. LHB. Cousin of Frank

Smart, Seth Joseph (1876-77) b. Saffron Walden 17.3.1835, d

Smith, A. (1882)

Spencer, Richard Stacey (1882) b. Bishops Stortford, Herts. 1849, d. South Africa 26.1.1905. ed. Bishops Stortford College. Hertfordshire

Spencer, T.A. (1876)

Spencer, W. J. (1888)

Stevens, Charles Richard (1877-80) b. Surrey 9.3.1851, d. Isle of Wight 16.8.1910. ed. Felsted

Stevens, Francis Hewitt (1884-92) b. Witham 1865, d. Eastbourne, Sussex 9.11.1948. ed. Felsted

Sworder, Henry (1876) b. Bishops Stortford, Herts. 1850, d. Albury, Herts. 7.4.1928. ed. Bishops Stortford College; Forest Sch. Hertfordshire

Taberer, Henry Melville (1891-93) b. Keiskama Hoek, Cape Province, S. Africa 7.10.1870, d. Colesburg, S. Africa 5.6.1932. RHB RF, ed. St. Andrew's. Grahamstown, S. Africa. OU (no Blue) SA (1) Natal, Transvaal (not fc), Rhodesia (not fc)

Tompson, C. H. (1877-82)

Tween, H. H. (1882)

Ward, Henry Francis (1885-87)

Waters, Arthur Henry Capel (1876) b. 1855, d. Epping 10.12.1931. ed. Shrewsbury. Shropshire

Watts, J. (1885)

Webster, W. (1882)

Welldon, James Turner (1876-78) b. Felsted 3.8.1847, d. Ashford, Kent 6.2.1927. RHB. ed. Tonbridge CU (no Blue) Kent

Wheble, James William St. Lawrence (1877) b. Wokingham, Berks. 1853, d. Earley, Berks. 1.4.1925. Berkshire

Whittaker, Robert Linney (1892) b. Preston, Lancs 26.12.1867, d. Ludlow, Shropshire 20.3.1938

Wilkes, John (1876-78) b. Elmdon 12.10.1848, d. Wenden Lofts 27.6.1887. ed. Rugby

Williams, A. W. (1881)

Womersley, Dale (1882-92) b. Snaresbrook 28.7.1860, d. Brentwood 22.8.1942. WK, ed. Marlborough. Father of A. D. & L. D. (Essex II)

Wood, Sir Matthew (1879-80) b. Isle of Wight 21.9.1857, d. Westminster, London 13.7.1908. RHB RSLobs, ed. Winchester. Hampshire

Wren, W. (1884)

Wyatt, Albert C. (1881) b. 1855, d. Romford 1919

ABBREVIATIONS AND SYMBOLS

LFM	Left arm fast medium bowler
LHB	Left hand batsman
LM	Left arm medium pace bowler
occ.	Occasional
RF	Right arm fast bowler
RFM	Right arm fast medium bowler
RFMLB	Right arm fast medium leg break bowler
RHB	Right hand batsman
RLB	Right arm leg break bowler
RLBG	Right arm leg break and googly bowler
RM	Right arm medium pace bowler
RMF	Right arm medium fast bowler
ROB	Right arm off break bowler
RRF	Right hand round arm fast bowler
RRFM	Right hand round arm fast medium bowler
RS	Right arm slow bowler
RSM	Right arm slow medium bowler
RSLobs	Right arm slow lob bowler
SLA	Slow left arm bowler
SLC	Slow left arm Chinaman bowler
WK	Wicket-keeper
b.	born
d.	died
fc.	First class
NZ	New Zealand
SA	South Africa
WI	West Indies
YC	Young Cricketers
ed.	educated
CHS	County High School
GS	Grammar School
HS	High School
RGS	Royal Grammar School
Sec.	Secondary
Sch(s)	School(s)
SMS	Secondary Modern School
*	In career records denotes not out
MCC(1)	MCC tour overseas involving first class matches, number of such tours in brackets
Eng(1)	Number of official Test Matches for England. Similar information for other countries playing official Test Matches
CU(1)	Appeared for Cambridge in the University Match, number of years in brackets
OU(1)	Appeared for Oxford in the University Match, number of years in brackets.

CAREER RECORDS

In the details set out below the first line against a player's name shows his career record in first class matches for Essex. Players who appeared in first class matches other than for Essex have two lines of statistics, the second line being the player's record in all first class matches. Career records are complete to the end of the 1986 English season.

Name	*From*	*To*	*M*	*I*	*NO*	*Runs*	*HS*	*Avge*	*100*	*Runs*	*Wkts*	*Avge*	*BB*	*5i/10m*	*Ct*	*St*
D. L. Acfield	1966	1986	378	353	191	1259	38	7.77	0	23509	855	27.49	8-55	30/ 4	120	
	1966	1986	420	417	212	1677	42	8.18	0	26800	950	28.21	8-55	34/ 4	137	
F. Appleyard	1946	1947	14	19	11	55	15*	6.87	0	817	19	43.00	5-14	1	6	
	1939	1950	18	25	14	74	15*	6.72	0	1210	30	40.33	5-14	2	10	
H. A. Arkwright	1894	1895	3	6	0	35	19	5.83	0	109	4	27.25	3-25	0	2	
	1893	1903	23	40	4	436	38	12.11	0	1659	71	23.36	8-40	5/ 1	15	
C. T. Ashton	1921	1938	89	146	10	3193	118	23.47	3	2923	97	30.13	7-51	3	72	
	1921	1938	127	204	15	4723	118	24.98	4	4299	139	30.92	7-51	5/ 1	113	
H. Ashton	1921	1939	21	35	1	819	90	24.08	0						21	
	1920	1939	71	115	11	4025	236*	38.70	8	14	0				72	
P. Ashton	1924		1	2	0	52	31	26.00	0	55	1	55.00	1-55	0	0	
A. V. Avery	1935	1954	268	453	35	14045	224	33.60	25	627	9	69.66	1-11	0	119	
	1935	1954	269	455	35	14137	224	33.65	25	627	9	69.66	1-11	0	119	
G. W. Ayres	1899		12	17	1	263	83	16.43	0	139	5	27.80	1-2	0	12	
	1892	1899	38	52	2	672	83	13.44	0	166	5	33.20	1-2	0	22	
J. A. Bailey	1953	1958	71	88	24	295	27*	4.60	0	4553	198	22.99	7-32	11/ 0	49	
	1953	1968	112	148	38	641	29*	5.82	0	7504	347	21.62	8-24	20/ 2	67	
T. E. Bailey	1946	1967	482	774	152	21460	205	34.50	22	35042	1593	21.99	10-90	91/10	320	
	1945	1967	682	1072	215	28641	205	33.42	28	48170	2082	23.13	10-90	110/13	428	
K. K. Baker	1972		1	1	1	14	14*	-	0						2	0
	1972	1974	20	34	3	505	59*	16.29	0						25	1
A. E. Banfield	1921		1	2	1	0	0*	0.00	0	62	2	31.00	2-62	0	0	
A. N. Barber	1925		2	4	0	46	31	11.50	0	76	1	76.00	1-42	0	2	
G. Barker	1954	1971	444	797	46	21895	181*	29.15	30	200	5	40.00	2-34	0	232	
	1954	1971	451	809	46	22288	181*	29.21	30	200	5	40.00	2-34	0	236	
J. D. Barnfather	1924		5	5	3	50	28*	25.00	0	355	13	27.30	6-32	1	1	
P. L. Barrow	1922		1	1	0	0	0	0.00	0	43	1	43.00	1-21	0	0	
J. F. Bawtree	1895	1896	5	9	1	96	47	12.00	0	66	2	33.00	1-16	0	5	
M. J. Bear	1954	1968	322	562	44	12564	137	24.25	9	53	0				113	
B. H. Belle	1935	1937	26	42	3	776	63	19.89	0						20	
	1934	1950	43	72	5	1235	70	18.43	0	33	1	33.00	1-10	0	29	
C. E. Benham	1904	1909	57	80	11	985	65*	14.27	0	2176	65	33.47	7-60	4	31	
	1904	1912	59	84	11	1047	65*	14.34	0	2338	70	33.40	7-60	4	33	
M. Berkley	1894		2	3	1	6	5	3.00	0	103	7	14.71	6-50	1	2	
F. D. Billham	1924		2	3	1	12	12*	6.00	0	72	0				0	

Name	From	To	M	I	NO	Runs	HS	Avge	100	Runs	Wkts	Avge	BB	5i/10m	Ct	St
J. W. Bonner	1896	1898	16	27	1	339	59	13.03	0						5	
A. R. Border	1986		20	32	4	1385	150	49.46	4	120	1	120.00	1-8	0	17	
	1976/7	1986	194	324	48	14820	200	53.69	45	2013	55	36.60	4-61	0	180	
O. R. Borradaile	1894		1	2	0	7	5	3.50	0						1	
N. F. Borrett	1937	1946	3	4	2	33	15*	16.50	0	43	0				2	
C. S. R. Boswell	1932	1936	30	46	8	406	69	10.68	0	1345	36	37.36	4-22	0	12	
K. D. Boyce	1966	1977	211	319	18	6848	147*	22.75	3	15704	662	23.72	9-61	30/ 6	181	
	1964/5	1977	285	420	27	8800	147*	22.39	4	21324	852	25.02	9-61	35/ 7	215	
M. J. H. Boyers	1969		1	2	0	2	2	1.00	0						0	
A. Bradfield	1922		5	7	3	7	4*	1.75	0						2	3
C. Bray	1927	1937	95	154	14	3474	129	24.81	5	104	2	52.00	1-1	0	54	
O. C. Bristowe	1913	1914	11	16	1	249	81	16.60	0	901	22	40.95	4-74	0	2	
	1913	1914	21	33	2	567	81	18.29	0	1751	74	23.66	6-81	4	6	
V. C. G. Brooks	1970	1971	3	5	0	53	22	10.60	0						1	
A. Brown	1921		2	4	0	59	52	14.75	0	44	1	44.00	1-25	0	1	
G. R. R. Brown	1924	1932	23	35	10	302	38*	12.08	0	834	30	27.80	5-55	1	14	
	1924	1945/6	29	46	12	396	38*	11.64	0	1358	46	29.52	5-55	1	15	
H. J. Brunwin	1937		1	1	1	2	2*	-	0	5	1	5.00	1-5	0	0	
C. P. Buckenham	1899	1914	258	394	63	4882	124	14.74	2	24629	934	26.36	8-33	72/16	143	
	1899	1914	307	468	79	5641	124	14.50	2	29110	1150	25.31	8-33	85/17	172	
F. G. Bull	1895	1900	88	125	31	1171	41*	12.45	0	7923	365	21.70	9-93	29/ 5	41	
	1895	1905	95	138	35	1274	51	12.36	0	9042	416	21.73	9-93	34/ 7	46	
J. Burns	1894	1896	26	47	1	713	114	15.50	1	310	6	51.66	3-24	0	11	
	1890	1901	41	70	4	1134	114	17.18	1	460	15	30.66	6-41	1	15	
N. D. Burns	1986		2	3	0	54	29	18.00	0						2	2
	1985/6	1986	5	8	0	84	29	10.50	0						10	2
Rev. H. J. E. Burrell	1895		2	4	0	15	10	3.75	0	0	0				0	
	1889	1895	3	5	0	15	10	3.00	0	78	2	39.00	1-37	0	0	
R. J. Burrell	1894	1895	6	9	0	127	40	14.11	0						1	
	1894	1897	10	17	1	200	40	12.50	0						2	
C. N. Calnan	1919	1929	4	8	0	49	24	6.12	0	25	0				1	
P. Campbell	1911	1919	13	21	2	270	35	14.21	0	26	0				6	
G. N. Capel-Cure	1929		1	2	0	6	6	3.00	0	58	2	29.00	2-58	0	0	
N. J. O. Carbutt	1923		2	1	1	12	12*	-	0	202	2	101.00	2-23	0	0	
	1920	1928	15	19	5	135	45	9.64	0	1386	36	38.50	5-20	2	7	
H. A. Carpenter	1894	1920	262	466	24	13043	199	29.50	22	2163	46	47.02	4-57	0	220	
	1893	1920	310	551	26	14939	199	28.45	25	2246	50	44.92	4-57	0	257	
R. B. Carr	1960		1	1	1	7	7*	-	0	62	0				0	
	1960	1964/5	2	3	2	35	28*	35.00	0	107	0				2	
G. Carter	1921	1923	7	11	1	163	44*	16.30	0	18	0				3	
G. R. Cass	1964	1967	45	77	11	1447	104*	21.92	1						27	5
	1964	1975	155	231	34	4304	172*	21.84	2						213	28
B. K. Castor	1932		1	1	0	13	13	13.00	0						0	
I. Chapman	1929		1	1	0	9	9	9.00	0	18	0				0	

Name	From	To	M	I	NO	Runs	HS	Avge	100	Runs	Wkts	Avge	BB	5i/10m	Ct	St
J. H. Childs	1985	1986	28	27	8	231	34	12.15	0	1977	94	21.03	8-58	5/ 3	5	
	1975	1986	193	178	80	766	34*	7.81	0	15445	515	29.99	9-56	26/ 5	68	
H. G. Clark	1923		2	3	0	13	11	4.33	0						0	
L. S. Clark	1946	1947	24	44	3	745	64	18.17	0	15	0				11	
R. D. Clark	1912	1919	7	11	1	61	14	6.10	0						10	1
Dr. C. B. Clarke	1959	1960	18	27	14	177	39	13.61	0	1353	58	23.32	7-130	3	6	
	1937/8	1961	97	145	40	1292	86	12.30	0	8782	333	26.37	7-75	20/ 1	42	
D. F. Cock	1939	1946	14	20	2	355	98	19.72	0						5	
E. C. Coleman	1912		2	3	0	10	6	3.33	0						1	1
	1911	1912	3	5	1	14	6	3.50	0						2	1
E. J. Connor	1905		2	4	0	43	26	10.75	0	131	2	65.50	2-21	0	0	
R. M. O. Cooke	1973	1975	40	66	5	1373	139	22.50	2	149	3	49.66	2-55	0	24	
	1972	1976	42	70	5	1450	139	22.30	2	184	4	46.00	2-55	0	25	
A. V. Cooper	1923		1	2	0	14	12	7.00	0						0	
F. J. Cooper	1921	1923	8	14	1	111	32	8.53	0	341	7	48.71	5-71	1	2	
W. Cooper	1905	1910	3	6	0	32	18	5.33	0	69	0				1	
F. Cottam	1922		1							25	0				0	
P. Cousens	1950	1955	39	50	26	72	13	3.00	0	1707	44	38.79	4-63	0	3	
H. P. Crabtree	1931	1947	24	41	1	1281	146	32.02	4	63	0				12	
C. L. Crawley	1929		1	2	0	3	3	1.50	0						1	
L. G. Crawley	1926	1936	56	91	4	2949	222	33.89	6	39	0				17	
	1922	1939	109	177	9	5227	222	31.11	8	57	0				42	
S. J. Cray	1938	1950	99	172	6	4062	163	24.46	7	40	1	40.00	1-0	0	22	
	1938	1950	102	177	6	4218	163	24.66	7	40	1	40.00	1-0	0	24	
J. A. Cutmore	1924	1936	342	593	36	15937	238*	28.61	15	687	11	62.45	2-31	0	121	
A. G. Daer	1925	1935	100	141	42	1469	59	14.83	0	6183	195	31.70	6-38	3	48	
H. B. Daer	1938	1939	9	12	3	60	17	6.66	0	387	11	35.18	3-21	0	4	
G. B. Davies	1912	1914	32	51	8	757	118	17.60	2	1769	68	26.01	6-51	2	27	
	1912	1914	54	90	9	1487	118	18.35	2	2935	141	20.81	8-67	4/ 1	43	
W. Davis	1920		4	6	0	26	13	4.33	0	69	1	69.00	1-67	0	2	
M. H. Denness	1977	1980	83	137	9	4050	195	31.64	6	0	0				38	
	1959	1980	501	838	65	25886	195	33.48	33	62	2	31.00	1-7	0	411	
J. N. Dennis	1934	1939	22	33	3	530	53	17.66	0						13	
H. W. de Zoete	1897		2	2	2	2	2*	-	0	91	3	30.33	2-44	0	0	
	1897	1898	18	26	4	151	29	6.86	0	1033	55	18.78	6-53	3	7	
W. J. Dines	1947	1949	20	30	7	431	69*	18.73	0	980	15	65.33	3-35	0	7	
S. C. Dinsdale	1970		5	7	0	97	29	13.85	0						4	
	1969/70	1975/6	15	26	2	581	88	24.20	0	160	8	20.00	4-24	0	8	
J. G. Dixon	1914	1922	93	148	12	2214	173	16.27	3	6484	206	31.47	7-61	9/ 2	48	
T. C. Dodds	1946	1959	380	663	17	18565	157	28.73	17	1053	35	30.08	4-34	0	176	
	1943/4	1961	396	693	18	19407	157	28.75	17	1126	36	31.27	4-34	0	187	
C. H. Douglas	1912	1919	21	27	0	326	78	12.07	0	350	6	58.33	3-46	0	4	
J. W. H. T. Douglas	1901	1928	459	746	108	17915	210*	28.07	18	33653	1443	23.32	9-47	93/21	265	
	1901	1930	651	1035	156	24531	210*	27.90	26	44159	1893	23.32	9-47	113/23	364	

Name	From	To	M	I	NO	Runs	HS	Avge	100	Runs	Wkts	Avge	BB	5i/10m	Ct	St
W. D. F. Dow	1958	1959	2	3	2	9	9*	9.00	0	171	4	42.75	4-51	0	0	
	1956	1967	13	16	4	107	18	8.91	0	1015	38	26.71	6-56	2/ 1	2	
A. W. Durley	1957		5	8	0	38	16	4.75	0						3	
D. E. East	1981	1986	141	190	27	3433	131	21.06	3	12	0				361	43
R. E. East	1965	1984	405	513	111	7103	113	17.66	1	25804	1010	25.54	8-30	49/10	251	
	1965	1984	410	517	112	7178	113	17.72	1	26210	1019	25.72	8-30	49/10	256	
G. F. Eastman	1926	1929	48	66	28	265	34*	6.97	0						29	21
L. C. Eastman	1920	1939	442	679	49	12965	161	20.57	7	26102	975	26.77	7-28	29/ 3	254	
	1920	1939	451	693	50	13385	161	20.81	7	26940	1006	26.77	7-28	30/ 3	259	
B. E. A Edmeades	1961	1976	335	555	69	12593	163	25.91	14	9688	374	25.90	7-37	10/ 1	105	
G. J. Edwards	1907		2	3	0	45	21	15.00	0						2	
H. D. E. Elliott	1913		2	4	0	3	3	0.75	0	107	1	107.00	1-67	0	1	
R. E. Evans	1950	1957	17	29	0	482	79	16.62	0						8	
V. J. Evans	1932	1937	62	96	37	469	23*	7.94	0	3843	129	29.79	6-47	5/ 1	12	
S. C. Eve	1949	1957	32	51	4	1041	120	22.14	1						17	
F. L. Fane	1895	1922	292	512	30	12599	217	26.13	18	32	0				141	
	1895	1924	417	721	44	18548	217	27.39	25	49	2	24.50	2-17	0	194	
H. A. Faragher	1949	1950	6	9	2	274	85*	39.14	0						4	
K. Farnes	1930	1939	79	94	31	590	97*	9.36	0	7086	367	19.30	8-38	28/ 5	42	
	1930	1939	168	201	59	1182	97*	8.32	0	14804	690	21.45	8-38	44/ 8	84	
G. G. Farnfield	1921		12	20	1	252	41	13.26	0						5	
W. F. O. Faviell	1908		7	12	4	104	27	13.00	0	13	0				4	
	1903/4	1909/10	14	24	5	241	66*	12.68	0	261	10	26.10	3-40	0	11	
K. W. R. Fletcher	1962	1986	538	871	116	28206	228*	37.35	44	1259	29	43.41	5-41	1	498	
	1962	1986	694	1118	164	36437	228*	38.19	62	2287	51	44.84	5-41	1	623	
M. K. Fosh	1976	1978	14	23	0	481	66	20.91	0						5	
	1976	1978	30	48	2	1069	109	23.23	1						9	
N. A. Foster	1980	1986	75	84	23	1260	63	20.65	0	7242	305	23.74	6-46	19/ 2	35	
	1980	1986	100	119	31	1567	63	17.80	0	9544	384	24.85	6-30	24/ 3	43	
B. C. Francis	1971	1973	47	84	7	2962	188*	38.46	7						10	
	1968/9	1974/5	109	192	10	6183	210	33.97	13	15	1	15.00	1-10	0	42	
H. W. F. Franklin	1921	1931	73	104	14	1757	106	19.52	2	1596	36	44.33	4-40	0	36	
	1921	1931	92	134	19	2212	106	19.23	2	2002	46	43.52	4-40	0	41	
R. C. Franklin	1924		1	2	0	1	1	0.50	0	41	1	41.00	1-20	0	1	
A. J. Freeman	1920		1	2	1	1	1	1.00	0	95	0				0	
E. C. Freeman	1894	1896	5	9	0	95	35	10.55	0	40	0				1	
E. J. Freeman	1904	1912	55	91	3	1280	84	14.54	0	50	1	50.00	1-6	0	14	
J. R. Freeman	1905	1928	336	577	56	14507	286	27.84	26	365	10	36.50	3-31	0	230	46
	1905	1928	337	579	56	14602	286	27.91	26	365	10	36.50	3-31	0	231	46
W. T. Garrett	1900	1903	15	25	1	516	92	21.50	0	142	1	142.00	1-72	0	4	
J. S. B. Gentry	1925		1							20	0				0	
	1919	1925	12	12	4	68	13	8.50	0	794	36	22.05	4-36	0	3	

Name	From	To	M	I	No	Runs	HS	Avge	100	Runs	Wkts	Avge	BB	5i/10m	Ct	St
P. A. Gibb	1951	1956	145	250	12	6328	141	26.58	8	4	0				273	63
	1934	1956	287	479	33	12520	204	28.07	19	161	5	32.20	2-40	0	425	123
A. L. Gibson	1895	1910	23	36	3	492	71	14.90	0	16	0				6	
	1895	1926/7	25	39	3	504	71	14.00	0	18	0				9	
K. L. Gibson	1909	1912	36	55	6	795	75	16.22	0	9	1	9.00	1-9	0	53	9
	1909	1920	42	63	6	959	75	16.82	0	9	1	9.00	1-9	0	62	11
F. W. Gilligan	1919	1929	79	108	27	1808	78*	22.32	0	6	0				87	33
	1919	1935	129	174	46	3024	110	23.62	1	6	0				153	68
Rev. F. H. Gillingham	1903	1928	181	307	21	9160	201	32.02	19	13	0				91	0
	1903	1928	210	352	24	10050	201	30.64	19	13	0				111	1
C. Gladwin	1981	1986	57	97	5	2614	162	28.41	1	71	0				26	
A. K. Golding	1983		1	2	2	8	6*	-	0	97	2	48.50	1-44	0	0	
	1983	1986	16	26	5	385	47	18.33	0	1604	18	89.11	3-51	0	4	
G. A. Gooch	1973	1986	232	381	32	15610	227	44.72	41	4501	150	30.00	7-14	3	222	
	1973	1986	341	576	45	22835	227	43.00	57	5776	179	32.26	7-14	3	329	
C. H. Gosling	1930		2	4	0	61	33	15.25	0						2	
	1929	1930	5	8	0	132	37	16.50	0						3	
R. C. Gosling	1894	1896	4	8	1	55	21*	7.85	0						1	
	1888	1896	26	48	5	584	61	13.58	0	11	0				18	
L. Graham	1926		2	3	1	14	12	7.00	0						2	
D. A. A. Gray	1947		1	1	0	6	6	6.00	0	63	1	63.00	1-34	0	0	
	1947		3	5	0	22	8	4.40	0	182	3	60.66	2-67	0	1	
W. J. Gray	1894		1	2	0	4	3	2.00	0						0	
M. A. Green	1930		2	4	0	27	13	6.75	0						1	
	1912	1934	107	183	20	2629	127	16.12	1	65	0				55	
W. T. Greensmith	1947	1963	371	550	149	8042	138*	20.05	1	20711	720	28.76	8-59	21/ 2	147	
	1947	1963	379	566	151	8249	138*	19.87	1	21206	733	28.93	8-59	21/ 2	149	
C. Griffiths	1951	1953	27	41	3	615	105	16.18	1	22	0				4	
A. S. Grimwood	1925		4	6	0	26	15	4.33	0	5	0				0	
T. G. Grinter	1909	1921	8	13	1	201	49*	16.75	0						2	
W. C. Gunary	1929		1	1	0	0	0	0.00	0	58	0				1	
S. Hadden	1912	1920	6	5	2	29	17*	9.66	0						5	1
H. Hailey	1894	1895	13	22	5	301	66*	17.70	0						5	
B. R. Hardie	1973	1986	305	494	62	14678	162	33.97	20	173	3	57.66	2-39	0	279	
	1970	1986	309	501	63	14836	162	33.87	20	173	3	57.66	2-39	0	282	
S. N. Hare	1921		3	5	0	117	98	23.40	0						1	
J. Harris	1905		2	3	1	0	0*	0.00	0						4	0
J. G. W. Harrold	1923	1928	11	19	3	88	17	5.50	0	123	3	41.00	1-15	0	13	
R. C. Harvey	1952		1	2	2	12	12*	-	0	88	3	29.33	3-88	0	0	
F. C. Hawker	1937		1	2	0	26	16	13.00	0						0	
A. F. G. Hayzelden	1929	1931	2	3	1	5	4*	2.50	0	110	6	18.33	3-30	0	3	
E. W. Hazelton	1919		1	2	0	8	8	4.00	0	77	0				0	
	1919	1930	8	16	4	77	43	6.41	0	621	23	27.00	6-45	2/ 1	6	
A. E. Heatley	1894		1	2	1	20	13*	20.00	0	10	0				4	

Name	From	To	M	I	NO	Runs	HS	Avge	100	Runs	Wkts	Avge	BB	5i/10m	Ct	St
R. M. Heaven	1939		1	1	1	5	5*	-	0						4	
P. A. Hector	1977		3	5	1	75	40	18.75	0	190	7	27.14	3-56	0	0	
R. Herbert	1976	1980	6	9	1	62	14*	7.75	0	148	3	49.33	3-64	0	5	
	1976	1986	8	12	1	138	43	12.54	0	262	6	43.66	3-64	0	6	
J. P. Herringshaw	1921	1922	9	14	5	94	18	10.44	0	498	9	55.33	2-48	0	7	
G. F. Higgins	1894	1895	9	17	0	306	118	18.00	1						2	
H. M. Hills	1912	1919	14	21	4	139	26	8.17	0	738	15	49.20	5-63	1	7	
C. Hilton	1964		24	23	9	128	29*	9.14	0	1999	58	34.46	6-86	1	12	
	1957	1964	115	133	44	665	36	7.47	0	9038	321	28.15	6-38	8/ 1	40	
A. B. Hipkin	1923	1931	231	326	55	4239	108	15.64	2	13377	518	25.82	8-71	18/ 3	209	
	1923	1931	232	326	55	4239	108	15.64	2	13435	522	25.73	8-71	18/ 3	210	
R. N. S. Hobbs	1961	1975	325	429	102	4069	100	12.44	2	19844	763	26.00	8-63	32/ 5	222	
	1961	1981	440	546	138	4940	100	12.10	2	29776	1099	27.09	8-63	50/ 8	295	
G. W. Hockey	1928	1931	19	33	5	305	23	10.89	0	20	0				4	
G. W. Horrex	1956	1957	7	13	0	141	41	10.84	0						0	
R. Horsfall	1947	1955	207	349	25	9583	206	29.59	17	41	1	41.00	1-4	0	85	
	1947	1956	214	361	25	9777	206	29.09	17	41	1	41.00	1-4	0	88	
W. G. Hubble	1923		1	1	0	0	0	0.00	0	60	2	30.00	2-3	0	0	
M. G. Hughes	1983		1	2	0	10	10	5.00	0	162	6	27.00	4-71	0	0	
	1981/2	1985/6	30	30	8	229	47	10.40	0	3330	88	37.84	5-53	2	6	
F. E. Hugonin	1927	1928	6	8	3	42	17	8.40	0						8	1
	1927	1937	14	19	6	167	44	12.84	0						26	6
A. Hurd	1958	1960	35	34	14	115	20*	5.75	0	2221	84	26.44	6-15	5/ 1	5	
	1958	1960	90	106	36	376	21	5.37	0	7671	249	30.80	6-15	13/ 1	16	
G. C. Hurst	1962		1	2	1	0	0*	0.00	0						1	
R. W. J. G. Hyndson	1919		1	2	0	7	6	3.50	0	71	0				0	
J. H. Inns	1898	1904	10	14	3	73	28	6.63	0	15	0				8	0
D. J. Insole	1947	1963	345	574	54	20113	219*	38.67	48	4061	119	34.12	5-22	1	279	1
	1947	1963	450	743	72	25241	219*	37.61	54	4680	138	33.95	5-22	1	366	6
B. L. Irvine	1968	1969	54	89	12	2674	109	34.72	1	70	1	70.00	1-39	0	40	
	1962/3	1976/7	157	271	26	9919	193	40.48	21	142	1	142.00	1-39	0	240	7
V. E. Jarvis	1925		2	4	0	44	37	11.00	0	23	0				0	
C. V. Jenkinson	1922	1923	5	6	2	9	8	2.25	0						4	4
L. C. S. Jerman	1950	1951	3	2	0	8	8	4.00	0	222	1	222.00	1-39	0	2	
A. S. Johnston	1894	1896	7	12	1	235	63	21.36	0						3	
	1886	1896	10	18	2	259	63	16.18	0						5	
A. M. Jorden	1966	1970	60	85	20	704	59*	10.83	0	3501	117	29.92	4-29	0	36	
	1966	1970	89	130	31	1112	67*	11.23	0	5347	176	30.38	5-95	1	47	
R. C. G. Joy	1922	1928	13	16	2	142	35	10.14	0	398	12	33.16	3-41	0	10	
	1922	1931/2	21	29	4	315	36	12.60	0	916	41	22.34	5-70	1	14	
H. D. Keigwin	1906	1907	4	6	0	69	20	11.50	0	179	4	44.75	1-23	0	1	
	1905	1909	11	18	0	351	77	19.50	0	472	15	31.46	5-83	1	3	

Name	From	To	M	I	NO	Runs	HS	Avge	100	Runs	Wkts	Avge	BB	5i/10m	Ct	St
R. P. Keigwin	1903	1919	20	32	3	455	75	15.68	0	639	14	45.64	4-49	0	3	
	1903	1923	74	129	12	2316	116	19.79	1	2614	87	30.04	8-79	3/ 1	41	
C. J. M. Kenny	1950	1953	18	14	6	26	16	3.25	0	1212	39	31.07	5-80	1	4	
	1950	1962	40	38	16	75	16	3.40	0	3348	117	28.61	7-45	6/ 1	17	
T. Kent	1960	1962	10	10	4	74	23*	12.33	0	561	15	37.40	4-54	0	5	
I. M. King	1957		28	36	21	131	33	8.73	0	1146	34	33.70	4-25	0	29	
	1952	1957	81	96	39	476	33	8.35	0	3706	129	28.72	5-59	1	60	
R. J. S. King	1928		1	1	0	3	3	3.00	0	20	0				0	
B. R. Knight	1955	1966	239	399	42	8798	165	24.64	8	17162	761	22.55	8-69	39/ 8	171	
	1955	1969	379	602	83	13336	165	25.69	12	26205	1089	24.06	8-69	45/ 8	263	
C. J. Kortright	1894	1907	160	255	18	4182	131	17.64	2	9036	440	20.53	8-57	35/ 8	167	
	1893	1907	170	271	21	4404	131	17.61	2	10294	489	21.05	8-57	39/ 8	176	
J. C. Laker	1962	1964	30	29	8	248	28	11.80	0	2367	111	21.32	7-73	7/ 2	11	
	1946	1964/5	450	548	108	7304	113	16.60	2	35791	1944	18.41	10-53	127/32	270	
A. W. F. Lapham	1921		3	5	0	31	16	6.20	0	90	5	18.00	2-25	0	0	
A. E. Lashbrooke	1908		1	2	0	9	9	4.50	0	61	1	61.00	1-26	0	0	
A. B. Lavers	1937	1953	25	44	2	695	42*	16.54	0	483	13	37.15	4-68	0	6	
	1937	1953	26	46	3	734	42*	17.06	0	497	13	38.23	4-68	0	6	
T. P. Lawrence	1933	1935	7	14	0	133	39	9.50	0						3	
J. M. Leiper	1950		2	4	0	50	44	12.50	0	79	1	79.00	1-38	0	1	
R. J. Leiper	1981	1982	2	4	0	53	49	13.25	0						2	
J. K. Lever	1967	1986	406	414	165	2661	91	10.68	0	31716	1370	23.15	8-37	74/11	151	
	1967	1986	492	509	189	3509	91	10.96	0	38817	1619	23.97	8-37	82/12	178	
D. C. Levick	1950	1951	3	6	0	14	6	2.33	0						1	
A. W. Lilley	1978	1986	62	100	6	2295	100*	24.41	1	309	7	44.14	3-116	0	29	
P. J. Lindsey	1964		1	1	1	7	7*	-	0	50	1	50.00	1-8	0	0	
Rev. C. G. Littlehales	1896	1904	6	10	1	109	23	12.11	0						4	1
J. Littlewood	1905		1	1	1	5	5*	-	0	36	0				1	
G. M. Locks	1928		2	4	2	5	3*	2.50	0	227	3	75.66	2-86	0	0	
G. M. Louden	1912	1927	82	125	33	844	74	9.17	0	9066	415	21.84	8-36	33/ 5	54	
	1912	1927	94	140	39	931	74	9.21	0	10081	451	22.35	8-36	36/ 5	62	
F. A. Loveday	1921	1923	7	14	0	321	81	22.92	0						2	
A. P. Lucas	1894	1907	98	153	21	3554	135	26.92	2	90	1	90.00	1-17	0	50	0
	1874	1907	256	435	46	10263	145	26.38	8	2849	155	18.38	6-10	4	152	0
R. A. G. Luckin	1962	1963	29	46	3	735	82	17.09	0						8	
R. V. Lynch	1954		3	3	2	7	6*	7.00	0	107	4	26.75	4-64	0	2	
L. W. Lywood	1930		2	3	0	12	7	4.00	0	83	2	41.50	1-7	0	0	
	1927	1930	4	5	0	19	7	3.80	0	260	3	86.66	1-7	0	0	
M. S. A. McEvoy	1976	1981	43	74	1	1371	67*	18.78	0	103	3	34.33	3-20	0	42	
	1976	1984	69	113	2	2128	103	19.17	1	103	3	34.33	3-20	0	70	
K. S. McEwan	1974	1985	282	458	41	18088	218	43.37	52	301	4	75.25	1-0	0	197	0
	1972/3	1985/6	389	642	58	23645	218	40.48	63	309	4	77.25	1-0	0	339	7
C. P. McGahey	1894	1921	400	685	61	19079	277	30.57	29	9481	306	30.98	7-27	12/ 3	140	
	1894	1921	437	751	65	20723	277	30.20	31	10300	330	31.21	7-27	12/ 3	151	

Name	From	To	M	I	NO	Runs	HS	Avge	100	Runs	Wkts	Avge	BB	5i/10m	Ct	St
C. D. McIver	1902	1922	59	101	6	2544	134	26.77	4	25	1	25.00	1-4	0	47	13
	1902	1934	134	227	18	4651	134	22.25	5	40	1	40.00	1-4	0	98	24
M. Mackinnon	1927		3	4	0	55	31	13.75	0						0	
	1927	1934/5	6	10	0	122	31	12.20	0						3	
S. J. Malone	1975	1978	2							101	2	50.50	1-28	0	0	
	1975	1985	57	46	15	182	23	5.87	0	4236	118	35.89	7-55	3/ 1	13	
J. W. Marston	1923	1924	2	4	1	12	6	4.00	0	112	2	56.00	2-47	0	1	
A. D. Martin	1920	1921	3	3	0	0	0	0.00	0	210	5	42.00	3-43	0	1	
E. G. Martin	1928		2	4	0	25	13	6.25	0	140	2	70.00	1-63	0	1	
O. Martyn	1922		1	1	0	0	0	0.00	0						1	
W. H. J. Mayes	1914		1	2	0	2	2	1.00	0	69	0				0	
H. Mead	1913	1914	4	8	2	19	8*	3.16	0	194	3	64.66	2-84	0	3	
W. Mead	1894	1913	332	469	125	3843	119	11.17	1	28423	1472	19.30	9-40	117/30	151	
	1892	1913	429	618	148	4991	119	10.61	1	36388	1916	18.99	9-40	152/39	194	
G. C. Melluish	1926		4	3	1	18	16*	9.00	0	115	3	38.33	1-17	0	0	
C. F. Mercer	1929		2	4	0	26	8	6.50	0						0	
A. H. Meston	1926	1927	12	17	4	143	41	11.00	0	352	4	88.00	2-18	0	9	
S. P. Meston	1907	1908	17	29	2	476	130	17.62	1	48	1	48.00	1-10	0	7	
	1906	1908	20	35	2	516	130	15.63	1	65	1	65.00	1-10	0	11	
J. Milner	1957	1961	66	117	12	2688	135	25.60	3	14	0				57	
	1957	1961	67	119	12	2767	135	25.85	3	14	0				57	
E. S. Missen	1921		1	2	0	20	12	10.00	0						0	
G. F. Mitchell	1926		1	1	0	4	4	4.00	0	45	1	45.00	1-25	0	0	
K. F. Moore	1961		1	1	0	2	2	2.00	0	43	4	10.75	4-21	0	2	
H. M. Morris	1919	1932	240	383	29	6974	166	19.70	3	839	14	59.92	2-16	0	78	
	1919	1932	246	393	30	7086	166	19.52	3	885	16	55.31	2-16	0	80	
P. E. Morris	1909	1924	28	43	5	418	55*	11.00	0	1848	83	22.26	8-106	6/ 1	13	
W. B. Morris	1946	1950	48	78	10	1219	68	17.92	0	1975	43	45.93	4-90	0	18	
H. C. Mortlock	1912	1921	4	4	0	32	26	8.00	0	380	7	54.28	5-104	1	6	
A. S. Moule	1921	1924	17	31	5	317	64	12.19	0	6	0				5	
W. Naylor	1906		1	2	0	2	2	1.00	0						2	0
F. W. H. Nicholas	1912	1929	63	101	2	2255	140	22.77	1						41	13
	1912	1929/30	76	122	5	2634	140	22.51	1						51	16
M. S. Nichols	1924	1939	418	664	66	15736	205	26.31	20	34201	1608	21.26	9-32	108/22	279	
	1924	1939	483	756	85	17827	205	26.56	20	39666	1833	21.63	9-32	118/23	326	
G. J. Nolan	1968		1	2	0	14	11	7.00	0						0	
G. Norman	1920		4	5	1	44	21	11.00	0	18	0				1	
R. O. G. Norman	1932		1	2	0	20	10	10.00	0						0	
J. O'Connor	1921	1939	516	866	76	27819	248	35.21	71	17523	537	32.63	7-52	17/ 2	215	1
	1921	1939	540	903	79	28764	248	34.90	72	18325	557	32.89	7-52	18/ 2	226	1
C. E. L. Orman	1896		2	2	0	16	12	8.00	0						1	
H. G. P. Owen	1894	1902	133	222	17	4459	134	21.75	3	321	9	35.66	2-37	0	38	
	1882	1902	136	228	17	4510	134	21.37	3	332	9	36.88	2-37	0	38	

Name	From	To	M	I	NO	Runs	HS	Avge	100	Runs	Wkts	Avge	BB	5i/10m	Ct	St
E. J. Palmer	1957		4	6	5	39	11*	39.00	0	225	7	32.14	2-35	0	1	
H. J. Palmer	1924	1932	53	65	23	257	25*	6.11	0	3477	142	24.48	6-68	6	19	
	1924	1936	58	74	27	278	25*	5.91	0	4053	160	25.33	6-68	7	21	
L. F. Parslow	1946		1	2	0	9	5	4.50	0						0	
C. H. Pascoe	1909		1	1	1	3	3*	-	0	16	0				0	
R. F. T. Paterson	1946		25	40	5	680	80	19.42	0	464	13	35.69	4-98	0	12	3
	1946	1958	28	45	5	884	88	22.10	0	464	13	35.69	4-98	0	16	3
J. H. Pawle	1935	1938	6	11	0	194	68	17.63	0						4	
	1935	1947	34	59	4	1544	125	28.07	3	13	0				14	
T. N. Pearce	1929	1950	231	376	48	11139	211*	33.96	20	927	15	61.80	4-12	0	144	
	1929	1952	250	406	54	12061	211*	34.26	22	927	15	61.80	4-12	0	153	
P. A. Perrin	1896	1928	525	894	88	29172	343*	36.19	65	740	16	46.25	3-13	0	284	
	1896	1928	538	918	91	29709	343*	35.92	66	753	16	47.06	3-13	0	293	
P. J. Phelan	1958	1965	154	192	70	1505	63	12.33	0	8510	300	28.36	8-109	17/ 2	67	
	1958	1965	160	199	71	1693	63	13.22	0	9006	314	28.68	8-109	17/ 2	67	
N. Phillip	1978	1985	144	201	22	3784	134	21.13	1	10638	423	25.14	6-4	18/ 1	45	
	1969/70	1985	230	334	37	7013	134	23.61	1	17032	688	24.75	7-33	30/ 2	75	
L. J. Phillips	1919	1922	4	5	1	38	19	9.50	0	31	0				0	
H. G. Pickering	1938		3	6	0	62	17	10.33	0						0	
	1938	1947	8	16	0	297	79	18.56	0						0	
H. Pickett	1894	1897	52	80	34	387	35	8.41	0	2780	114	24.38	10-32	4/ 1	19	
	1884	1898	62	94	38	450	35	8.03	0	3269	134	24.39	10-32	4/ 1	25	
S. G. Plumb	1975	1977	2	3	1	68	37*	34.00	0	47	2	23.50	2-47	0	0	
	1975	1986	5	8	1	216	69	30.85	0	124	3	41.33	2-47	0	2	
I. L. Pont	1985	1986	9	11	5	121	43	20.16	0	675	22	30.68	5-103	1	1	
	1982	1986	14	20	6	169	43	12.07	0	1039	27	38.48	5-103	1	2	
K. R. Pont	1970	1986	198	305	44	6558	125*	25.12	7	3189	96	33.21	5-17	2	92	
D. F. Pope	1928	1934	148	248	14	6443	161	27.53	7	272	4	68.00	1-11	0	35	
	1925	1934	159	268	19	6557	161	26.33	7	272	4	68.00	1-11	0	37	
A. G. Powell	1932	1937	23	35	7	495	62*	17.67	0						30	8
	1932	1957	53	82	12	1149	79	16.41	0						75	19
H. C. Preece	1895		2	4	0	74	49	18.50	0						0	
E. R. Presland	1962	1970	30	41	4	625	51	16.89	0	761	13	58.53	2-19	0	24	
K. C. Preston	1948	1964	391	460	165	3024	70	10.25	0	30288	1155	26.22	7-55	37/ 2	344	
	1948	1964	397	468	169	3053	70	10.21	0	30533	1160	26.32	7-55	37/ 2	350	
E. J. Price	1948	1949	43	56	16	214	26*	5.35	0	3013	92	32.75	8-125	4	24	
	1946	1949	80	95	31	558	54	8.71	0	5722	215	26.61	8-125	10/ 2	40	
P. J. Prichard	1984	1986	67	107	9	3009	147*	30.70	2	5	0				44	
D. R. Pringle	1978	1986	101	144	25	2743	121*	23.05	2	6371	239	26.65	7-32	8	57	
	1978	1986	162	239	46	5335	127*	27.64	7	10489	381	27.53	7-32	11/ 1	91	
G. C. Pritchard	1965	1966	10	11	2	19	8	2.11	0	406	7	58.00	4-24	0	3	
	1962	1966	35	42	15	111	18	4.11	0	2058	56	36.75	6-51	2	13	
S. Proffitt	1937		7	14	0	170	39	12.14	0	32	0				1	
S. C. Puddefoot	1922	1923	8	8	2	101	42	16.83	0	105	1	105.00	1-34	0	2	
G. R. Pullinger	1949	1950	18	20	11	53	14*	5.88	0	1557	41	37.97	5-54	1	14	

Name	From	To	M	I	NO	Runs	HS	Avge	100	Runs	Wkts	Avge	BB	5i/10m	Ct	St
J. H. Purves	1960	1961	5	7	0	36	14	5.14	0						1	
	1960	1964	11	19	0	474	74	24.94	0						5	
A. B. Quick	1936	1952	19	32	1	433	57	13.96	0	10	0				12	
	1936	1952	20	33	1	439	57	13.71	0	10	0				13	
S. E. V. Quin	1924		1	1	0	0	0	0.00	0	13	0				0	
	1924	1931/2	3	5	0	3	3	0.60	0	60	0				0	
M. Raison	1928	1930	17	27	2	451	57	18.04	0	575	14	41.07	5-104	1	6	
L. H. R. Ralph	1953	1961	174	262	39	3763	73	16.87	0	11053	460	24.02	7-42	19/ 3	143	
A. H. Read	1904	1910	22	30	6	419	70	17.45	0	1192	38	31.36	7-75	1	7	
H. D. Read	1933	1935	32	41	15	104	17*	4.00	0	2765	131	21.10	7-35	7/ 1	14	
	1933	1948	54	70	27	158	25*	3.67	0	5022	219	22.93	7-35	13/ 2	21	
D. Reese	1906		8	15	2	198	70	15.23	0	165	6	27.50	4-55	0	0	
	1895/6	1920/1	72	134	8	3182	148	25.25	4	3893	196	19.86	7-53	11/ 1	36	
W. Reeves	1897	1921	271	422	34	6451	135	16.62	3	16137	581	27.77	7-33	37/ 5	115	
	1897	1921	280	436	35	6656	135	16.59	3	16526	601	27.49	7-33	38/ 5	121	
R. J. Richards	1970		1												0	0
C. S. Richardson	1914		1	1	0	15	15	15.00	0						1	
J. V. Richardson	1924	1926	14	18	3	300	82	20.00	0	253	7	36.14	2-55	0	8	
	1924	1926	35	53	9	1038	89	23.59	0	838	27	31.03	3-25	0	21	
P. J. Richardson	1912		2	2	0	34	21	17.00	0	12	0				1	
	1912		3	4	0	44	21	11.00	0	12	0				2	
K. R. Rickards	1953		1	2	0	25	13	12.50	0						0	
	1945/6	1958/9	37	60	7	2065	195	38.96	2	128	1	128.00	1-66	0	10	
H. W. Riding	1921		1	2	0	23	16	11.50	0						0	
G. V. N. Ridley	1922	1926	6	11	0	113	54	10.27	0						3	
F. H. Rist	1934	1953	65	108	9	1496	62	15.11	0	8	1	8.00	1-8	0	35	5
D. C. Robinson	1908		7	12	1	148	37	13.45	0						12	1
	1905	1926	155	267	14	4376	150*	17.29	1						123	39
R. H. Robinson	1912		4	7	2	25	11*	5.00	0						9	4
C. J. Round	1921		2	4	0	9	8	2.25	0	62	1	62.00	1-49	0	0	
F. E. Rowe	1894	1895	3	5	0	32	19	6.40	0						1	
	1890	1895	4	7	1	53	19	8.83	0						2	
Sir G. W. Rowley	1926		5	7	1	53	23	8.83	0	29	0				0	
	1926	1932/3	6	9	1	73	23	9.12	0	29	0				0	
A. E. Russell	1898	1910	130	196	42	2025	100	13.14.	1						163	44
C. A. G. Russell	1908	1930	379	628	51	23610	273	40.91	62	7480	276	27.10	5-25	5	280	
	1908	1930	437	717	59	27358	273	41.57	71	7637	283	26.98	5-25	5	314	
T. M. Russell	1894	1905	162	246	45	3106	139	15.45	3						246	88
	1894	1905	170	260	46	3273	139	15.29	3						251	89
Sadiq Mohammad	1970		1	1	0	20	20	20.00	0						0	
	1959/60	1986	387	684	40	24160	203	37.51	50	7476	235	31.81	7-34	8	326	
G. E. Sainsbury	1979	1980	3	2	2	2	2*	-	0	268	8	33.50	4-85	0	1	
	1979	1986	60	53	30	151	14*	6.56	0	4780	153	31.24	7-38	7	11	

Name	From	To	M	I	NO	Runs	HS	Avge	100	Runs	Wkts	Avge	BB	5i/10m	Ct	St
N. H. Saint	1920	1923	44	72	7	757	36	11.64	0	800	17	47.05	3-32	0	10	
L. A. Savill	1953	1961	125	200	16	3919	115	21.29	4	26	1	26.00	1-26	0	50	
G. J. Saville	1963	1974	124	214	29	4265	126*	23.05	2	59	3	19.66	2-30	0	101	
	1963	1974	126	218	29	4474	126*	23.67	3	76	3	25.33	2-30	0	103	
D. Sayers	1967		1	1	1	0	0*	-	0	64	1	64.00	1-22	0	0	
F. J. Scoulding	1912	1920	22	28	11	92	21	5.41	0	1252	32	39.12	4-50	0	6	
C. J. Searle	1947		1	1	1	5	5*	-	0						1	1
L. D. Sears	1925		2	4	0	18	16	4.50	0						0	
D. J. Semmence	1962		1	2	0	33	24	16.50	0	31	0				0	
	1956	1968	39	63	2	890	108	14.59	1	123	1	123.00	1-43	0	24	
E. H. D. Sewell	1902	1904	55	91	5	1822	107	21.18	2	388	7	55.42	2-79	0	45	
	1892/3	1922	87	147	7	3430	181	24.50	5	807	17	47.47	3-73	0	70	
R. H. Sharp	1925	1928	16	25	7	169	36*	9.38	0	696	16	43.50	5-66	1	16	
J. R. Sheffield	1929	1936	177	272	40	3822	108	16.47	1	28	0				194	54
	1929	1938/9	180	277	40	3914	108	16.51	1	28	0				196	54
H. R. Sherman	1967	1969	13	21	3	448	66	24.88	0	23	0				4	
R. N. Shorter	1927	1929	23	29	11	104	21	5.77	0	695	15	46.33	3-14	0	12	
I. J. Skinner	1950		13	21	7	28	7*	2.00	0	808	21	38.47	4-56	0	5	
G. J. Smith	1955	1966	239	412	30	8519	148	22.30	4	913	33	27.66	5-39	1	131	
	1955	1966	243	419	30	8796	148	22.61	5	951	33	28.81	5-39	1	133	
G. W. O. Smith	1929	1930	10	18	3	206	39*	13.73	0						2	
H. T. O. Smith	1929	1935	23	36	5	361	38	11.64	0	1618	61	26.52	6-56	3	19	
	1929	1936	25	40	5	400	38	11.42	0	1740	63	27.61	6-56	3	20	
H. W. Smith	1912	1922	20	31	12	195	22	10.26	0	1055	35	30.14	5-59	1	12	
N. Smith	1973	1981	178	226	47	3225	126	18.01	2						381	47
	1970	1981	187	239	53	3336	126	17.93							395	51
R. Smith	1934	1956	419	646	81	11125	147	19.69	6	39817	1317	30.23	8-63	73/10	179	
	1934	1956	445	682	88	12041	147	20.27	8	41265	1350	30.56	8-63	73/10	191	
T. P. B. Smith	1929	1951	434	647	115	9652	163	18.14	8	42314	1610	26.28	9-77	117/27	330	
	1929	1952	465	690	123	10142	163	17.88	8	45059	1697	26.55	9-77	120/28	346	
W. G. Spencer	1938	1948	3	5	1	52	25	13.00	0	8	1	8.00	1-8	0	0	
P. A. Spicer	1962	1963	17	29	2	526	86	19.48	0	55	2	27.50	2-1	0	4	
E. F. Spinks	1926		2	3	1	2	2	1.00	0	81	0				1	
H. Spurr	1923		1	2	0	13	9	6.50	0						0	
E. A. W. Stanley	1950	1952	13	21	3	226	35	12.55	0	8	0				2	
A. R. Stanyard	1960		2	3	0	47	26	15.66	0						0	
B. Stead			Selected for one match for Essex in 1962 but absent													
	1959	1976	231	253	77	2166	58	12.30	0	18318	653	28.05	8-44	24/2	59	
J. P. Stephenson	1985	1986	15	27	1	661	85	25.42	0	5	0				7	
J. W. A. Stephenson	1934	1939	61	93	21	1050	65	14.58	0	4156	174	23.88	8-46	10/1	30	
	1928/9	1948	103	158	37	2582	135	21.33	2	7521	312	24.10	9-46	16/2	60	
E. A. W. Steward	1964	1965	15	23	2	272	47	12.95	0						17	
	1964	1967/8	18	27	3	310	47	12.91	0						20	0
F. Street	1898	1899	9	11	0	246	76	22.36	0	14	0				4	
B. T. Strutton	1914	1919	4	6	1	64	19	12.80	0	197	0				1	

Name	From	To	M	I	NO	Runs	HS	Avge	100	Runs	Wkts	Avge	BB	5i/10m	Ct	St
G. Sutton	1912		1	1	0	0	0	0.00	0						0	
C. F. Swann	1912		1	1	0	0	0	0.00	0						0	
B. J. Swyer	1923		1	2	0	12	7	6.00	0	56	0				0	
A. G. Taylor	1923		2	3	0	7	7	2.33	0	77	1	77.00	1-40	0	0	
B. Taylor	1949	1973	539	901	69	18240	135	21.92	9	21	1	21.00	1-16	0	1040	191
	1949	1973	572	949	73	19094	135	21.79	9	30	1	30.00	1-16	0	1083	211
J. F. Taylor	1960	1961	14	23	6	436	86	25.64	0						19	3
	1960	1967	15	24	7	461	86	27.11	0						22	5
R. M. Taylor	1931	1946	206	349	21	6755	193	20.59	5	2933	92	31.88	7-99	3	185	
E. C. Tedder	1946		8	14	0	208	55	14.85	0						3	
E. C. Thompson	1926	1929	44	61	17	696	45*	15.81	0	938	17	55.17	2-12	0	10	
H. W. Thorn	1928		1	2	0	12	7	6.00	0	42	1	42.00	1-42	0	0	
P. Toone	1912	1922	29	42	13	215	24	7.41	0	1954	62	31.51	6-51	2/ 1	23	
T. D. Topley	1985	1986	13	14	3	122	45	11.09	0	1144	47	24.34	5-52	2	9	
	1985	1986	14	15	4	128	45	11.63	0	1208	49	24.65	5-52	2	10	
G. Tosetti	1898	1905	41	63	6	1054	132*	18.49	1	891	16	55.68	3-67	0	15	
E. M. O'B. Toulmin	1899	1912	2	2	0	1	1	0.50	0	57	2	28.50	2-16	0	2	
	1899	1912	5	8	0	134	59	16.75	0	250	17	14.70	6-60	1/ 1	4	
A. F. M. Townsend	1910		1												0	
	1903	1910	10	14	0	200	28	14.28	0	171	3	57.00	1-23	0	6	
C. J. H. Treglown	1922	1928	34	55	3	792	77	15.23	0						11	
B. Tremlin	1900	1919	132	193	63	1776	61	13.66	0	11734	452	25.96	9-126	23/ 4	62	
	1900	1919	136	200	64	1843	61	13.55	0	12058	467	25.82	9-126	23/ 4	64	
S. A. Trick	1905	1919	5	9	0	69	26	7.66	0						1	
A. J. Turner	1897	1910	68	116	12	3730	124	35.86	11	438	12	36.50	3-47	0	26	2
	1897	1914	77	134	15	4053	124	34.05	11	484	15	32.26	3-47	0	31	2
S. Turner	1965	1986	354	503	98	9264	121	22.87	4	20987	810	25.90	6-26	27/ 1	215	
	1965	1986	361	513	101	9411	121	22.84	4	21351	821	26.00	6-26	27/ 1	217	
W. M. F. Turner	1899	1926	48	81	7	2004	172	27.08	2	180	3	60.00	2-12	0	58	
	1899	1926	51	86	7	2090	172	26.45	2	205	5	41.00	2-12	0	62	
P. W. Turrall	1927		1	1	0	45	45	45.00	0						0	
E. J. Unwin	1932	1939	7	14	0	152	48	10.85	0	103	0				2	
F. St. G. Unwin	1932	1950	52	85	8	1125	60	14.61	0	41	0				33	
	1932	1951	53	87	9	1138	60	14.58	0	41	0				33	
J. Valiant	1912		1	2	1	3	3	3.00	0	20	0				0	
H. H. van Straubenzee	1938		1	1	1	4	4*	-	0	12	0				0	
	1938	1939	4	4	2	56	38	28.00	0	185	10	18.50	4-96	0	0	
N. Vere Hodge	1936	1939	23	38	6	713	108	22.28	2						11	0
F. H. Vigar	1938	1954	256	397	62	8660	144	25.58	11	8958	236	37.95	8-128	8	195	
	1938	1954	257	399	62	8858	145	26.28	12	9135	241	37.90	8-128	8	197	
J. E. W. Waddington	1931		1	1	0	8	8	8.00	0						0	

Name	From	To	M	I	NO	Runs	HS	Avge	100	Runs	Wkts	Avge	BB	5i/10m	Ct	St
T. H. Wade	1929	1950	318	472	135	4972	96	14.75	0	1391	47	29.59	5-64	1	413	177
	1929	1950	321	476	135	5024	96	14.73	0	1418	48	29.54	5-64	1	414	178
H. Wagstaff	1920	1921	5	6	4	19	17*	9.50	0	135	2	67.50	1-19	0	0	
K. W. Wallace	1967	1972	10	16	0	219	55	13.68	0						2	
B. Ward	1967	1972	128	222	19	4799	164*	23.64	4	68	5	13.60	2-5	0	60	
G. H. Ward	1950		1	2	0	4	2	2.00	0						1	0
	1949	1950	3	6	2	23	6*	5.75	0						3	1
B. Warsop	1931	1932	5	10	2	128	51	16.00	0	18	0				1	
A. G. Waterman	1937	1938	10	15	1	380	103	27.14	1	348	11	31.63	4-79	0	7	
D. Watkins	1949	1954	12	17	4	210	32	16.15	0	421	8	52.62	2-45	0	5	
A. C. Watson	1913	1914	2	4	0	89	37	22.25	0						2	
	1913	1928	106	178	15	2724	111	16.71	1	209	5	41.80	3-42	0	38	
C. J. M. Watts	1928		8	11	0	119	41	10.81	0	4	0				2	2
H. P. Waugh	1919	1929	8	14	0	213	128	15.21	1	135	3	45.00	1-6	0	8	
	1919	1937	9	16	0	251	128	15.68	1	168	4	42.00	1-6	0	9	
G. H. S West	1949	1953	2	4	0	79	55	19.75	0						0	
L. H. West	1928		3	5	0	33	30	6.60	0						0	
H. M. Whitcombe	1922		3	4	2	13	7*	6.50	0	199	1	199.00	1-34	0	1	
P. S. Whitcombe	1922		1	2	0	9	5	4.50	0	22	0				0	
	1922	1930/1	4	7	2	81	32*	16.20	0	37	0				1	
D. R. Wilcox	1928	1947	118	186	8	5482	142	30.79	8	117	1	117.00	1-46	0	88	
	1928	1951	179	296	11	8399	157	29.47	15	136	3	45.33	1-0	0	130	
J. W. T. Wilcox	1964	1967	19	30	5	596	87	23.84	0						11	
	1961	1967	31	54	7	903	87	19.21	0						15	
C. C. P. Williams	1954	1959	40	68	3	1518	119	23.35	1	5	0				23	
	1952	1959	87	153	8	4090	139*	28.20	6	61	1	61.00	1-33	0	60	
H. R. H. Williams	1919	1920	10	12	2	67	23*	6.70	0						18	7
A. D. Womersley	1910		1	2	0	9	9	4.50	0						0	
A. E. Wright	1931	1934	3	5	1	45	14	11.25	0	86	0				1	
J. V. Wright	1962	1967	4	6	0	60	40	10.00	0						2	
R. W. Wrightson	1965	1967	12	20	4	332	84	20.75	0						8	
N. G. Wykes	1925	1936	30	42	3	879	162	22.53	1	52	0				5	
	1925	1936	42	60	6	1277	162	23.64	2	150	1	150.00	1-5	0	13	
H. I. Young	1898	1912	128	186	50	1413	44	10.38	0	9092	368	24.70	8-54	18/ 3	59	
	1898	1912	171	257	65	2303	81	11.99	0	12014	514	23.37	8-54	27/ 4	80	

NOTES

1. The figures are compiled in accordance with the ACS Guides to First-Class Matches for British Isles, Australia, New Zealand, South Africa, West Indies and India. Copies of these Guides can be purchased from the Association Office at 4 Croft End, Little Eaton, Derby, DE2 5DP.

2. This means that the match between Sir Julien Cahn's XI and Essex at West Bridgford in September 1930 is excluded as it is not now regarded as first class.

3. The Essex only statistics do not include appearances for Middlesex & Essex v. Surrey & Kent at Kingston in 1947. These details are in the records for all first class matches.

4. Only ten players appeared for Essex in the match against Oxford University at Oxford in 1962. B. Stead was selected but failed to appear chosing instead to play for Nottinghamshire II v. Worcestershire II at Halesowen. He subsequently joined the Nottinghamshire staff.

5. In the match against Somerset at Leyton in 1920 A. D. Martin was allowed to replace the injured F. W. Gilligan who kept wicket in the early stages of the match, J. R. Freeman assuming the duties of wicket-keeper. The match is counted for both players in the first column of the career figures as in effect twelve players appeared for Essex in the match.

6. The career figures of A. Brown and F. J. Cooper are shown separately. This matter is dealt with in the Introduction.

7. Following the decision of the International Cricket Conference with effect from the 1985 season in the British Isles wides and no balls are debited against the bowler's analysis. It follows that the "runs" column in the career bowling averages actually consists of runs conceded plus wides plus no balls from which no runs were scored in such matches from 1985 onwards. There is the further complication that the date of introduction of the new system has varied in different parts of the world, namely 1983-84 in Australia, India and West Indies; 1984-85 in New Zealand, Pakistan, Sri Lanka and Zimbabwe. This affects the career figures of A. R. Border, N. A. Foster, M. G. Hughes, N. Phillip, D. R. Pringle and Sadiq Mohammad. South Africa is not a member of the Conference and the system has not yet been introduced there.

DERBYSHIRE CRICKETERS 1871-1981

Compiled and published by
The Association of Cricket Statisticians
Haughton Mill,
Retford, Notts.

Price £1.50

Tranter **Printing** Services, Bridge Works, London Road, Derby.

Previous booklets in this series are:

- Warwickshire Cricketers 1843-1973
- Worcestershire Cricketers 1899-1974
- Somersetshire Cricketers 1875-1974
- Middlesex Cricketers 1850-1976
- Leicestershire Cricketers 1879-1977
- Victorian Cricketers 1850-1978
- Nottinghamshire Cricketers 1835-1978
- Queensland Cricketers 1892-1979
- Gloucestershire Cricketers 1870-1979
- Irish Cricketers 1855-1980
- Scottish Cricketers 1905-1980
- Surrey Cricketers 1839-1980
- New South Wales Cricketers 1855-1981

Companion booklets are:

- A Guide to First Class Cricket Matches in the British Isles 1864 to date
- A Guide to Important Cricket Matches in the British Isles 1709-1863
- A Guide to First Class Cricket Matches in Australia
- A Guide to First Class Cricket Matches in New Zealand
- A Guide to First Class Cricket Matches in South Africa

Also published by the Association is a series of books containing the full score cards of every first-class match both in the British Isles and overseas. Each book contains on average 150 matches and the seasons so far published are 1864 to 1885 inclusive.

For details of publications in stock and of membership, write to K.S.C.Trushell, Hon. Treasurer, 127 Davenport Drive, Cleethorpes, S.Humberside.

INTRODUCTION

The present Derbyshire County Cricket Club was founded at a meeting in the Guildhall, Derby on November 4th, 1870. The newly formed Club played its first inter-county match on May 26 and 27, 1871 against Lancashire at Old Trafford and contemporary cricket annuals rated this game and the others played by Derbyshire in 1871 as first-class. The biographical and statistical details given in this booklet therefore commence in May 1871.

In 1888 Derbyshire fell victim to the rationalisation programme undertaken by certain sporting journalists and the County was demoted from first class status - 'league mania' was sweeping the country and the haphazard system of deciding the Champion County, a system which had lasted many years, was too much for the zealous Pardons. Derbyshire, with no opportunity to appeal, was unceremoniously dumped into the *Second Class Counties* League.

The County regained its first-class status in May 1894. Players whose careers were confined to the period between 1888 and 1893 are given separately in this work and these players' performances are not included in the career records.

The Committee of the Association wish to express their thanks to Frank Peach for providing the biographical details in this booklet, and to Philip Bailey, who with Mr Peach's help, provided the statistical details.

Any addenda or errata to this work will be gratefully received by the Committee and will be published in subsequent works in this series.

A.Woodhouse
Chairman

P.Wynne Thomas
Hon. Secretary

Derwent
GLOSSOP
Charlesworth
Ashop
Hayfield
NEW MILLS
Edale
Stanage Edge
Chinley
Castleton
Hope
Aston
Brough
Bradwell
Whaley Bridge
CHAPEL-EN-LE-FRITH
Peak Forest
Little Hucklow
Great Hucklow
Hathersage
Combs
Dove Holes
Peak Dale
Wheston
Wormhill
Tideswell
Litton
Wardlow
Grindleford Bridge
Eyam
Stoney Middleton
Calver
Froggatt
BUXTON
Burbage
Wye
Taddington
Great Longstone
Ashford
Hassop
BASLOW
Chelmorton
Sheldon
Flagg
BAKEWELL
Pilsley
Edensor
Haddon Hall
Monyash
Hurdlow
Great Rowsley
Youlgreave
Alport
Stanton in the Peak
Darley
Middleton
Birchover
Smerrill
Elton
Winster
Hartington
MATLOCK
Tansley
Matlock Bath
Bonsall
Lea
Cromford
Middleton
Alsop-en-le-Dale
Brossingtone
Wirksworth
Whatstandwell
Hopton
Callow
Alderwasley
Ambergate
Tissington
Ilam
Thorpe
Kirk Ireton
Mappleton
Dove
ASHBOURNE
Atlow
Hulland
Bradley
Hazelwood
Windley
Clifton
Osmaston
Snelston
Edlaston
Norbury
Wyaston
Shirley
Mercaston
Brailsford
Weston-Underwood
Duffield
Kedleston
Yeaveley
Rodsley
Hollington
Kirk Langley
Great Cubley
Alkmonton
Longford
Osleston
Marston Montgomery
Boylestone
Doveridge
Church Broughton
Sutton-on-the Hill
Sydbury
Foston
Etwall
Dove
Hatton
Hilton
Findern
Marston-on-Dove
Willington
Tutbury
Repton
Stretton
BURTON-UPON-TRENT
Bretby
Drakelow
Church Gresley
Castle Gresley
Rosliston
Linton
Overseal
Trent
Lullington
Netherseal
SWADLINCOTE
Woodville
Hartshorne
Calke
Ticknall
MELBOURNE
Swarkestone
Chellaston
Shardlow
Elvaston
Alvaston
Littleover
Mickleover
DERBY
Mackworth
Darley Abbey
Allestree
Breadsall
Chaddesden
Spondon
Ockbrook
Borrowash
Risley
Draycott
Sawley
Long Eaton
Sandiacre
Stanton by Dale
Dale Abbey
Stanley
West Hallam
Morley
Little Eaton
Horsley
Stanley
Milford
Holbrook
Kilburn
HEANOR
ILKESTON
BELPER
Hazelwood
Heage
Hartshay
RIPLEY
Ironville
Swanwick
ALFRETON
South Wingfield
Wessington
South Normanton
Shirland
Higham
Stonebroom
Tibshelf
Morton
Stretton
Pilsley
Handley
Ashover
Milltown
Clay Cross
Tupton
N. Wingfield
Wingerworth
Grassmoor
Temple Normanton
Doe Lea
Glapwell
Pleasley
Shirebrook
Holymoor Side
CHESTERFIELD
Hasland
Calow
Duckmanton
Arkwright Town
Bolsover
Scarcliffe
Brampton
Brimington
Barlow
Holmesfield
Whittington
STAVELEY
Clowne
Cresswell
Elmton
Whaley
Barlborough
Whitwell
Renishaw
Eckington
DRONFIELD
Dronfield Woodhouse
Ridgeway
Mosbrough
Beighton

DERBYSHIRE

CRICKETERS WHO HAVE APPEARED IN A FIRST CLASS MATCH FOR THE COUNTY BETWEEN 1871 AND 1981

Ackroyd, Archibald. b Heanor 18.5.1897. du Dudley, Worcs 25.6.1968. rhb rfm. Scotland.

Alderman, Albert Edward. b Alvaston 30.10.1907. rhb occ.wk.

Allen, Michael Henry John. b Bedford 7.1.1933. rhb sla. Northants.

Allsop, Richard. b Wirksworth 10.6.1849. du Burton-on-Trent, Staffs 20.3.1908 rhb.

Anderson, Iain Stuart. b Derby 24.4.1960. rhb ob.

Antliff, William Norris. b Bottesford, Leics 23.8.1848. du Draycott 29.4.1909. rhb.

Armishaw, Christopher John. b Willington 22.9.1952. rhb rm. (One JPL only).

Armstrong, Thomas Riley. b Clay Cross 13.10.1909. lhb sla.

Ashcroft, Edward Maynard (Dr). b Chorlton, Manchester 27.9.1875. d Upton-by-Chester, Cheshire 26.2.1955. rhb ob. Ed Owens College. Gents of England. Joint capt 1904-05.

Attenborough, Thomas. b Ilkeston 7.1833. du Ilkeston 21.1.1907. rhb sla.

Baggallay, Robert Romer Claude. b Kensington, London 4.5.1884. d Kensington, London 12.12.1975. rhb. Ed Marlborough. Cousin of T.W.B.(Surrey). Capt 1913-14, Joint 1919.

Bagguley, William. b Ruddington, Notts 9.9.1866. du Nottingham 18.4.1936. Brother of Robert B.(Notts). **Birth** not registered until 8.2.1930.

Bagshaw, Henry. b Foolow 1.9.1859. d Crowden, Cheshire 31.1.1927. lhb rfm/ob/lb. Players.

Barber, Frederick Arthur. b Ilkeston 13.5.1887. du Mickleover 4.6.1943.

Barlow, Edgar John. b Pretoria, S.Africa **9.10.1850** rhb rm. South Africa(30). W.Prov., E.Prov., Transvaal. Tours(2). Rest of World. Capt 1976-78.

Barnes, Alan Sedgwick. b West Derby, Liverpool 9.10.1950. du (Brentford) 17.5.1915. rhb. M.C.C., Hants. Ed Cambr U.

Barnett, Kim John. b Stoke-on-Trent, Staffs 17.7.1960. rhb lb. D.H.Robins XI 1980-81 in N.Z.

Barrington, George Bainbridge. b Pimlico, London 20.4.1857. d Kirk Langley 29.3.1942. rhb r slow round. Birth registered as George Bainbridge Bainbridge. Ed Repton. Gents of North.

Barrs, Frank Arthur. b Repton 24.3.1871. du Vancouver, Canada 16.12.1963.

Barton, Arthur. b Shipley, Ilkeston 30.9.1874. du Ealing, Middx 19.1.1949. rhb.

Bedford, Edward Henry Rilands. b Aston, Birmingham 7.6.1903. d Chelmsford, Essex 9.10.1976. rhb. Ed Winchester, Midland Counties Agricultural College.

Beet, George. b Somercotes 24.4.1886. d Somercotes 13.12.1946. rhb wk. M.C.C.

Beet, Gordon Albert. b Heanor 5.5.1939. rhb ob. Grandson of George Beet.

Beet, George Hector Cook. b Somercotes 30.5.1904. du Somercotes 22.8.1949. rhb wk. Son of George Beet. M.C.C.

Bell, Geoffrey Foxall. b Stapenhill, Staffs 16.4.1896. rhb. Ed Repton, OU 1919. Cousin of the Eversheds.

Bennett John William. b Lower Whitfield, Glossop 22.2.1864. du Stockport, Cheshire 10.11.1928. rhb lm/sla. registered at death as William Bennett.

Bentley, Michael. b Rotherham, Yorks 14.2.1934. lhb.

Berry, Robert. b Manchester 29.1.1926. lhb sla. M.C.C.(1), Eng(2). Lancashire, Worcestershire.

Berwick, John Albert (Alf) b Northampton 30.7.1867. du Glossop 31.7.1946. lhb lfm.

Bestwick, Robert Saxton. b Heanor 29.9.1899. rhb rfm. Son of W.B.

Bestwick, William. b Heanor 24.2.1875. d Nottingham 3.5.1938. rhb rfm.

Billyeald, James. b Hyson Green, Nottingham c 1835. du Nottingham 8.7.1890. rhb.

Bingham, Frank Miller (Dr). b Alfreton 17.9.1874. d Sanctuary Wood, Ypres, Belgium 22.5.1915. rm. Ed St Peter's York.

Birkett William (also known as Burkitt) b Coal Aston 27.2.1874.

Blacklidge, Henry George. b Stoughton, Surrey 14.7.1884. d Amara, Mesopotamia 23.5.1917 lhb sla. Appointed County Coach 1914 and when qualified would have played for Derbyshire. Surrey.

Blackwell, Henry. b Wirksworth 16.12.1876. du Wirksworth 24.1.1900. rhb rm.

Blaxland, Lionel Bruce. b Lillieshall, Salop 25.3.1898. d Temple Ewell, Kent 29.4.1976. rhb rfm. Ed Shrewsbury, OU.

Blount, Albert. b Morton 8.8.1889. du Rossington, Yorks 11.11.1961. rhb sla.

Boden, Timothy Walter. b Sherborne, Dorset 19.5.1901. d Axminster, Devon 5.9.1969. Great nephew of W.B. Ed Eton.

Boden, Walter. b Derby 6.8.1837. d Mickleover 16.9.1905. rhb. Ed Rugby.

Boissier, Arthur Paul. b Bloxham, Oxon 25.1.1881. d Aberdeen 2.10.1953. Ed Leatherhead, OU.

Bolus, John Brian. b Whitkirk, Leeds 31.1.1934. rhb lm. Capt 1973-75. Eng(7), MCC(1). Yorkshire, Nottinghamshire.

Boot, Jesse. b South Normanton 18.3.1860. du (Chesterfield) 1.3.1940. rhb wk.

Borrington, Anthony John. b Spondon 8.12.1948. rhb occ wk. ob.

Bostock, Herbert. b Ilkeston 4.5.1869. d Ilkeston 20.2.1954. rhb.

Bottom, Daniel. b Whitwell 2.10.1864. d Bulwell, Nottingham 16.2.1937. rhb rm. Nottinghamshire.

Bourne, John James. b Church Gresley 2.11.1872. du Burton-on-Trent 23.12.1952. lm.

Bowden, Joseph. b Glossop 8.10.1884. d Glossop 1.3.1958. rhb.

Bowmer, Herbert Edgar. b Wirksworth 4.7.1891. du Derby 1.6.1966. rhb rfm. Ed Wellingborough.

Bracey, Frederick. b Derby (?) 20.6.1887. d Derby 28.3.1960. lhb sla.

Bradbury, Leslie. b Matlock 19.4.1938. rfm.

Bradley, George. b Derby 29.4.1850. du Derby 24.4.1887. rhb.

Brailsford, Frank Colliss (Jim) b Chesterfield 26.8.1933. rhb.

Brelsford, James. b Brimington 19.12.1855. du Hale, Cheshire 24.12.1924. (registered at death as Bralsford). rhb rm. Cheshire.

Brooke-Taylor, David C. b Bakewell 15.6.1920. rhb. Ed Cheltenham.

Brooke-Taylor, Geoffrey Parker. b Bakewell 25.10.1895. d Buenos Aires, Argentina 15.1.1968. lhb wk. Ed Cheltenham CU 1919-20. Argentine.

Brooks, Joseph. b South Normanton 10.9.1870. du Shuttlewood 15.5.1937. lfm.

Brooks, Kevin Graham. b Reading, Berks 15.10.1959. rhb rm.

Buckley, George Arthur. b Skegby, Notts 3.2.1889. du Norton Lees, Yorks 1.12.1935. rhb rfm. Cheshire.

Buckston, George Moreton. b Hope 12.3.1881. d Sutton-on-the-Hill 24.11.1942. rhb wk. Ed Eton, **M.C.C., CU 1903. Capt 1921.**

Buckston, Robin Henry Rowland. b Kensington, London 10.10.1908. d Burton-on-Trent 16.5.1967. rhb wk. Ed Eton, CU. **M.C.C.. Capt 1937-39**

Burnham, George Joseph. b Nottingham 5.11.1878. du Nottingham 7.3.1971. rhb.

Burnham, John William. b Nottingham 6.6.1839. d Derby 20.4.1914. rhb.

Burrows, Matthew. b Chesterfield 18.8.1855. du Beeston, Leeds 29.5.1893. rhb rfm. Yorkshire.

Burton, Joseph Parkin. b Somercotes 10.12.1873. du Somercotes 25.1.1940. rhb.

Burton, Oswald. b Gorton, Lancs 21.8.1874. du Bristol 4.7.1944. rhb rmf.

Butterfield, Walter. b Dewsbury, Yorks 16.8.1870. du West Bridgford, Nottingham 19.7.1954. rhb rm.

Buxton, Ian Ray. b Cromford 17.4.1938. rhb rm/ob. Capt 1970-72.

Buxton, Noah. b Codnor 26.11.1876. du Pontefract, Yorks 26.5.1967. rhb rfm. **Uncle of** J.H.B.(Notts).

Cadman, Samuel William (plus Anthony at death) b Gibraltar Lane, Denton, Lancs 29.1.1877. d Glossop 6.5.1952. rhb rm.

Carlin, Robert McKenzie. b Eastwood, Notts 24.1.1871. du **Conisborough, Yorks** 10.3.1950. rhb rm.

Carr, Donald Brice. b Wiesbaden, Germany 28.12.1926. rhb sla. Ed Repton OU 1949-51. Capt 1950. Eng(2) MCC(1). Capt 1955-62.

Carrington, Elijah. b Blackwell 25.3.1914. rhb.

Carter, Horatio Stratton. b Hendon, Sunderland, co.Durham 21.12.1913. rhb rm. Football International.

Carter, Reginald. b Whitwell 7.11.1933. rhb sla.

Carter, Wilfred. b Annesley, Notts 19.6.1896. d Watford, Herts 1.11.1975. rhb lb.

Cartledge, J (or W.) b c 1857

Cartwright, Harold. b Halfway 12.5.1951. rhb.

Chapman, John. b Frocester Court, Glos 11.3.1877. d Dunford Bridge, Yorks 12.8.1956. **rhb. Ed Uppingham. Capt 1910-12. Joint 1919-20.**

Charlesworth, Alfred. b Simmondley, Glossop 9.5.1865. du St Annes on Sea, Lancs 4.12.1928.

Chatterton, Joseph. b Thornsett 14.2.1867. d Derby 7.11.1886. rhb rm. **Brother of W.C.**

Chatterton, William. b Thornsett 27.12.1861. d Hyde, Ches 19.3.1913. rhb slow bowler. Capt 1887(part), 1888-89. M.C.C. SA(1). Read to S.Africa 1891-92.

Chester, Charles. b Langley Mill 7.2.1869. du Langwith 9.2.1940. rhb rm.

Clarke, Charles Cyril. b (Burton-on-Trent), Staffs 22.12.1910. rhb. Sussex. Staffs. Ed Repton.

Clayton, John Morton. b Chesterfield 17.11.1857. du Bournemouth, Hants 1.4.1938. rhb rfm.

Cochrane, Alfred Henry John. b Mauritius 26.1.1865. d Batheaston, Somerset 14.12.1948. rhb lmf/ob. Ed Repton OU 1885-6,1888.

Cole, Terence George Owen. b Llanrhaiadr, Denbighshire 14.11.1877. d Taunton, Somerset 15.12.1944. rhb sla. Ed Harrow, CU. Lancashire, Somerset, Cambs, Denbighs.

Cook, Enoch. b Sandiacre 23.4.1845. du Long Eaton 14.4.1927. rhb.

Cooke, John. b Wirksworth 7.3.1851. du Wirksworth 22.11.1908. rhb wk.

Cooper, Archibald Henry Hedges. b Cowley, Oxon 14.8.1878. du Chesterfield 13.1.1922.

Cooper, Herbert. b Dukinfield, Cheshire 25.12.1883. du Oldham, Lancs 6.12.1963. rhb.

Copson, William Henry. b Stonebroom 27.4.1908. d Clay Cross 14.9.1971. rhb rfm. Eng(3). MCC(1).

Corbett, Bertie Oswald. b Thame, Oxon 15.5.1875. d Portesham, Dorset 30.11.1967. rhb. Bucks.

Corbett, Cornelius John. b Thame, Oxon 8.3.1883. du Chandlers Ford, Hants 10.4.1944. ((Registered at Death as John Cornelius Corbett.) **Brother of B.O.C.**

Coup, Edwin (known as Coupe). b Ripley 9.6.1861. du Mickleover 2.7.1892. lhb.

Cresswell, James Arthur. b Marehay 16.3.1903. rhb lfm. Related to Joseph C.(Warwicks).

Crommelin-Brown, John Louis. b Delhi, India 20.10.1888. d Minehead, Somerset 11.9.1953. rhb. Ed Winchester, CU.

Cropper, William. b Brimington 27.12.1862. d Grimsby, Lincs 13.1.1889. rhb lm.

Cross, James.

Cupitt, Joseph. b Barrow Hill 25.9.1867. du South Kirkby, Yorks 6.5.1932. sla/lm

Curgenven, Gilbert. b Derby 1.12.1882. d Birmingham 26.5.1934. rhb slow round. Ed Repton. **Brother of H.G.C. and son of W.G.C.**

Curgenven, Henry Grafton. b Derby 22.12.1875. du Bridgend, Glamorgan 14.2.1959. rhb rfm. Ed Repton, CU.

Curgenven, William Grafton (Dr). b Plymouth, Devon 30.11.1841. d Fareham, Hants 18.3.1910. rhb. Ed Wellingborough.

Cursham, Arthur William. b Wilford, Notts 14.3.1853. d Florida 24.12.1884. rhb slow round. Nottinghamshire. Brother of H.A.C.(Notts).

Davidson, Frank. b Brimington 1.10.1872. du (Chesterfield) 7.6.1951. rhb rm. **Brother of G.A.D., son of J.D.**

Davidson, George Arthur. b Brimington 29.6.1866. d Dudley, Worcs 8.2.1899. rhb rfm. M.C.C.

Davidson, Joseph. b Brimington 9.8.1846. d Brimington 3.12.1901. rhb rm/ob

Davis, John William. b Ironville 10.4.1882. du Ripley 29.10.1963. rhb.

Dawkes, George Owen. b Leicester 19.7.1920. rhb wk. Leicestershire.

Deakin, Michael. b Bury, Lancs 6.5.1957. rhb wk.

Dearnaley, Irvine. b Glossop 18.2.1877. d Ashton-under-Lyne, Lancs 14.3.1965. rhb.

Delacombe, William Barclay. b Ascension Is 20.7.1860. d Nottingham 15.10.1911. Ed King's School, Bruton.

De Ville, Roger Thomas. b Uttoxeter, Staffs 21.1.1935 rhb lb.

Dickinson, Stanley Patrick. b Norton 7.3.1890 **d Wern, N.Wales** 25.6.1972. (registered at death as Stanley Dickinson). rhb rfm. Ed Haileybury.

Disney, James Joseph. b Butterley 20.11.1859. d Ripley 24.6.1934. rhb wk. Cheshire.

Dixon, Francis (Dr). b Derby 31.6.1855. du Eastwood, Notts 20.8.1943. rhb ob. **Shrewsbury's Notts XI**

Dobson, Kenneth William Cecil. b Barrow-on-Trent 28.8.1900. d Newton Abbot, Devon 3.3.1960. rhb rm. Ed Repton. Warwickshire.

Docker, Frank Dudley. b Smethwick, Staffs 26.8.1862. du (Amersham) 8.7.1944.

Docker, Ludford b Smethwick, Staffs 26.11.1860. d Stratford-on-Avon, Warw 1.8.1940. (Registered at death as Ludford Charles Docker). rhb rmf. Ed K.E.S. Birmingham. Capt 1884. Warwickshire. Shrewsbury/Lillywhite to Australia 1887-88.

Docker, Ralph. b Harborne, Staffs 31.8.1855. du (Tonbridge), Kent 7.7.1910.

Doughty, Stephen. b Staveley 16.10.1855. du Halton East, Skipton, Yks 11.11.1929. rhb rm/ob.

Eadie, John (Thom Clarke). b Burton-on-Trent 25.9.1861. du (Lichfield), Staffs 9.8.1923. **Brother of W.S.E. Registered at b & d as John Eadie.**

Eadie, William Stewart. b Burton-on-Trent 27.11.1864. d Barrow-on-Trent 20.9.1914. Ed Dollar Academy, Edinburgh Univ.

Earl, George Burril. b Melbourne 7.8.1859. du Melbourne 20.4.1933 (registered at Death as Earle). rhb rfm.

Eato, Alwyn. b Duckmanton 15.2.1929. rhb rfm.

Eggar, John Drennan. b Nowshera, N.W.F.P., India 1.12.1916. rhb. Ed Winchester, OU 1938. Hampshire.

Elliott, Charles Standish. b Bolsover 24.4.1912. rhb ob.

Elliott, Harry. b Scarcliffe 2.11.1891. d Derby 2.2.1976. rhb wk. Eng(4) MCC(2).

Ellis, William. b Whitwell 28.8.1876. du Huddersfield, Yorks 22.1.1931.

Else, Robert. b Leawood, Matlock 17.11.1876. du Sheffield, Yorks 16.9.1955. lhb.

Estridge, Edward. b Hounslow, Middx 28.4.1843. d Abingdon, Berks 30.8.1919. Ed Tonbridge, OU.

Evans, Charles. b Whittington Moor 19.2.1866. d Chesterfield 14.1.1956. rhb rfm.

Evans, Henry. b Stoneyford, Codner 8.7.1857. du Spondon 20.7.1920. rhb rfm.

Evans, Thomas. b Stoneyford, Codnor 3.6.1852. du Heaton Moor, Stockport 2.12.1916. rhb rm to slow. **Brother of H.E. Liverpool.**

Evershed, Edward. b Stapenhill 3.11.1867. d Birmingham 18.2.1957. rhb. Ed Amersham Hall, OU. **Brother of F.E., S.H.E., and W.E.**

Evershed, Sidney Herbert. b Burton-on-Trent 13.1.1861. d Burton-on-Trent 7.3.1937. (Registered as Evershead at birth) rhb rm. Ed Clifton. Capt 1891-98.

Evershed, Wallis (W). b Stapenhill 10.5.1863. d Kendal, Westmorland 8.5.1911. rhb. Ed Clifton. **Registered at b & d as Wallis Evershed.**

Exham, Percy George. b Cork, Ireland 26.6.1859. d Repton 7.10.1922. Ed Repton, CU.

Eyre, John Arthur. b North Wingfield 25.7.1885. du Bolton-upon-Dearne, Yorks 12.6.1964. rhb.

Eyre, John Richard. b Glossop 13.6.1944. rhb rm.

Eyre, Thomas John Peter. b Brough 17.10.1939. lhb rmf.

Fisher, John. b Hodthorpe 4.8.1897. du Castleford, Yorks 22.6.1954. lhb rm.

Fleming, Charles Barnett. b Derby 28.2.1887. du Grevillers, France 22.9.1918. rhb.

Fletcher, Henry. b Clay Cross 25.7.1882. du Derby 27.10.1937.

Fletcher, Thomas. b Heanor 15.6.1881. d Derby 29.9.1954. rhb rm.

Flint, Joseph. b Wirksworth 23.4.1840. d Wirksworth 2.11.1912. **rhb & slow bowler.**

Flint, Louis Edward. b Ripley 10.1.1895. du Mansfield, Notts 3.4.1958. lhb rfm.

Foley, Edward Francis Walwyn. b Derby 6.10.1851. du Kensington, London 21.10.1923. Ed Repton, OU.

Ford, Neville Montague. b Repton 18.11.1906. rhb. Ed Harrow, OU 1928-30. Middlesex.

Forrester, Thomas (known as Forester, Thomas). b Clay Cross 21.9.1873. d Nottingham 27.12.1927. lhb rmf. Ed Saltley College. Warwickshire.

Forman, Arthur Emilius Francis. b Gibraltar 26.7.1850. d Repton 13.2.1905. rhb. Ed Sherborne, OU. Dorset.

Forman, Frederick Gerald. b Chellaston 30.8.1884. d Penzance, Cornwall 8.12.1960.

Foster, Thomas. b Newton, Ches. 15.12.1848. du Glossop 23.3.1929. rhb wk ra. North.

Foulke, William Henry. b Dawley, Salop 12.4.1874. d Sheffield, Yorks 1.5.1916. (registered at birth as Foulk, but as Foulkes at death).

Frederick, Michael. b Barbados 6.5.1927. West Indies(1).

Freeman, Charles Redfern. b Overseal 22.8.1887. du Fulham, Middx 16.3.1956. rhb.

Frost, George. b Wirksworth 16.10.1848. d Wirksworth 12.2.1913. rhb. **Brother of J.H.F.**

Frost, John Henry. b Wirksworth 30.1.1847. du Ashover 1.11.1916.

Fullwood, Walter. b Holmewood 8.2.1907. rhb wk.

Furniss, John Brian. b Baslow 16.11.1934. rhb rfm.

Genders, William Roy. b Dore 21.1.1913. rhb. Ed King's School, Ely. Somerset, Worcesters.

Gibbs, Peter John Keith. b Buglawton, Ches. 17.8.1944. rhb. **ob. Ed Hanley G.S.,OU 1964-66**

Gibson, Ian (Dr). b Glossop 15.8.1936. d Bowdon, Ches 3.5.1963. rhb lbg. Ed Manchester G.S., OU 1955-58.

Gilbert, John Dudley Harwood. b Chellaston 8.10.1910. Ed Repton.

Gladwin, Clifford. b Doe Lea 3.4.1916. rhb rfm. Eng(8) MCC(1). **Son of J.G.**

Gladwin, Joseph. b Doe Lea 6.9.1890. d Chesterfield 8.9.1962. rhb rfm.

Glenn, Michael. b Belper 14.6.1956. rhb rfm.

Goodall, John. b London 19.6.1863. du Watford, Herts 20.5.1942. Football International.

Goodwin, George William. b Chesterston, Staffs 7.9.1898. sla Ed Rossall, Sheffield Univ.

Gothard, Edward James. b Burton-on-Trent 1.10.1904. d Birmingham 17.1.1979. rhb rm. Capt 1947-48. Staffordshire.

Gould, Thomas. b Brassington 26.9.1863. du Burton-on-Trent 30.3.1948.

Graham-Brown, James Martin Hilary. b Thetford, Norfolk 11.7.1951. rhb rm. Ed Sevenoaks, Univ of Kent. Kent.

Grainger, George. b Morton 11.11.1887. d Walton, Chesterfield 17.8.1977. lhb sla/lm.

Green, David J. b Burton-on-Trent 18.12.1935. rhb. Ed Burton G.S., CU 1957-59, Capt 1959.

Green, George. b Hasland 13.4.1880. du (Chesterfield) 25.11.1940. lm.

Gregory, George Robert. b Pilsley 22.8.1878. du Scarborough, Yorks 28.11.1958. **rhb lb.**

Gregory, Dove. b Sutton-in-Ashfield, Notts 9.2.1840. du Derby 21.5.1873. rhb rf.

Hall, Bert

Hall, Derek. b Creswell 21.2.1932. **rhb, rfm.**

Hall, Ian William. b Sutton Scarsdale 27.12.1939. rhb. occ wk

Hall, John Peter. b Worksop, Notts 20.8.1874. du Worksop, Notts 6.11.1925. rhb rfm.

Hall, Thomas Auckland. b Durham, co. Durham 19.8.1930. rhb rfm. Ed Uppingham. Somerset.

Hall, Walter. b Whitfield 27.11.1861. probably died Halifax, Yorks 23.4.1919.

Hallam, Thomas Haydn. b Pilsley 12.4.1882. du Christchurch NZ 24.11.1958.

Hamer, Arnold. b Huddersfield, Yorks 8.12.1916. rhb ob. Yorkshire.

Hancock, Joseph. b Old Tupton 26.11.1876. du Rotherham, Yorks 23.5.1939 (Registered at death as Joseph William Hancock). lm. Scotland.

Handford, James. b Hayfield 1.2.1890. du (Stockport) 14.5.1948.

Hanson, Raymond Leslie. b Chesterfield 12.4.1951. rhb wk.

Hardy, Solomon. b Ilkeston 18.5.1863. du Ilkeston 5.7.1931. rhb wk.

Harvey, John Frank. b Cambridge 27.9.1939. rhb ob. M.C.C., Cambridgeshire, Berkshire.

Harvey-Walker, Ashley John. b East Ham, Essex 21.7.1944. rhb rm/ob. Ed Strathallan.

Hay, George. b Staveley 28.1.1851. d Staveley 4.10.1913. rhb rfm. North.

Headley, Ronald George Alphonso. b Kingston, Jamaica 29.6.1939. lhb. West Indies(2). Worcestershire. Only One day matches for Derbyshire.

Heath, Frederick Rhead. b Swadlincote 30.10.1894. du Seaford, Sussex 19.9.1967.

Heath, John Stanley. b Woodville 30.8.1891. India(Dom). Staffordshire.

Hendrick, Michael. b Darley Dale 22.10.1948. rhb rfm. Eng(28) MCC(5).

Hickton, William. b Hardstoft 14.12.1842. d Lower Broughton, Manchester 27.2.1900. Lancashire. rhb rfm.

Higson, Thomas Atkinson. b Stockport, Ches 18.11.1873. d Grange-over-Sands, Lancs 3.8.1949. Ed Rossall, CU. rhb ob. Father of T.A.H. jun.

Higson, Thomas Atkinson. b Whaley Bridge 25.3.1911. Ed Cheltenham, CU. Lancashire.

Hill, Alan. b Buxworth 29.6.1950. rhb ob. O.F.S.

Hill, Maurice. b Scunthorpe, Lincs 14.9.1935. rhb. Nottinghamshire, Somerset.

Hill-Wood, Basil Samuel Hill. b Chelsea, London 5.2.1900. d Farley Hill, Reading 3.7.1954. rhb rfm. Ed Eton, CU.

Hill-Wood, Charles Kerrison Hill. b Hoxne, Norfolk 5.6.1907. Ed Eton, OU 1928-30.

Hill-Wood, Denis John Charles Hill. b Hoxne, Norfolk 25.6.1906. Ed Eton, OU 1928. d Hartley Witney, Hants 4.5.1982.

Hill-Wood, Wilfred William Hill. b Chelsea, London 8.9.1901. d Kensington, London 10.10.1980. rhb lb/ob. (Later Sir Wilfred Hill-Wood). Ed Eton, Cu 1922. MCC(1). India(Dom).

Hind, Amos. b Calverton, Notts 1.2.1849. du Calverton, Notts 27.4.1931. rhb ram.

Hodgkinson, Gilbert Frank. b Derby 19.2.1913. rhb. Capt 1946. Ed Derby School. (Reported missing in *Wisden* 1941 and dead in 1943 - incorrect. Removed from death list in *Wisden* 1944).

Hodgkinson, J.

Hogg, Arthur. b Greenwich, Ripley 2.7.1877. du Ripley 21.4.1956. rhb.

Holden, Stanley Mitton. b Chesterfield 25.1.1886. du Coventry, Warwicks 10.5.1971. rhb lfm with lb.

Horsley, James. b Melbourne 4.1.1890. d Derby 13.2.1976. rhb rfm. Nottinghamshire.

Hounsfield, Thomas Douglas. b Hackenthorpe 28.4.1910.

Houseman, Edward Outram. b Dronfield 19.3.1869. du Westhoughton, Lancs 10.4.1942. rhb.

Howarth, Thomas. b 10.5.1845. du (Fylde) 12.10.1897.

Howcroft, Albert. b Cliffe, Yks 27.12.1882. du Belper 7.3.1955. lhb.

Hughes-Hallett, Norton Montresor. b Melbourne 18.4.1895. Ed Haileybury. India(Dom).

Hulme, John Joseph. b Church Gresley 30.6.1862. du Nelson, Lancs 11.7.1940. M.C.C.

Humble, William John (Rev). b Sutton Scarsdale 9.12.1846. d Waldron, Sussex 1.7.1924. (**Registered ar death as Humble-Crofts). Ed Newark Magnus,OU.**

Humphries, Joseph. b Stonebroom 19.5.1876. d Chesterfield 8.5.1946. rhb wk. Eng(3) MCC(1).

Hunt, Samuel Walter. b Doe Lea 9.1.1909. du Rochdale, Lancs 2.8.1963. **rhb lb**

Hunter, Frederick Cecil. b (Hayfield) 23.8.1886. du Australia 21.7.1926. lb. Cheshire.

Hurt, Colin Noel Bickley. b Darley Dale 16.12.1893. d Bexhill-on-Sea, Sussex 31.12.1972. rhb rm. Ed Malvern, OU.

Hutchinson, James (Metcalfe). b New Tupton 29.11.1896. rhb rmf. **(Registered at birth as James H.)**

Inman, Clive Clay. b Colombo, Ceylon 29.1.1936. lhb ob. Leicestershire, Ceylon. Ceylon to India Only One Day matches for Derbyshire.

Jackson, Albert Brian. b Kettleshulme, Ches 21.8.1933. rhb rfm. M.C.C.

Jackson, Anthony Henry Mather. b London 9.11.1899. rhb rfm. Ed Harrow. Now Sir Anthony Mather-Jackson. Cousin to G.L. and G.R.J.

Jackson, Geoffrey Laird, M.C. b Birkenhead, Ches 10.1.1894. d Faimpoux, Arras, Belgium 9.4.1917. rhb rm. Ed Harrow, OU. Brother of G.R.J.

Jackson, Guy Rolfe. b Ankerbold, Tupton 23.6.1896. d Chesterfield 21.2.1966. lhb. Ed Harrow. Capt 1922-30. M.C.C.

Jackson, Herbert Leslie. b Whitwell 5.4.1921. rhb rf. Eng(2).

Jackson, Leonard. b Norton Woodseats 8.4.1848. du Sheffield, Yorks 21.3.1887. rf - round.

Jelf, Henry Francis Donhoff. b Aldershot, Hants 27.8.1877. d (Southport) 18.4.1944.

Jervis, William Monk. b London 25.1.1827. d Quarndon 25.3.1909. rhb. Ed Eton, OU.

Johnson, Hubert Laurence. b Barbados 8.11.1927. rhb ob occ wk.

Johnston, Duncan Alexander. b Edinburgh 25.6.1847. d Edinburgh 22.10.1931. Father of A.C.J.(Hants). KCMG 1906.

Jordan, Henry Guy Bowen. b Buxton 10.6.1898. d Tonbridge, Kent 5.10.1981. rhb. Ed Marlborough.

Keeton, Frederick William. b Mosborough 26.10.1855. du Bolton, Lancs 27.11.1911. rhb ra (roundarm).

Kelly, John Martin. b Bacup, Lancs 19.3.1922. d Rochdale, Lancs 13.11.1979. rhb. Lancs.

Kenward, Richard. b Hastings, Sussex 23.5.1875. du Croydon, Surrey 24.12.1957. Ed Hurstpierpont. Sussex.

Kirsten, **Peter Noel. b Pietermaritzburg,** S.Africa 14.5.1955. rhb ob. Sussex. W.Province.

Langdale, George Richmond. b Thornaby-on-Tees, Yorks 11.3.1916. lhb rob. Somerset.

Langton, Samuel Thomas. b Parkgate, Doncaster, Yorks 24.1.1886. du Bentley, Doncaster, Yorks 10.7.1918. rhb.

Lawton, Albert Edward. b Dukinfield, Ches 31.3.1879. d Manchester 25.12.1955. rhb rm to slow. Capt 1902-03,1909, Joint 1904-06, 1908. Lancashire, Cheshire.
Ed Rugby.

Lee, Charles. b Rotherham, Yorks 17.3.1924. rhb rm. Capt 1963-64. Yorkshire.

Lee, Garnett Morley. b Calverton, Notts 7.6.1887. d Newark, Notts 29.2.1976. rhb lbg. Nottinghamshire. Tennyson to Jamaica.

Leech, Colin. b Hayfield 30.8.1889. du Frome, Somerset 6.3.1961. rhb.

Limb, Thomas. b Eastwood, Notts 25.2.1850. du Eastwood, Notts 21.2.1901. middle paced round.

Linathan, Douglas Valentine. b Woodhouse, Sheffield 29.5.1885. du Derby 17.12.1932. lhb sla.

Lister, John Wilton. b Darlington, co Durham 1.4.1959. rhb.

Locker, William. b Long Eaton 16.2.1866. d Derby 14.8.1952. rhb.

Loney, Escott Frith. b Bristol 21.7.1903. Ed Derby School. Canada. lhb rmf.

Lowe, Charles. b Whitwell 23.6.1890. rfm.

Lowe, George. b Mastin Moor 25.5.1915. rhb.

Lyon, Charles Henry. b Rocester, Staffs 18.3.1878. du Ightfield, Salop 3.12.1959. rhb.

McCurdy, Rodney John. b Melbourne, Australia 30.12.1959. rhb rfm. Shropshire, Tasmania.

McDonald, John Archibald. b Belper 29.5.1882. d Blackburn, Lancs 4.6.1961. rhb.

McLellan, Alan James. b Ashton-under-Lyne, Lancs 2.9.1958. rhb wk. occ ob.

McMillan, Stuart Thomas. b Leicester 17.9.1896. du Ashbourne 27.9.1963. rhb rmf.

Maher, Bernard Joseph Michael. b Hillingdon, Middx 11.2.1958. rhb wk. Ed Loughborough U of Tech.

Maltby, George. b South Normanton 1.10.1876. du Huthwaite 30.7.1924. rhb.

Malthouse, Samuel. b Whitwell 13.10.1857. d (Worksop) 7.2.1931. lhb rm/ob. Father of W.N.

Malthouse, William Norman. b Whitwell 16.12.1890. d South Kirkby, Yorks 10.5.1961. rhb ob. Son of Samuel M.

Marks, Christopher Peter. b Hanley, Staffs 17.7.1946. rhb rm. Ed Worksop. Staffordshire.

Marlow, Joseph. b Bulwell, Notts 12.12.1854. du Bulwell, Notts 8.6.1923. rhb rm.

Marple, George (Smith). b Chester, Ches 14.8.1868. du Ecclesall or Millhouses 12.8.1932.

Marples, George. b Attercliffe, Yorks 30.5.1883. du (Chesterfield) 30.12.1947. lfm.

Marsden, Arthur. b Buxton 28.10.1880. d London 31.7.1916 (of wounds received on the Somme). rhb. Ed Cheethams Hospital, Manchester.

Marsden, George Allen. b Wirksworth 28.6.1869. du Diep River, Cape Province 7.1.1938. rhb lb. Ed Denstone.

Marsh, Frederick Eric. b Bolsover 17.7.1920. lhb sla. Nephew of T.S.Worthington.

Marshall, Joseph. b Mosborough 25.7.1862. d Derby 15.1.1913. rhb

Maynard, Edmund Anthony Jefferson. b Chesterfield 19.2.1861. d Hoon, Hilton 10.1.1931. rhb. Capt 1885-86, part 1887. Ed Harrow, CU.

Mellor, Alan. b Horninglow, Staffs 4.7.1959. rhb sla.

Middleton, Charles. b Leeds 21.12.1869. du Chesterfield 5.2.1938. rhb lb.

Miller, Geoffrey. b Chesterfield 8.9.1952. rhb ob. Capt part 1979, 1980 and part 1981. Eng(25) MCC(5).

Millner, David. b Dove Holes 24.7.1938. rhb ob.

Mir, Parvez Jamil. b Dacca, Pakistan 24.9.1953. rhb rfm. Glamorgan. Pakistan (One Day only). Habib Bank.

Mitchell, Thomas Bignall. b Creswell 4.9.1902. rhb lbg. Eng(5) MCC(1).

Mohan, Keith Frederick. b Glossop 11.6.1935. rhb.

Moir, Dallas Gordon. b Malta 13.4.1957. rhb sla. Scotland.

Morgan, Derek Clifton. b Muswell Hill, London 26.2.1929. rhb rfm. Ed Berkhamsted. Capt 1965-69. M.C.C.

Morris, Alan. b Staveley 23.8.1953. rhb lb. Griqualand West.

Morton, Arthur. b Salford, Lancs 27.3.1882. du Sheffield, Yorks 21.2.1970. rhb rfm.

Morton, Arthur. b Mellor 7.5.1884. d (Hayfield) 19.12.1935. rhb rm/ob. M.C.C.

Moses, Eric Claude. b South Africa (Johannesburg?) 18.7.1893. du Durban, S.Africa 10.7.1971. (changed name to E.C.Murray). rhb ob. Ed Repton. Transvaal.

Mycroft, Frank. b Furnace, Shirland 30.6.1873. du Leicester 26.9.1900. lhb wk.

Mycroft, Thomas. b Brimington 28.3.1848. d Mickleover 13.8.1911. lhb wk. occ rm round. M.C.C. Half brother of William M.

Mycroft, William. b Brimington 1.2.1841. d Derby 19.6.1894. rhb lf occ wk. M.C.C. A.E.E. Half brother of Thomas M.

Needham, Ernest. b Newbold Moor, Chesterfield 21.1.1873. d Chesterfield 7.3.1936. lhb rm occ. wk.

Needham, Joseph. b Flagg 9.1.1862. du Taddington 30.8.1889. rhb.

Newcombe, Charles Niel. b (Yarmouth) 16.3.1891. d Fleuraix, France 27.12.1915. rhb lmf.

Newman, Paul Geoffrey. b Leicester 10.1.1959. rhb rfm.

Newton, Frederick Arthur. b Denaby, Yorks 16.9.1890. d Warsop, Notts 8.8.1924. rhb.

Nornable, Ernest. b Norton 25.12.1886. d Sheffield 21.4.1970. rhb rfm.

Oates, William Farrand. b Aston, Sheffield 17.6.1929. rhb ob. Yorkshire.

O'Connor, John. b Pinxton 23.2.1867 du Cambridge 13.7.1936. rhb rm/ob. Cambridgeshire. Father of J.O'Connor (Essex); brother-in-law of Herbert Carpenter (Essex).

Oldham, Stephen. b High Green, Sheffield 26.7.1948. rhb rfm. Yorkshire.

Oldknow, James. b Denby 12.3.1873. du Belper 10.9.1944. rhb rm.

Oliver, Leonard. b Glossop 18.10.1886. d Glossop 26.1.1948. lhb rm. Capt 1920.

Ollivierre, Charles Augustus. b Kingston, Jamaica 20.7.1876. d Pontefract, Yorks 25.3.1949. rhb. Trinidad.

Osborne, George.

Page, Michael Harry. b Blackpool, Lancs 17.6.1941. rhb ob.

Page, William. b Caverswall, Staffs 29.4.1847. d Derby 27.9.1904. rhb.

Parrington, William Ferguson. b Sunderland, co.Durham 1.11.1889. du Northallerton, Yorks 7.5.1980. rhb rm. Ed Rossall, CU. Durham.

Payton, Wilfred Ernest Granville (Rev). b Beeston, Notts 27.12.1913. rhb. Ed Nottingham H.S., CU 1937. Nottinghamshire. Combined Services. Son of W.R.D.P.(Notts).

Peach, Frederick George. b Repton 2.11.1882. d Stapenhill, Staffs 15.1.1965. rhb lb occ. wk.

Peach, William. b Timberland Fen, Lincs 6.5.1875. du Chesterfield 29.1.1959. rhb rfm.

Pearson, Laurence Ivor (Jack). b Darnall, Yorks 25.1.1922. lhb.

Pink, Hubert Selwyn. b Chapel-en-le-Frith 12.11.1878. du Chapel-en-le-Frith 26.11.1946. rhb. Ed St Edmunds School, Canterbury, CU.

Platts, John Thomas Brown Dumelow. b Chellaston 5.12.1848. d Derby 6.8.1898. lhb rf round/sra. M.C.C.

Pope, Alfred Vardy. b Tibshelf 15.8.1909. rhb rfm/ob.

Pope, George Henry. b Tibshelf 27.1.1911. rhb rfm. Eng(1).

Pope, Harold. b Chesterfield 10.5.1919. rhb lb.

Porter, George. b Kilburn 3.12.1861. d Spondon 15.7.1908. rhb rfm.

Pratt, Richard. b Lower Broughton, Manchester 23.6.1896. rhb wk.

Prince, William. b Somercotes 28.3.1868. du Ollerton, Notts 1.6.1948. rhb rmf.

Purdy, Henry Fox. b Brimington 17.1.1884. du Chesterfield 21.2.1943. rhb rfm. Nephew of John Henry P.

Purdy, John Henry (also known as Purdew). b Brimington 23.9.1871. du Mansfield, Notts 19.5.1938. rhb rmf. Brother of Thomas P.

Radford, Henry William. b Derby 19.6.1896. du Banbury, Oxon 29.11.1972. lm.

Ratcliffe, George. b Ilkeston 1856. d (Nottingham) 7.3.1928. rhb.

Ratcliffe, George. b Nov 1885. du Ollerton, Notts 31.12.1952. rhb.

Reader-Blackton, Walter. b Shirland 4.7.1895. d Derby 1.1.1976. rhb rm. (Played as Reader, W. in 1914).

Regan, Charles. b Barnsley, Yorks 11.5.1842. du Southend-on-Sea, Essex 17.3.1921. rhb occ wk. Ed Hammersmith College.

Revill, Alan Chambers. b Sheffield, Yorks 27.3.1923. rhb ob. Leicestershire. Son of T.F.R.

Revill, Thomas Frederick. b Bolsover 9.5.1892. d Mansfield, Notts 29.3.1979. lhb lbg.

Rhodes, Albert Ennion Groucott. b Tintwhistle, Ches 10.10.1916. rhb rfm/lb. M.C.C. MCC(1). Father of H.J.R.

Rhodes, Harold James. b Glossop 22.7.1936. rhb rf. Eng(2).

Richardson, Arthur Walker. b Quarndon 4.3.1907. rhb. Ed Winchester. Capt 1931-36. Father of G.W.R.

Richardson, Bertram Harold. b Ashton-under-Lyne 12.3.1932. lhb sla.

Richardson, George William. b Marylebone, London 26.4.1938. rhb lfm. M.C.C. Ed Winchester. **Son of A.W.R.**

Richardson, John. b Duckmanton 17.3.1856. du Brimington 19.2.1940. rhb rfm round.

Richardson, Samuel. b Derby 24.5.1844. d Madrid, Spain March 1938. rhb wk. Capt 1871-75.

Richardson, Thomas Haden. b Tutbury, Staffs 4.7.1865. d Tutbury, Staffs 10.12.1923. rhb. Staffordshire.

Rickman, Reginald Binns. b Doncaster, Yorks 6.5.1881. du Chelsea, London 22.11.1940. rhb rm. Ed Sherborne. Devon. Joint Capt 1908. (Registered at death as Rickman, James, but this was later corrected by statutory declaration to Rickman, Reginald Binns.)

Rigley, William. b Eastwood, Notts 24.3.1852. du Nottingham 15.3.1897. rhb rm.

Rimmer, Joseph. b Langwith 26.1.1925. rhb rfm.

Root, Charles Frederick. b Somercotes 16.4.1890. d Wolverhampton 20.1.1954. rhb rm. Eng(3) MCC(1). Worcestershire.

Rose, Alfred. b Glossop 15.2.1894. rhb.

Rowe, Lawrence George. b Kingston, Jamaica 8.1.1949. rhb rm. Jamaica. W.I.(30).

Rumsey, Frederick Edward. b Stepney, London 4.12.1935. rhb lfm. Eng(5). Somerset. Worcestershire.

Russell, Philip Edgar. b Ilkeston 9.5.1944. rhb rm/ob.

Ryder, Reginald Thomas. b (Nantwich) 18.6.1875. du (Stockport) 6.11.1923.

Sale, Richard. b Broughty Ferry, Scotland 21.6.1889. d East Hannay, Berks 7.9.1970. lhb rfm. Ed Repton, OU 1910. Father of Richard S jun.

Sale, Richard. b Shrewsbury, Salop 4.10.1919. lhb. Ed Repton, OU 1939,1946. Warwickshire.

Selby, Thomas Gothard. b North Wingfield 19.2.1851. du Shirebrook 6.11.1924. rhb rf round.

Severn, Arthur. b Alfreton 23.6.1893. d Stainforth, Yorks 10.1.1949.

Shacklock, Francis Joseph. b Crich 22.9.1861. d Christchurch, N.Z. 3.5.1937. rhb rf. Nottinghamshire. Otago.

Shardlow, Wilfred. b Clowne 30.9.1902. du Burton-on-Trent 21.6.1956. lhb rfm.

Sharpe, Philip John. b Shipley, Yorks 12.12.1936. rhb ob. Eng(12). MCC(1). Ed Bradford G.S., Worksop. Yorkshire.

Shaw, Henry. b Mansfield, Notts 21.5.1854. du Derby 8.11.1932. rhb rm round. Staffordshire.

Shearwood, Kenneth Arthur. b Derby 5.9.1921. rhb wk. OU.

Sherwin, Arthur West. b Derby 22.7.1879. du Duffield 10.10.1947. rhb rm. Brother of C.B.S.

Sherwin, Charles Bakewell. b Derby 9.8.1877. du Derby 8.6.1950. rhb.

Sherwin, Howard. b (Chesterfield) 22.7.1911. **lhb**

Shipton, William Louis. b Buxton 9.3.1861. d Buxton 21.10.1941. rhb rf round. Ed Repton, CU.

Short, John David. b Chesterfield 13.6.1934. rhb ob. Ed Denstone.

Shuker, Abraham. b Stockton, Salop 6.7.1848. d Tunstall, Staffs 11.2.1909. rhb. Ed Brewood, CU.

Skinner, Alan Frank. b Brighton, Sussex 22.4.1913. d Bury St Edmunds, Suffolk 28.2.1982. rhb. Ed Leys School, CU. Northants. Brother of D.A.S.

Skinner, David A. b Duffield 22.3.1920. rhb ob. Ed Leys School. Capt 1949.

Slater, Archibald Gilbert. b Pilsley 22.11.1890. d Manchester 22.7.1949. rhb rm. Son of Henry, brother of Herbert S.

Slater, Henry. b Heanor 23.2.1855. d (Worksop) 20.11.1916. rhb. **rm**

Slater, Herbert. b Langley Mill 11.11.1881. d Creswell 2.12.1958. rhb rfm/ob.

Smith, Alfort. b Bury, Lancs 7.7.1846. d Glossop 21.12.1908. rhb wk. Lancashire.

Smith, Denis. b Somercotes 24.1.1907. d Derby 12.9.1979. Eng(2), MCC(1). **lhb rm**

Smith, David Henry Kilner. b Shipley, Yorks 29.6.1940. lhb occ wk. O.F.S.

Smith, Edwin. b Grassmoor 2.1.1934. rhb ob. M.C.C.

Smith, Harry Watson. b Chesterfield 30.9.1886. d Ruthin, Denbighshire 24.6.1955. rhb wk. Ed Worksop, Sheffield Univ. Warwickshire.

Smith, John. b Clifton 27.10.1841. d Derby 26.11.1898. rhb slow round.

Smith, Lemuel Strutt Tugby. b Tibshelf 5.6.1880. du South Kirkby, Yorks 30.12.1927. rhb wk

Smith, Robert (Posnett). (later Stevens, Robert Posnett). b Sawley 1.11.1848. d Staunton, Notts 1.5.1899. rhb rf round/lobs. Capt 1876-83.

Smith, Willie. b Gringley-on-the-Hill, Notts 12.5.1885. du Scawsby, Yorks 8.5.1964. rhb.

Snape, Maurice Desmond. b Creswell 7.7.1923. rhb.

Southern, John Dunlop (Guy). b Derby 5.11.1899. d Melksham, Wilts 7.2.1972. rhb.

Sowter, Unwin. b Derby 22.4.1839. d Derby 14.4.1910. rhb. Ed Derby School.

Sparrow, Guy Ratcliff. b Aston, Birmingham 2.7.1877. du Burton-on-Trent 6.1.1958. rhb.

Spencer, Harry/Henry.

Stapleton, Ernest. b New Basford, Notts 15.1.1869. du Nottingham 14.12.1938. rhb. Married a sister of George Gunn (Notts).

Steele, David Stanley. b Stoke-on-Trent, Staffs 29.9.1941. rhb sla. Northants. Eng(8). Capt 1979 part.

Steeples, Albert. b Somercotes 28.7.1870. du Derby 14.8.1945. rfm

Steeples, Richard. b Somercotes 30.4.1873. du Somercotes 2.8.1946. rfm

Stephenson, George Robert. b Derby 19.11.1942. rhb wk. Ed Derby School. Hampshire.

Stevenson, George Stanley. b Derby 20.7.1876. du (Belper) 25.7.1938.

Stevenson, Keith. b Derby 6.10.1950. rhb rfm. Hampshire.

Stevenson, Michael Hamilton. b Chinley 13.6.1927. rhb sla. Ed Rydal, CU 1949-52. M.C.C. Ireland.

Storer, Harry. b Butterley 24.7.1870. d Holloway 25.4.1908. rhb. Brother of William S., Father of Harry S. jun.

Storer, Harry. b Liverpool 2.2.1898. d Derby 1.9.1967. rhb lb occ. wk.

Storer, William. b Butterley 25.1.1867. d Derby 5.3.1912. rhb wk lb. Eng(6), Stoddart (1) M.C.C.

Street, Henry. b Riddings 18.4.1863. du Riddings 12.3.1953. rhb

Stubbings, James (Registered as Stubbins at birth) b Whitwell 27.4.1856. d Huddersfield 17.7.1912. rhb rf. Father of Walter S.

Stubbings, Walter. b Whitwell 4.9.1870. du Wakefield 28.11.1949.

Sugden, Albert Sidney. b Edmonton. Middx 31.10.1864. du Christchurch, N.Z. 1.10.1917. rhb. Brother of H.E.S. Only v Essex - not first-class.

Sugden, Henry Emanuel. b Edmonton, Middx 16.7.1859. du Chilworth, Hants 4.9.1935. rhb.

Sugg, Frank Howe. b Ilkeston 11.1.1862. d Liverpool 29.5.1933. rhb. Eng(2). Yorkshire. Lancashire.

Sugg, Walter. b Ilkeston 21.5.1860. d Dore, Yorks 21.5.1933. rhb rm. Ed Sheffield G.S. Yorkshire.

Swallow, Raymond. b Southwark, London 15.6.1935. rhb. M.C.C.

Swarbrook, Frederick William. b Derby 27.12.1950. lhb sla. Griq West. O.F.S.

Swindell, Robert Stephen. b Derby 22.1.1950. rhb ob.

Sykes, Eric. b Bolsover 23.6.1906. rhb. Son of E.C.S.(Hants).

Tate, Cecil Frederick. b Gillingham, Kent 1.5.1908. rhb sla. Warwickshire. Son of F.W.T. and brother of M.W.T.

Taylor, Francis Henry. b Wirksworth 14.6.1890. d Derby 6.12.1963. rhb. Brother of W.T.T.

Taylor, Robert William. b Stoke-on-Trent, Staffs 17.7.1941. rhb wk. Eng(29) MCC(8). Capt part 1975-76.

Taylor, William Thomas. b Wirksworth 14.4.1885. d Breadsall 17.8.1976. rhb rm. Ed Leeds Univ.

Thompson, William Holloway. b Spondon 24.6.1882. d Spondon 19.10.1954. rhb.

Thornhill, Frederick. b Beeston, Notts 25.9.1846. d Toton Sidings, Long Eaton 23.7.1876.

Tilson, John. b Ilkeston 27.3.1845. du Ilkeston 4.11.1895. rhb rm round.

Todd, Norman Douglas. b Hetton-le-Hole, co Durham 11.6.1884. du (Basford) 12.5.1959.

Tomlinson, John D. b South Normanton 26.3.1926. rhb.

Tomlinson, William James Vincent. b (Burton-on-Trent) 10.8.1901. rhb rm. Ed Felsted, CU 1923.

Topham, Henry Gillespie (Rev). b Ladbroke, Warwicks 16.2.1862. d Middleham, Yorks 28.2.1925. lhb sla. Ed Repton, CU 1883-84.

Townsend, Arnold Frederick. b Long Eaton 29.3.1912. rhb. Brother of L.F.T.

Townsend, Leslie Fletcher. b Long Eaton 8.6.1903. rhb rm/ob. Eng(4) MCC(2).

Trueman, Frederick Seawards. b Stainton, Yorks 6.2.1931 rhb rfm. Yorks. One Day matches only for Derbyshire.

Tunnicliffe, Colin John. b Derby 11.8.1951. rhb lfm.

Turland, Herbert. b Stapleford, Notts 29.8.1894. rhb lm. Nottinghamshire.

Turner, Allen. b Heath 24.10.1891. du Holmwood 15.1.1961. rhb rfm.

Tye, John. b Bulwell, Notts 10.7.1848. d Brighouse, Yorks 19.11.1905. rhb rf. Nottinghamshire.

Vaulkhard, Patrick. b Nottingham 15.9.1911. rhb wk lbg. Capt 1950. Ed Oakham. Cahn's XI, Nottinghamshire. Northumberland.

Venkataraghavan, Srinivasaraghavan. b Madras, India 21.4.1946. rhb ob. India(50). Tamil Nadu (Madras).

Walkden, George Godrey. b Derby 10.3.1883. d Derby 17.5.1923.

Walker, George Glossop. b Harthill, Yorks 14.6.1860. d Whitwell 11.1.1908. lhb sla (later rfm)

Walker, Niel Alexander McDonald. b Poona India 22.8.1895. d Spinkhill, Yorks 10.8.1960. rhb rm. India (Dom).

Walker, Stanley George. b Pinxton 18.5.1908. rhb lfm.

Wallis, William Alfred. b Long Eaton 14.12.1878. du (Ilkeston) 12.11.1939. rhb. Ed Trent Coll.

Wallroth, Conrad Adolphus. b Lee, Kent 17.5.1851. d Compton, Surrey 22.2.1926. Ed Harrow, OU 1872-74. Kent.

Walters, John. b Brampton, Yorks 7.8.1949. lhb.

Walton, William. b Glossop 7.8.1862. du Glossop 16.2.1925. rhb.

Ward, Alan. b Dronfield 10.8.1947. rhb rf. Leicestershire. Eng(5) MCC(1). Border.

Ward, John Michael. b Sandon, Staffs 14.9.1948. rhb. Ed Newcastle-under-Lyne H.S., OU 1970-73.

Ward, Joseph Preston. b Leeds, Yorks 10.4.1871. du Langford Budville, Somerset 21.2.1931. Staffordshire.

Ward, Leonard Foster (Rev). b Oldham 24.3.1866. du St Helier. Jersey 1.9.1945.

Warren, Arnold (R). b Codnor 2.4.1875. d Codnor 3.9.1951. rhb rf. Eng(1)

Wass, Horace. b (Chesterfield) 26.8.1903.

Watson, Richard Martin. b Bakewell 31.12.1921. lhb lb. Ed Trent College.

Webster, David. b Sheffield 22.5.1944. lhb rm.

Webster, Frederick. b (Ecclesall) 19.1.1885. du 23.3.1938.

Webster, William. b 1880. du Dinnington, Yorks 10.3.1931.

Whyatt, Christopher. b Old Whittington 12.6.1954. rhb wk.

Wickstead, Archibald. b Meltham Mills, Yorks 6.11.1884. du Mansfield, Notts 1.2.1966. lhb.

Widdowson, Albert. b Bingham, Notts 31.3.1864. du Duffield 28.4.1938.

Wild, Harold. b Hadfield 3.2.1891. d Glossop 8.8.1977. rhb rm.

Wilde, David. b Glossop 3.7.1950. lhb lfm.

Wilkins, Christopher Peter. b Kingwilliamstown, S.Africa 31.7.1944. rhb rm wk. Border,E.P.,Natal.

Willatt, Guy Longfield. b Nottingham 7.5.1918. lhb. Capt 1951-54. Ed Repton, CU 1946-47(Capt 47). Nottinghamshire. Scotland, M.C.C.

Wilmot, Arthur Alfred (Rev). b Chaddesden 14.2.1845. d Morley 12.5.1876.

Wilmot, William. b Denby 25.12.1869. d Leyland, Lancs 19.5.1957. rhb wk.

Wilson, Guy Denis. b Melbourne 30.11.1882. du France 30.11.1917. Ed Derby School.

Wincer, Robert Colin. b Portsmouth, Hants 2.4.1952 lhb rfm.

Wood, Arthur John. b Derby 7.2.1892. du Croydon, Surrey 1.3.1951. Ed Denstone, CU.

Wood, Arthur Machin. b Pye Bridge 21.2.1861. d Philadelphia, U.S.A. 25.8.1947. rhb. Nottinghamshire. Philadelphia. Toured Eng with Gts of Philad. 1897,03 and 08.

Wood, Barry. b Ossett, Yorks. 26.12.1942. rhb rm. Yorkshire. Lancashire. E.Province. Eng(12) MCC(2). Capt part 1981, 1982.

Wood, Samuel Hill. b Glossop 21.3.1872. d Westminster, London 4.1.1949. rhb. Ed Eton. Capt 1899-1901. Suffolk. (later Sir Samuel Hill Hill-Wood).

Woodland, Albert William. b Conisborough, Yorks 10.6.1895. du Mansfield 31.1.1955. rhb rfm.

Wood-Sims, William (registered at birth as Sims, William Wood). b Ironville 10.2.1858. du Lambeth, London 30.11.1926. rhb.

Woodward, Kenneth Alexander. b Liverpool 23.12.1874. d Charlton Kings, Glos 24.12.1950 rhb rm. Ed Harrow, OU. Hertfordshire.

Worthington, Thomas Stanley. b Bolsover 21.8.1905. d Kings Lynn, Norfolk 31.8.1973. rhb rfm. Eng(9), MCC(2).

Wright, Frank. b Ilkeston 4.5.1870. du Cotmanhay 9.12.1943. (Registered at death as Wright, Francis Moult). rhb.

Wright, Henry Fitzherbert. b Swanwick 9.10.1870. d Yeldersley, Ashbourne 23.2.1947. rhb rm. Ed Eton, CU.

Wright, James. b Newbold, Leics 25.3.1874. d Sheffield 20.8.1961. rhb.

Wright, John Geoffrey. b Darfield, N.Z. 5.7.1954. lhb rm. Northern Districts. N.Z.(17). N.Z. to Eng, N.Z. to Austr.

Wright, Levi George. b Oxford 15.1.1862. d Derby 11.1.1953. rhb Capt 1907, Joint 1906.

Wright, William John. b (Bakewell) 24.2.1909. rhb.

Wyatt, Gerry. b New Mills 4.6.1933. rhb wk.

Yates, George. Believed to be the Lancashire cricketer. b Haslingdon, Lancs 6.6.1856. d Bolsover 21.7.1933. rhb rf round.

Young, John Henry. b Melbourne 2.7.1876. d Melbourne 2.8.1913. rhb rfm.

Young, John William. b Clay Cross 24.5.1863. du Bolsover 9.5.1933. rhb.

DERBYSHIRE PLAYERS WHO APPEARED FOR THE COUNTY IN SECOND CLASS MATCHES.

The birth and death details are given only for those who did not appear in first-class cricket for the county.

Bagshaw, Henry 1888-1893

Bottom, Daniel

Burrows, Joseph Robert. b Belper 3.9.1868. du Belper 12.3.1954. rhb. 1889.

Charlesworth, Alfred. 1888.

Chatterton, William. 1888-93.

Cropper, Martin. b Brimington 16.7.1864. du (Staincross) 26.10.1943. 1892. Cousin of Wm.C.

Cropper, William.

Cupitt, Joseph.

Davidson, George. 1888-93.

Delacombe, William Barclay. 1892

Disney, James Joseph 1888-90.

Eadie, William Stewart. 1889-93.

Earl, George Burrill. 1888.

Evans, Charles. 1889-90.

Evershed, Edward. 1888-93.

Evershed, Frank. b Winshill 6.9.1866. d Winshill, Staffs 29.6.1954. rhb wk Ed Clifton, OU. 1889-1894.

Evershed, Sydney Herbert. 1888-93.

Eyre, Frederick. b North Winfield 20.2.1861. du Bolton-on-Dearne, Yorks 1.7.1932. rhb rm 1892 Father of J.A.E.

Hall, Walter. 1888-92.

Hindley, William Albert. b Eyam 19.5.1854. du Heaton Norris, Ches 30.1.1933. 1888.

Hodges, Walter (Dr). b Derby 30.9.1871. du London 8.2.1897. rhb. Ed Cheltenham.

Hulme, John Joseph. 1888-93

Keeton, Frederick William. 1888.

Maltby, George Albert. b Morton 19.6.1867. du Victoria, Brit Col 14.11.1963. rhb rm. 1889. Ed Harlow College.

Malthouse, Samuel. 1891-93

Marlow, Joseph. 1890.

Marshall, Joseph. 1890.

Morley, Haydn Arthur. b Derby 26.11.1860. d Hathersage 5.1953. rhb. Ed Repton. 1891.

Mosby, Herbert Christopher. b Normanton, Yorks 25.12.1863. d Leeds, Yorks 21.9.1898. 1888-92.

Mycroft, Frank. 1893.

Myton, William. b Oulton, Yorks 22.7.1867. du Breadsall 9.11.1944. 1891.

Pedley, William Everard. b Wingerworth 16.6.1858. du Riverside, Calif 9.7.1920. rhb rm. 1888. Ed Eastbourne.

Porter, George. 1888-93.

Purdy, Thomas (REgistered as Purdew at Birth and Death) b Elsecar, Yorks 3.7.1861. du Tibshelf 23.5.1945. rhb rfm. 1889-90.

Ratcliffe, George. 1888-89.

Raynor, Samuel. b Heanor 14.8.1861. d Heanor 14.9.1907. rhb rfm. 1891. Worcs.

Shipton, Herbert. b Buxton 19.6.1864. du Buxton 13.3.1925. rhb slow. 1885.

Shipton, William Louis. 1890-93

Slater, George Herbert. b Langley Mill 23.2.1875. du (Chesterfield) 20.2.1927. 1900.

Soult, Joseph. b Ripley 17.10.1866. du (Shardlow) 8.1944. rhb rm. 1893. Staffs.

Spofforth, Frederick Robert. b Balmain, N.S.W. 9.9.1853. d Surbiton, Surrey 4.6.1926. rhb rf/m 1889-91. Austr(18). N.S.W. Victoria. Austr to Eng 1878,80,82,84,86; to N.America 1878.

Storer, William 1888-93

Straw, John Henry. b Farnsfield, Notts 28.12.1864. du Burley-in-Wharfedale, Yorks 18.6.1939. rhb. 1888.

Stubbings, Joseph. 1892-93.

Sugg, Walter. 1888-93.
Thorpe, Stephen. b Tibshelf 16.11.1864. du Tibshelf 13.12.1930. rhb rmf. 1891-93.
Tomlinson, Robert George. b Winshill 30.3.1869. d Malvern, Worcs 13.1.1949. rhb r slow. 1891-93.
Walker, George Glossop. 1888-93.
Walton, William. 1893.
Ward, Joseph Preston. 1893.
Wood-Sims, William. 1891.
Wright, Henry Fitherbert. 1891.
Wright, Levi George. 1888-93.
Wright, Reuben. b Codnor 21.9.1864. du Heanor 22.8.1929. rhb rfm. 1891.
Young, William. b Staveley 8.3.186l. du Staveley 6.10.1933. wk. 1891.

Notes: Full details of players given in italics can be found in the first-class list. Certain places of birth or death which were in Derbyshire have passed into other counties e.g. Stapenhill and Winshill passed into Staffordshire and others in the North, North East and North West which were in Derbyshire are now in Cheshire and Yorkshire. Thus someone who was born at and died at the same place (e.g. F.Evershed of Winshill) could have been born in one county and died in another.When a place of birth or death is shown in brackets, the name of the registration district is indicated, though the event could have occurred at that place.

CAREER RECORDS

In the details set out below, the first line against each player's name shows his career record in first-class matches for Derbyshire; players who appeared in first-class matches other than for Derbyshire have two lines of statistics, the second of which shows the player's career record in all first-class matches.

Career records are complete to the end of the 1981 English season.

Name	*From*	*To*	*M*	*I*	*NO*	*Runs*	*HS*	*Avge*	*100*	*Runs*	*Wkts*	*Avge*	*BB*	*5wi*	*10wm*	*c*	*s*
Ackroyd, A.	1924	1925	11	18	0	70	15	3.89	0	646	19	34.00	4-63	0	0	5	
	1924	1937	12	20	1	79	15	4.16	0	707	20	35.35	4-63	0	0	5	
Alderman, A.E.	1928	1948	318	529	52	12376	175	25.95	12	171	4	42.75	3-37	0	0	202	2
Allen, M.H.J.	1964	1966	31	39	11	224	38*	8.00	0	1447	52	27.83	7-65	3	0	28	
	1956	1966	193	231	56	1723	59	9.85	0	11219	500	22.44	8-48	25	3	170	
Allsop, R.	1872	1874	3	5	0	42	33	8.40	0	did	not	bowl				3	
Anderson, I.S.	1978	1981	35	49	12	521	75	14.08	0	514	9	57.11	4-35	0	0	20	
Antliff, W.N.	1880		2	4	0	17	5	4.25	0	did	not	bowl			0		
Armstrong, T.R.	1929	1950	58	83	33	314	28*	6.28	0	3239	133	24.35	7-36	7	0	18	
Ashcroft, E.M.	1897	1906	100	169	13	4530	162	29.04	8	1186	24	49.42	5-18	1	0	31	
	1897	1906	101	170	13	4581	162	29.18	8	1186	24	49.42	5-18	1	0	33	
Attenborough, T.	1871	1874	6	9	0	72	27	8.00	0	29	2	14.50	1-9	0	0	2	
Baggallay, R.R.C.	1912	1919	31	59	1	688	88	11.86	0	did	not	bowl				25	
Bagguley, W.	1905		1	1	0	5	5	5.00	0	did	not	bowl				0	
Bagshaw, H.	1887	1902	123	215	9	5413	127*	26.28	7	2119	73	29.03	5-18	2	0	36	
	1887	1902	125	218	9	5456	127*	26.11	7	2119	73	29.03	5-18	2	0	36	
Barber, F.A.	1907	1920	5	10	1	30	10	3.33	0	267	9	29.67	2-19	0	0	3	
Barlow, E.J.	1976	1978	60	98	8	2813	217	31.26	3	2108	98	21.51	5-63	1	0	81	
	1959-60	1980-81	270	470	26	17156	217	38.64	40	13430	547	24.55	7-24	16	2	319	
Barnes, A.S.	1878		3	5	1	14	7*	3.50	0	did	not	bowl				0	
	1877	1879	13	20	2	107	16	5.94	0	did	not	bowl				4	
Barnett, K.J.	1979	1981	56	80	10	1557	96	22.24	0	1052	15	70.13	4-76	0	0	34	
	1979	1981	58	82	10	1606	96	22.31	0	1191	18	66.17	4-76	0	0	34	
Barrington, G.B.	1880	1887	24	46	1	440	50	9.78	0	27	1	27.00	1-27	0	0	7	
	1880	1887	25	48	1	455	50	9.68	0	27	1	27.00	1-27	0	0	7	
Barrs, F.A.	1900	1901	3	5	0	68	58	13.60	0	29	1	29.00	1-17	0	0	0	
Barton, A.	1901		3	6	0	24	7	4.00	0	61	0					0	
Bedford, E.H.R.	1924		1	2	0	3	3	1.50	0	did	not	bowl				0	
Beet, G.	1910	1925	47	87	9	1268	92*	16.26	0	27	0					58	11
	1910	1925	48	88	10	1277	92*	16.37	0	27	0					59	11
Beet, G.A.	1956	1961	6	7	2	36	17	7.20	0	100	2	50.00	1-42	0	0	3	
Beet, G.H.C.	1928	1932	5	9	1	102	35*	12.75	0	did	not	bowl				3	1
	1928	1938	11	19	2	277	61	16.29	0	did	not	bowl				14	2

Name	To	From	M	I	NO	Runs	HS	Avge	100	Runs	Wkts	Avge	BB	5wi	10wm	c	s
Bell, G.F.	1914	1920	5	9	0	69	20	7.67	0	did	not	bowl				2	
	1914	1920	12	21	0	336	64	16.00	0	did	not	bowl				6	
Bennett, J.W.	1895	1896	16	25	2	257	43	11.17	0	701	35	20.03	5-8	3	0	7	
Bentley, M.	1957		1	2	0	12	10	6.00	0	did	not	bowl				0	
Berry, R.	1959	1962	54	67	27	292	40	7.30	0	2906	97	29.96	6-100	3	0	35	
	1948	1962	273	305	112	1463	40	758	0	17389	703	24.74	10-102	33	5	138	
Berwick, J.A.	1895	1901	16	29	6	138	27	6.00	0	892	24	37.17	5-82	1	0	7	
Bestwick, R.S.	1920	1922	5	9	1	29	10	3.63	0	151	2	75.50	2-47	0	0	2	
Bestwick, W.	1898	1925	321	521	183	1605	39	4.75	0	30881	1452	21.27	10-40	104	27	89	
	1898	1925	323	524	183	1607	39	4.71	0	30998	1457	21.27	10-40	104	27	89	
Billyeald, J.	1871		1	2	1	15	11*	15.00	0	did	not	bowl				0	
Bingham, F.M.	1896		1	2	0	17	11	8.50	0	did	not	bowl				0	
Birkett, W.	1898	1901	4	7	0	20	10	2.86	0	115	3	38.33	2-28	0	0	0	
Blackwell, H.	1895	1898	4	6	2	41	15	10.25	0	105	4	26.25	2-23	0	0	1	
Blaxland, L.B.	1925	1947	19	31	1	483	64	16.10	0	18	0					7	
Blount, A.	1912	1926	7	11	2	52	17	5.78	0	215	7	30.71	4-53	0	0	3	
Boden, T.W.	1920		1	2	0	14	9	7.00	0	did	not	bowl				0	
Boden, W.	1874		1	2	1	2	2*	2.00	0	did	not	bowl				0	
	1859	1874	2	4	2	18	11	9.00	0	did	not	bowl				0	
Boissier, A.P.	1901	1906	2	4	0	13	6	3.25	0	32	2	16.00	2-32	0	0	0	
Bolus, J.B.	1973	1975	64	117	14	3279	151	31.83	4	did	not	bowl				17	
	1956	1975	469	833	81	25598	202*	34.04	39	886	24	36.92	4-40	0	0	201	
Boot, J.	1895		1	2	0	4	4	2.00	0	did	not	bowl				2	
Borrington, A.J.	1971	1980	122	203	24	4230	137	23.63	3	19	0					57	
Bostock, H.	1897		4	6	2	75	36	18.75	0	did	not	bowl				1	
Bottom, D.	1894	1901	3	5	0	22	9	4.40	0	62	1	62.00	1-50	0	0	1	
	1894	1901	6	10	0	42	9	4.20	0	250	9	27.78	5-34	1	0	2	
Bourne, J.J.	1898		1	1	0	6	6	6.00	0	103	3	34.33	2-63	0	0	0	
Bowden, J.J.	1909	1930	231	395	25	7613	120	20.58	4	54	1	54.00	1-0	0	0	75	
Bowmer, H.E.	1909	1911	3	6	0	6	3	1.00	0	did	not	bowl				1	
Bracey, F.	1906	1914	77	132	54	562	28	7.21	0	3122	132	23.65	6-36	5	1	20	
Bradbury, L.	1971		1	did	not	bat				53	1	53.00	1-53	0	0	1	
Bradley, G.	1875		1	2	0	1	1	0.50	0	17	0					0	
Brailsford, F.C.	1958		3	5	0	41	14	8.20	0	2	1	2.00	1-2	0	0	1	
Brelsford, J.	1883	1886	8	14	1	56	16	4.31	0	481	24	20.04	5-31	1	0	4	
Brooke-Taylor, D.C.	1947	1949	15	26	1	375	61*	15.00	0	did	not	bowl				6	
Brooke-Taylor, G.P.	1920		1	2	0	44	30	22.00	0	did	not	bowl				0	
	1919	1929-30	25	40	1	778	84	19.95	0	did	not	bowl				13	3
Brooks, J.	1895	1896	5	7	4	8	6	2.67	0	190	2	95.00	1-22	0	0	1	
Brooks, K.G.	1980		1	2	0	11	8	5.50	0	did	not	bowl				2	
Buckley, G.A.	1921		1	2	0	10	8	5.00	0	48	0					1	
Buckston, G.M.	1905	1921	33	65	2	829	96	13.16	0	did	not	bowl				1	
	1903	1921	39	75	3	852	96	11.83	0	did	not	bowl				8	1
Buckston, R.H.R.	1928	1939	72	101	22	912	60*	11.54	0	10	0					16	1
	1928	1939	74	104	24	944	60*	11.80	0	10	0					18	2
Burnham, G.J.	1912		5	6	1	30	15	6.00	0	did	not	bowl				3	

Name	From	To	M	I	NO	Runs	HS	Avge	100	Runs	Wkts	Avge	BB	5wi	10wm	c	s
Burnham, J.W.	1871	1876	6	11	0	55	31	5.00	0	did	not	bowl				2	
Burrows, M.	1884		1	2	0	13	13	6.50	0	10	0					0	
	1880	1884	7	12	0	95	23	7.93	0	10	0					2	
Burton, J.	1901		7	12	1	200	51*	18.18	0	did	not	bowl				4	
Burton, O.	1901	1905	3	4	4	21	9*	-	0	156	5	31.20	2-44	0	0	2	
Butterfield, W.	1896		2	4	0	11	7	2.75	0	20	1	20.00	1-10	0	0	0	
Buxton, I.R.	1959	1973	350	579	86	11803	118*	23.94	5	12742	483	26.38	7-33	12	2	199	
Buxton, N.	1902	1911	7	14	2	40	7	3.33	0	171	5	34.20	2-14	0	0	1	
Cadman, S.W.A.	1900	1926	375	689	33	14055	126	21.43	8	20281	803	25.26	8-70	30	2	277	
	1900	1926	377	690	34	14077	126	21.46	8	20370	807	25.24	8-70	30	2	277	
Carlin, R.M.	1905	1908	15	28	1	306	37	11.33	0	208	5	41.60	2-53	0	0	5	
Carr, D.B.	1946	1963	337	564	52	14656	162*	28.63	18	7786	232	33.56	7-53	4	0	404	
	1945	1968	447	745	72	19257	170	28.61	24	11396	328	34.74	7-53	5	0	499	
Carrington, E.	1934	1937	50	77	4	1470	80	20.14	0	32	0					18	
Carter, H.S.	1946		3	4	0	8	7	2.00	0	46	2	23.00	2-39	0	0	1	
Carter, R.	1953	1955	17	22	4	130	25	7.22	0	752	30	25.07	7-46	1	0	6	
Carter, W.	1920	1926	65	112	10	1812	145	17.76	2	707	16	44.19	3-12	0	0	26	
Cartledge, J.	1878		1	2	0	1	1	0.50	0	did	not	bowl				0	
Cartwright, H.	1973	1979	82	128	16	2384	141*	21.28	1	11	0					31	
Chapman, J.	1909	1920	113	210	15	3624	198	18.58	2	241	1	241.00	1-42	0	0	35	
Charlesworth, A.	1898		7	10	1	92	23	10.22	0	47	0					2	
Chatterton, J.	1884	1886	11	22	2	108	21	5.40	0	119	5	23.80	1-9	0	0	3	
Chatterton, W.	1882	1902	196	351	31	7587	169	23.71	6	3078	128	24.05	6-46	3	0	176	4
	1882	1902	289	510	39	10914	169	23.17	8	4466	208	21.48	6-42	4	1	239	4
Chester, C.	1899		1	2	0	0	0	0.00	0	9	1	9.00	1-9	0	0	1	
Clarke, C.C.	1929	1933	25	37	2	441	35*	12.60	0	did	not	bowl				8	
	1929	1947	28	43	3	472	35*	11.80	0	did	not	bowl				8	
Clayton, J.M.	1881	1883	2	3	0	3	2	1.00	0	11	0					1	
Cochrane, A.H.J.	1884	1886	4	8	0	96	50	12.00	0	207	11	18.82	6-51	1	0	0	
	1884	1888	28	48	15	347	61*	10.52	0	1956	103	18.99	7-66	4	0	16	
Cole, T.G.O.	1913		6	11	0	171	36	15.55	0	did	not	bowl				3	
	1898	1922	20	35	3	499	68	15.59	0	17	0					9	
Cook, E.	1878	1879	8	15	2	92	23*	7.08	0	did	not	bowl				3	
Cooke, J.	1874		1	2	0	6	6	3.00	0	did	not	bowl				0	
Cooper, A.H.H.	1902		1	1	0	0	0	0.00	0	12	0					1	
Cooper, H.	1905	1910	15	28	4	216	23	9.00	0	did	not	bowl				7	
Copson, W.H.	1932	1950	261	341	99	1601	43	6.62	0	19380	1033	18.76	8-11	64	6	91	
	1932	1950	279	359	108	1711	43	6.80	0	20752	1094	18.97	8-11	65	6	103	
Corbett, B.O.	1910		1	2	0	1	1	0.50	0	did	not	bowl				0	
Corbett, C.J.	1911	1924	27	48	4	633	61	14.39	0	54	0					7	
Coup, E.	1885	1887	13	26	3	195	33	8.48	0	did	not	bowl				2	
Cresswell, J.A.	1923	1927	21	34	13	160	28	7.62	0	1022	25	40.88	4-65	0	0	17	
Crommelin-Brown, J.L.	1922	1926	16	28	2	659	74	25.35	0	70	1	70.00	1-29	0	0	9	
Cropper, W.	1882	1887	56	107	4	1601	93	15.54	0	2844	170	16.73	7-25	8	0	26	
	1882	1888	60	113	4	1636	93	15.01	0	2930	171	17.13	7-25	8	0	26	

Name	From	To	M	I	NO	Runs	HS	Avge	100	Runs	Wkts	Avge	BB	5wi	5wm	c	s
Cross, J.	1897		9	15	4	82	29*	7.45	0	634	22	28.82	4-68	0	0	4	
Cupitt, J.	1905		2	4	2	19	13	9.50	0	145	3	48.33	2-24	0	0	0	
Curgenven, G.	1901	1922	95	169	5	3440	124	20.98	3	1163	25	46.52	3-32	0	0	40	
Curgenven, H.G.	1896	1897	9	12	0	102	26	8.50	0	180	4	45.00	2-25	0	0	6	
	1896	1897	11	14	1	125	26	9.62	0	223	7	31.86	2-9	0	0	6	
Curgenven, W.G.	1872	1878	17	30	0	376	71	12.53	0	did	not	bowl				5	
Cursham, A.W.	1879	1880	9	15	0	106	40	7.07	0	did	not	bowl				3	
	1876	1880	21	35	0	314	67	8.97	0	49	1	49.00	1-39	0	0	10	
Davidson, F.	1897	1899	14	23	4	129	43	6.79	0	1094	43	25.44	6-49	1	0	11	
Davidson, G.A.	1886	1898	95	157	13	3881	274	26.95	3	7859	449	17.50	9-39	31	9	79	
	1886	1898	158	260	27	5546	274	23.80	3	11341	621	18.26	9-39	43	10	135	
Davidson, J.	1871	1874	4	6	3	14	8	4.67	0	96	6	16.00	3-33	0	0	2	
Davis, J.W.	1920		1	2	0	9	8	4.50	0	did	not	bowl				2	
Dawkes, G.O.	1947	1961	392	608	86	9868	143	18.90	1	20	0					770	106
	1937	1961	482	736	105	11411	143	18.08	1	20	0					895	148
Deakin, M.J.	1981		4	6	0	45	15	7.50	0	did	not	bowl				9	
Dearnaley, I.	1905	1907	4	8	0	51	34	6.38	0	did	not	bowl				3	
Delacombe, W.B.	1894	1900	10	13	3	95	23*	9.50	0	44	0					2	
De Ville, R.T.	1963	1964	3	5	2	26	17	8.67	0	146	2	73.00	2-47	0	0	0	
Dickinson, S.P.	1909		2	3	1	13	10*	6.50	0	45	1	45.00	1-38	0	0	0	
Disney, J.J.	1881	1887	53	94	28	370	27*	5.61	0	did	not	bowl				93	9
	1881	1887	57	101	30	377	27*	5.31	0	did	not	bowl				97	12
Dixon, F.	1885		1	2	0	15	15	7.50	0	did	not	bowl				0	
	1885	1891	2	4	0	23	15	5.75	0	7	0					1	
Dobson, K.W.C.	1920		3	6	2	6	3	1.50	0	99	1	99.00	1-25	0	0	0	
	1920	1925	5	10	3	33	12*	4.71	0	123	1	123.00	1-25	0	0	0	
Docker, F.D.	1881	1882	2	3	0	33	25	11.00	0	did	not	bowl				3	
Docker, L.C.	1881	1886	48	90	2	1769	107	20.10	1	280	9	31.11	3-38	0	0	16	
	1881	1895	77	136	8	2665	107	20.82	1	280	9	31.11	3-38	0	0	41	
Docker, R.	1879		2	4	0	9	6	2.25	0	did	not	bowl				2	
Doughty, S.	1880	1886	4	7	1	40	13*	6.67	0	79	4	19.75	3-28	0	0	1	
Eadie, J.	1882		1	2	1	8	8*	8.00	0	6	1	6.00	1-6	0	0	0	
Eadie, W.S.	1885	1899	23	41	3	399	62	10.50	0	13	0					7	
Earl, G.B.	1883		1	1	0	4	4	4.00	0	did	not	bowl				1	
Eato, A.	1950	1955	25	28	5	220	44	9.57	0	1429	50	28.58	5-14	1	0	7	
Eggar, J.D.	1946	1954	31	47	3	1385	219	31.48	3	149	1	149.00	1-2	0	0	16	
	1938	1954	41	64	6	1847	219	31.85	4	193	1	193.00	1-2	0	0	20	
Elliott, C.S.	1932	1953	275	468	29	11965	215	27.26	9	526	11	47.82	2-25	0	0	210	1
Elliott, H.	1920	1947	520	754	219	7480	94	13.98	0	5	0					889	294
	1920	1947	532	764	220	7580	94	13.93	0	5	0					904	302
Ellis, W.	1898	1906	18	32	2	361	58	12.03	0	120	0	-				7	
Else, R.	1901	1903	5	10	2	59	28	7.38	0	61	1	61.00	1-56	0	0	3	
Estridge, E.	1874		1	1	0	4	4	4.00	0	did	not	bowl				0	
Evans, C.	1894	1895	9	14	2	157	31	13.08	0	526	19	27.68	4-46	0	0	7	

Name	From	To	M	I	NO	Runs	HS	Avge	100	Runs	Wkts	Avge	BB	5wi	10wm	c	s
Evans, H.	1878	1882	5	10	0	41	10	4.10	0	252	19	13.26	7-47	2	0	4	
Evans, T.	1883		2	4	0	78	35	19.50	0	91	3	30.33	1-22	0	0	1	
	1883	1889	4	7	0	91	35	13.00	0	150	6	25.00	2-27	0	0	2	
Evershed, E.	1898		1	1	0	1	1	1.00	0	did	not	bowl				2	
Evershed, S.H.	1880	1901	75	127	2	3126	153	25.01	4	117	5	23.40	5-19	1	0	33	
	1880	1901	76	129	2	3137	153	24.70	4	122	5	24.40	5-19	1	0	35	
Evershed, W.	1882	1884	13	24	0	357	92	14.88	0	8	3	2.67	3-8	0	0	6	
Exham, P.G.	1883		1	1	0	12	12	12.00	0	did	not	bowl				1	
	1880	1883	6	10	0	88	43	8.80	0	did	not	bowl				3	
Eyre, J.A.	1908		1	2	1	2	1*	2.00	0	did	not	bowl				0	
Eyre, J.R.	1963	1967	48	84	4	1194	106	14.93	1	248	1	248.00	1-6	0	0	17	
Eyre, T.J.P.	1959	1972	197	264	49	3436	102	15.98	1	10305	359	28.70	8-65	8	0	83	
Fisher, J.	1921	1922	3	6	1	52	39*	10.40	0	15	0					0	
Fleming, C.B.	1907		1	2	0	5	3	2.50	0	did	not	bowl				0	
Fletcher, H.	1907	1908	5	10	2	17	4	2.13	0	did	not	bowl				2	
Fletcher, T.	1906		1	1	0	28	28	28.00	0	3	0					0	
Flint, J.	1872	1879	14	24	3	143	24	6.81	0	601	44	13.66	6-28	2	0	11	
Flint, L.E.	1919	1920	7	11	0	100	35	9.09	0	291	8	36.38	3-30	0	0	1	
Foley, E.F.W.	1871		1	2	0	0	0	0.00	0	did	not	bowl				1	
Ford, N.M.	1926	1934	31	49	1	762	65	15.88	0	73	1	73.00	1-19	0	0	5	
	1926	1935	75	121	9	2925	183	26.12	5	117	1	117.00	1-19	0	0	15	
Forester, T.	1902	1920	105	176	20	2586	87	16.58	0	6691	270	24.78	7-18	15	3	48	
	1896	1920	131	212	33	2829	87	15.80	0	8920	347	25.59	7-18	17	3	62	
Forman, A.F.E.	1877	1882	5	7	0	90	36	12.86	0	3	0					0	
Forman, F.G.	1911		1	2	0	3	3	1.50	0	did	not	bowl				1	
Foster, T.	1873	1884	85	157	6	2485	101	16.46	1	208	8	26.00	2-18	0	0	61	
	1873	1884	90	167	6	2594	101	16.11	1	233	9	25.89	2-18	0	0	64	
Foulke, W.H.	1900		4	7	1	65	53	10.83	0	92	2	46.00	2-15	0	0	2	
M.Frederick	1949		2	3	0	98	84	32.67	0	did	not	bowl				1	
	1944-45	1953-54	6	10	0	294	84	29.40	0	did	not	bowl				3	
Freeman, C.R.	1911		1	2	0	7	4	3.50	0	did	not	bowl				1	
Frost, G.	1872	1880	36	65	4	771	52	12.64	0	did	not	bowl				10	
	1872	1880	37	67	4	771	52	12.24	0	did	not	bowl				10	
Frost, J.H.	1874		1	2	0	19	18	9.50	0	did	not	bowl				2	
Fullwood, W.	1946		6	10	1	41	13	4.56	0	did	not	bowl				5	1
Furniss, J.B.	1955	1956	4	5	1	9	6	2.25	0	259	7	37.00	3-52	0	0	2	
Genders, W.R.	1946		3	6	1	62	24	12.40	0	22	0					2	
	1946	1949	10	19	4	245	55*	16.33	0	98	3	32.67	2-43	0	0	6	
Gibbs, P.J.K.	1966	1972	145	260	13	7295	138*	29.53	9	288	4	72.00	2-54	0	0	77	
	1964	1972	178	319	14	8885	138*	29.13	11	321	4	80.25	2-54	0	0	96	
Gibson, I.	1957	1961	7	12	3	199	66*	22.11	0	128	3	42.67	1-6	0	0	7	
	1955	1961	51	92	7	1697	100*	19.96	1	1959	51	38.41	5-29	2	0	29	
Gilbert, J.D.H.	1930	1936	11	11	0	106	25	9.64	0	did	not	bowl				2	

Name	From	To	M	I	NO	Runs	HS	Avge	100	Runs	Wkts	Avge	BB	5wi	10wm	c	s
Gladwin, C.	1939	1958	332	457	130	5490	124*	16.79	1	27147	1536	17.67	9-41	99	17	123	
	1939	1958	374	510	148	6283	124*	17.36	1	30265	1653	18.31	9-41	101	18	133	
Gladwin, J.	1914	1919	3	5	2	8	5*	2.67	0	20	1	20.00	1-15	0	0	3	
Glenn, M.	1975	1976	7	7	4	23	11*	7.67	0	398	6	66.33	3-36	0	0	1	
Goodall, J.	1895	1896	2	3	0	38	32	12.67	0	did	not	bowl				2	
Goodwin, G.W.	1921		8	16	1	224	53	14.93	0	205	7	29.29	4-23	0	0	1	
Gothard, E.J.	1947	1948	45	63	19	543	50	12.34	0	730	18	40.56	3-84	0	0	10	
Gould, T.	1896	1897	7	10	2	63	16*	7.88	0	225	9	25.00	4-45	0	0	5	
Graham-Brown, J.M.H.	1977	1978	17	22	2	219	43	10.95	0	457	9	50.78	2-23	0	0	5	
	1974	1978	30	37	7	368	43	12.27		696	12	58.00	2-23	0	0	8	
Grainger, G.	1909	1921	5	9	3	36	10*	6.00	0	348	7	49.91	0	0	1		
Green, D.J.	1953	1960	37	60	3	883	69*	15.49	0	1	0					17	
	1953	1961	87	152	7	2929	134	20.20	1	99	1	99.00	1-19	0	0	61	
Green, G.	1903	1907	6	11	0	39	20	3.55	0	236	6	39.33	2-31	0	0	2	
Gregory, D.	1871	1872	4	7	3	19	10	4.75	0	255	25	10.20	6-9	3	0	3	
Gregory, G.R.	1899	1910	15	22	2	174	23	8.70	0	267	12	22.25	4-70	0	0	5	
Hall, B.	1902		1	2	0	10	7	5.00	0	did	not	bowl				0	
Hall, D.	1955	1958	20	29	16	43	10*	3.31	0	1386	48	28.88	4-57	0	0	6	
Hall, I.W.	1959	1972	270	483	32	11666	136*	25.87	9	23	0					189	
Hall, J.P.	1895	1897	4	7	1	3	2	0.50	0	112	3	37.33	1-12	0	0	3	
Hall, T.A.	1949	1952	28	44	10	354	52	10.44	0	1882	70	26.89	5-57	2	0	15	
	1949	1958	66	103	23	892	69*	11.13	0	5108	183	27.91	5-50	4	0	29	
Hall, W.	1882	1886	11	17	4	146	43	11.23	0	376	14	26.85	6-47	1	0	9	
Hallam, T.H.	1906	1907	10	19	0	224	68	11.79	0	did	not	bowl				5	
Hamer, A.	1950	1960	290	507	19	15277	227	31.31	19	2271	68	33.40	4-27	0	0	159	
	1938	1960	295	515	19	15465	227	31.18	19	2363	71	33.28	4-27	0	0	164	
Hancock, J.W.	1897	1900	47	75	18	446	43*	782	0	2753	93	29.60	5-61	1	0	19	
	1897	1906	48	77	19	459	43*	7.91	0	2795	94	29.73	5-61	1	0	21	
Handford, J.	1910		9	17	3	137	23	9.79	0	31	0					4	
Hanson, R.L.	1973		1	1	1	1	1*	-	0	did	not	bowl				1	
Hardy, S.	1898		1	2	0	10	9	4.50	0	did	not	bowl				2	
Harvey, J.F.	1963	1972	204	340	32	7425	168	24.11	4	21	1	21.00	1-0	0	0	84	
	1961	1972	206	344	32	7538	168	24.16	4	21	1	21.00	1-0	0	0	87	
Harvey-Walker, A.J.	1971	1978	81	143	10	3186	117	23.95	3	1150	34	33.82	7-35	1	1	31	
Hay, G.	1875	1886	47	80	11	517	49	7.49	0	2193	137	16.01	6-16	6	1	33	
	1875	1887	55	94	16	683	49	8.58	0	2444	148	16.51	6-16	7	1	34	
Heath, F.R.	1924		3	4	0	59	17	14.75	0	47	3	15.67	2-4	0	0	1	
Heath, J.S.	1924	1925	7	11	2	82	28	9.11	0	268	7	38.29	5-54	1	0	2	
	1918-19	1925	12	21	3	227	34	12.61	0	832	30	27.73	5-33	3	0	8	
M.Hendrick	1969	1981	167	168	64	1093	46	10.51	0	9968	497	20.06	8-45	21	3	110	
	1969	1981	231	229	91	1419	46	10.28	0	13960	666	20.96	8-45	24	3	149	
Hickton, W.	1871	1878	34	58	8	674	63	13.48	0	1846	129	14.31	6-15	9	2	18	
	1867	1878	60	103	17	1054	63	12.26	0	4019	284	4.15	10-46	24	7	32	
Higson, T.A. sen.	1899	1910	21	38	2	422	46	11.72	0	1048	36	29.11	4-74	0	0	11	
	1892	1923	29	50	4	584	46	12.70	0	1165	41	28.41	4-74	0	0	12	

Name	From	To	M	I	NO	Runs	HS	Avge	100	Runs	Wkts	Avge	BB	5wi	10wm	c	s
Higson, T.A. jun	1932	1935	6	12	0	173	51	14.42	0	did	not	bowl				2	
	1932	1946	26	32	1	326	51	10.52	0	302	6	50.33	1-14	0	0	8	
Hill, A.	1972	1981	163	286	26	7390	160*	28.42	8	128	2	64.00	1-15	0	0	58	
	1972	1981	168	295	27	7703	160*	28.74	9	133	5	26.60	3-5	0	0	64	
Hill, M.	1966	1967	32	52	4	921	61	19.19	0	6	0					21	
	1953	1971	272	484	39	10722	137*	24.09	7	311	5	62.20	2-60	0	0	151	
Hill-Wood, B.S.H.	1919	1925	22	35	4	505	61	16.29	0	1406	45	31.24	6-74	1	0	8	
Hill-Wood, C.K.H.	1928	1930	18	22	4	359	72	19.94	0	1206	34	35.47	5-76	1	0	9	
	1928	1935-36	58	77	13	1256	72	19.63	0	5547	185	29.98	7-68	10	1	20	
Hill-Wood, D.J.C.H.	1928	1929	5	8	1	81	36	11.57	0	45	1	45.00	1-22	0	0	2	
	1928	1929	12	21	1	453	85	22.65	0	123	3	41.00	1-4	0	0	6	
Hill-Wood, W.W.H.	1919	1936	35	60	1	1519	107	25.75	1	1523	49	31.08	5-62	1	0	18	
	1919	1939	63	107	4	2848	122*	27.65	3	2237	65	34.42	5-62	1	0	34	
Hind, A.	1876	1877	16	30	0	392	77	13.07	0	419	24	17.46	4-9	0	0	4	
Hodgkinson, G.F.	1935	1946	19	32	0	472	44	14.75	0	did	not	bowl				10	
Hodgkinson, J.	1882		1	2	0	5	5	2.50	0	83	1	83.00	1-83	0	0	1	
Hogg, A.	1905	1906	3	6	0	5	4	0.83	0	did	not	bowl				0	
Holden, S.M.	1910	1920	4	6	2	13	6*	3.25	0	111	3	37.00	3-72	0	0	1	
Horsley, J.	1914	1925	84	127	30	1349	66	13.90	0	5058	264	19.16	7-48	19	3	45	
	1913	1925	87	132	32	1367	66	13.67	0	5412	267	20.27	7-48	19	3	47	
Hounsfield, T.D.	1938	1939	16	24	3	274	56	13.04	0	did	not	bowl				7	
Houseman, E.O.	1897		1	2	0	4	4	2.00	0	did	not	bowl				2	
Howarth, T.	1873		1	2	0	7	5	3.50	0	did	not	bowl				1	
Howcroft, A.	1908	1910	4	8	0	46	19	5.75	0	did	not	bowl				2	
Hughes-Hallett, N.M.	1913	1914	6	11	1	178	67	17.80	0	27	1	27.00	1-16	0	0	4	
	1913	1926-27	10	17	1	255	67	15.94	0	312	17	18.35	8-81	2	1	4	
Hulme, J.J.	1887	1903	133	215	28	2336	59	12.49	0	12607	508	24.82	9-27	32	7	74	
	1887	1903	142	229	32	2433	59	12.35	0	13364	557	23.99	9-27	34	9	80	
Humble, W.J.	1873	1877	6	10	1	77	19*	8.56	0	did	not	bowl				6	
Humphries, J.	1899	1914	276	482	122	5134	68	14.26	0	43	3	14.33	1-5	0	0	531	95
	1899	1914	302	514	129	5464	68	14.19	0	43	3	14.33	1-5	0	0	564	110
Hunt, S.W.	1936		5	5	0	48	17	9.60	0	3	0					0	
Hunter, F.C.	1905	1907	28	49	3	564	51	12.26	0	684	17	40.24	2-18	0	0	8	
Hurt, C.N.B.	1914		3	5	0	23	13	4.60	0	6	0					1	
Hutchinson, J.M.	1920	1931	255	415	37	7042	143	18.63	5	1238	31	39.94	3-44	0	0	96	2
	1920	1931	256	416	38	7055	143	18.66	5	1238	31	39.94	3-44	0	0	97	2
Jackson, A.B.	1963	1968	148	160	83	647	27	8.40	0	8602	456	18.86	8-18	17	4	28	
	1963	1968	149	160	83	647	27	8.40	0	8656	457	18.94	8-18	17	4	29	
Jackson, A.H.M.	1920	1927	64	96	15	1199	75	14.80	0	1324	44	30.09	5-84	1	0	15	
Jackson, G.L.	1912	1914	4	7	0	39	19	5.57	0	126	7	18.00	3-52	0	0	4	
	1912	1914	7	12	0	150	50	12.50	0	238	10	23.80	3-52	0	0	4	
Jackson, G.R.	1919	1936	260	438	21	9741	140	23.36	9	195	3	65.00	1-10	0	0	104	
	1919	1936	280	468	22	10291	140	23.07	9	195	3	65.00	1-10	0	0	110	
Jackson, H.L.	1947	1963	394	460	139	1966	39*	6.12	0	28589	1670	17.12	9-17	114	20	121	
	1947	1963	418	489	153	2083	39*	6.20	0	30101	1733	17.37	9-17	115	20	136	

Name	From	To	M	I	NO	Runs	HS	Avge	100	Runs	Wkts	Avge	BB	5wi	10wm	c	s
Jackson, L.	1877	1882	5	10	1	97	28	10.78	0	189	7	27.00	2-19	0	0	2	
	1875	1882	6	12	1	109	28	9.91	0	198	10	19.80	3-9	0	0	4	
	1875	1882	6	12	1	109	28	9.91	0	198	10	19.80	3-9	0	0	4	
Jelf, H.F.D.	1910	1911	10	20	0	220	37	11.00	0	did	not	bowl				3	
Jervis, W.M.	1873		1	2	0	6	6	3.00	0	did	not	bowl				0	
	1848	1873	5	8	3	34	17	6.80	0	did	not	bowl				3	
Johnson, H.L.	1949	1966	350	604	65	14164	154	26.28	16	822	21	39.14	3-12	0	0	216	2
	1949	1966	351	606	65	14286	154	26.41	16	822	21	39.14	3-12	0	0	216	2
Johnston, D.A.	1882		4	8	0	65	31	8.13	0	did	not	bowl				0	
Jordan, H.G.B.	1926		1	2	0	0	0	0.00	0	did	not	bowl				0	
Keeton, F.W.	1876	1880	3	6	0	33	9	5.50	0	did	not	bowl				1	
Kelly, J.M.	1950	1960	253	426	26	9464	131	23.66	9	89	1	89.00	1-21	0	0	119	
	1947	1960	259	437	29	9614	131	23.56	9	103	1	103.00	1-21	0	0	122	
Kenward, R.	1899		11	19	0	333	56	17.53	0	did	not	bowl				3	
	1899	1905	18	29	0	434	56	14.97	0	did	not	bowl				6	
Kirsten, P.N.	1978	1981	85	144	18	5781	228	45.88	12	1521	40	38.03	4-44	0	0	55	
	1973-74	1981	151	263	26	10365	228	43.73	25	1933	51	37.90	4-44	0	0	94	
Langdale, G.R.	1936	1937	4	7	1	77	29	12.83	0	141	2	70.50	2-29	0	0	1	
	1936	1953	25	42	3	709	146	18.18	1	939	23	40.83	5-30	1	0	7	
Langton, S.T.	1909	1910	3	5	0	14	6	2.80	0	42	0					1	
Lawton, A.E.	1900	1910	131	226	5	5554	149	25.13	8	2891	87	33.23	4-19	0	0	79	1
	1900	1914	182	314	11	7509	168	24.78	11	3607	113	31.92	4-19	0	0	125	1
Lee, C.	1954	1964	268	466	16	12008	150	26.68	8	721	21	34.33	2-9	0	0	201	
	1952	1964	271	472	16	12129	150	26.60	8	721	21	34.33	2-9	0	0	202	
Lee, G.M.	1925	1933	229	386	26	9652	191	26.81	16	8002	313	25.57	7-67	18	1	87	
	1910	1933	373	624	47	14858	200*	25.75	22	11133	397	28.04	7-67	19	1	156	
Leech, C.	1922		1	2	0	38	26	19.00	0	did	not	bowl				1	
Limb, T.	1878		1	2	0	0	0	0.00	0	did	not	bowl				0	
Linathan, D.V.	1920		3	6	1	35	14*	7.00	0	78	1	78.00	1-15	0	0	2	
Lister, J.W.	1978	1979	5	10	0	205	48	20.50	0	did	not	bowl				1	
Locker, W.	1894	1903	16	30	0	511	76	17.03	0	did	not	bowl				4	
Loney, E.F.	1925	1927	25	37	7	511	39*	17.03	0	650	20	32.50	4-27	0	0	18	
Lowe, C.	1909	1912	5	8	2	25	17	4.17	0	90	2	45.00	1-20	0	0	0	
Lowe, G.	1949	1953	2	3	0	43	22	14.33	0	did	not	bowl				3	
Lyon, C.H.	1902		2	2	0	6	4	3.00	0	6	0					0	
McCurdy, R.J.	1979		1	did	not	bat				50	1	50.00	1-50	0	0	0	
	1979	1980-81	8	11	0	52	11	4.73	0	823	26	31.65	7-91	1	0	3	
McDonald, J.A.	1905	1906	3	6	0	57	21	9.50	0	did	not	bowl				0	
McLellan, A.J.	1978	1979	26	24	8	99	41	6.18	0	did	not	bowl				41	2
McMillan, S.T.	1922	1924	4	6	2	30	24	7.50	0	14	0					0	
Maher, B.J.N.	1981		2	3	1	6	4*	3.00	0	did	not	bowl				6	2
Maltby, G.	1905		3	6	1	22	7*	4.40	0	20	0					1	
Malthouse, S.	1894	1895	9	12	2	118	38	11.80	0	67	0					3	
Malthouse, W.N.	1919	1920	7	13	1	116	30	9.67	0	69	0					2	

Name	From	To	M	I	NO	Runs	HS	Avge	100	Runs	Wkts	Avge	BB	5wi	5wm	c	s
Marks, C.P.	1967	1969	14	21	2	216	39	11.37	0	did	not	bowl				6	
Marlow, J.	1879	1886	24	45	5	317	25	7.93	0	1237	60	20.62	7-46	4	1	23	
Marple, G.S.	1901		1	1	0	6	6	6.00	0	17	1	17.00	1-17	0	0	0	
Marples, G.	1905		2	4	0	11	6	2.75	0	116	1	116.00	1-53	0	0	1	
Marsden, A.	1910		1	2	0	6	6	3.00	0	did	not	bowl				1	
Marsden, G.A.	1894	1898	30	46	6	417	37	10.43	0	did	not	bowl				12	
Marsh, F.E.	1946	1949	66	109	20	1627	86	18.28	0	1698	44	38.59	6-37	1	0	32	
Marshall, J.	1887		2	4	0	50	31	12.50	0	did	not	bowl				1	
Maynard, E.A.J.	1880	1887	37	68	4	558	84	8.72	0	53	2	26.50	2-34	0	0	12	
	1880	1887	47	85	4	720	84	8.89	0	53	2	26.50	2-34	0	0	18	
Mellor, A.	1978	1980	13	15	6	26	10*	2.89	0	653	17	38.41	5-52	1	0	4	
Middleton, C.	1896	1903	4	8	1	47	21	6.71	0	21	0					0	
Miller, G.	1973	1981	145	219	26	4627	95	23.97	0	9409	382	24.63	7-54	19	4	100	
	1973	1981	203	297	43	6560	98	25.83	0	12439	507	24.53	7-54	24	5	135	
Millner, D.	1960	1963	31	56	1	701	80	12.75	0	27	0					6	
Mir, Pervez J.	1975		1	2	1	61	57*	61.00	0	58	2	29.00	2-37	0	0	0	
	1970-71	1980-81	63	106	11	3080	155	32.42	5	3716	146	25.45	6-39	8	1	56	
Mitchell, T.B.	1928	1939	303	390	102	2342	57	8.13	0	18630	1417	20.20	10-68	115	29	120	
	1928	1939	328	412	107	2431	57	7.97	0	30543	1483	20.60	10-68	118	30	132	
Mohan, K.F.	1957	1958	10	17	2	163	49	10.87	0	23	0					4	
Moir, D.G.	1981		3	4	1	26	16	8.67	0	203	2	101.50	1-20	0	0	0	
	1980	1981	4	6	1	96	44	19.20	0	281	6	46.83	4-43	0	0	1	
Morgan, D.C.	1950	1969	540	857	143	17842	147	24.99	9	30523	1216	25.10	7-33	35	5	562	
	1950	1969	556	882	146	18356	147	24.94	9	31302	1248	25.08	7-33	35	5	572	
A.Morris	1974	1978	47	77	4	1174	74	16.08	0	118	0					29	
	1974	1979-80	49	81	5	1188	74	15.63	0	118	0					31	
Morton, A.	1901		1	2	0	0	0	0.00	0	14	0					0	
Morton, A.	1903	1926	350	610	56	10813	131	19.52	6	21958	966	22.73	9-71	62	11	124	
	1903	1926	357	623	56	10957	131	19.32	6	22352	981	22.78	9-71	63	11	128	
Moses, E.C.	1911		3	6	0	16	9	2.67	0	40	1	40.00	1-16	0	0	3	
	1911	1913-14	7	13	1	60	12	5.00	0	108	8	13.50	3-14	0	0	9	
Mycroft, F.	1894	1895	2	4	0	7	4	1.75	0	did	not	bowl				4	
Mycroft, T.	1877	1885	16	31	9	159	24*	7.22	0	5	0					24	10
	1877	1887	24	46	14	249	24*	7.78	0	16	0					43	16
Mycroft, W.	1873	1885	78	138	44	499	44*	5.31	0	6294	534	11.79	9-24	55	18	46	
	1873	1886	138	234	86	789	44*	5.32	0	10442	863	12.10	9-24	87	28	94	
Needham, E.	1901	1912	186	340	15	6550	159	20.15	7	82	0					135	1
Needham, J.	1883		1	2	1	9	6*	9.00	0	did	not	bowl				0	
Newcombe, C.N.	1910		1	2	0	1	1	0.50	0	32	0					0	
Newman, P.G.	1980	1981	18	19	7	153	29*	12.75	0	12.86	51	25.22	5-51	1	0	6	
	1980	1981	19	19	7	153	29*	12.75	0	1347	54	24.94	5-51	1	0	6	
Newton, F.A.	1909	1910	20	37	6	422	87	13.61	0	21	0					7	
Nornable, E.	1909		1	1	0	8	8	8.00	0	72	5	14.40	3-24	0	0	0	
Oates, W.F.	1959	1965	121	211	14	4568	148*	23.19	2	577	13	44.38	6-47	1	0	54	
	1956	1965	124	214	14	4588	148*	22.94	2	577	13	44.38	6-47	1	0	54	

Name	From	To	M	I	NO	Runs	HS	Avge	100	Runs	Wkts	Avge	BB	5wi	10wm	c	s
O'Connor, J.	1900		9	14	5	55	17	6.11	0	619	24	25.79	5-56	2	1	4	
Oldham, S.	1980	1981	34	24	9	103	33	6.87	0	2406	64	37.59	4-41	0	0	10	
	1974	1981	83	55	23	222	50	6.94	0	5450	172	31.69	5-40	2	0	25	
Oldknow, J.	1901		2	4	1	7	4*	2.33	0	162	4	40.50	3-123	0	0	2	
Oliver, L.	1908	1924	174	322	13	6303	170	20.40	6	328	5	65.80	2-20	0	0	69	
Ollivierre, C.A.	1901	1907	110	201	4	4670	229	23.71	3	414	10	41.40	3-34	0	0	108	
	1894-95	1907	114	209	4	4830	229	23.61	3	664	29	22.90	6-51	3	1	109	
Osborne, G.	1879	1883	7	13	1	45	14	3.75	0	23	1	23.00	1-23	0	0	3	
	1877	1883	8	15	1	60	14	4.28	0	39	1	39.00	1-23	0	0	3	
Page, M.H.	1964	1975	254	451	47	11538	162	28.56	9	527	7	75.29	1-0	0	0	248	
Page, W.	1881	1882	3	6	0	50	19	8.33	0	did	not	bowl				0	
Parrington, W.F.	1926		6	11	1	148	47	14.80	0	did	not	bowl				1	
Payton, W.E.G.	1949		2	4	1	93	35*	31.00	0	did	not	bowl				1	
	1935	1953	27	52	4	995	98	20.73	0	did	not	bowl				11	
Peach, F.G.	1907	1925	12	24	1	258	61*	11.22	0	170	4	42.50	3-50	0	0	3	
Peach, W.	1905		1	2	0	10	10	5.00	0	46	4	11.50	4-46	0	0	1	
Pearson, L.I.	1946		2	4	0	24	18	6.00	0	did	not	bowl				0	
Pink, H.S.	1900		3	5	0	24	11	4.80	0	33	0					0	
Platts, J.T.B.D.	1871	1884	90	167	6	2064	115	12.82	1	3433	183	18.76	6-39	6	0	52	
	1871	1884	97	180	6	2247	115	12.91	1	3673	195	18.84	6-39	6	0	56	
Pope, A.V.	1930	1939	211	312	46	4928	103	18.53	1	12144	542	22.41	7-84	21	3	96	
	1930	1939	214	316	46	4963	103	18.38	1	12512	555	22.54	7-84	22	3	98	
Pope, G.H.	1933	1948	169	265	33	6606	207*	28.47	8	11240	567	19.82	8-38	32	7	126	
	1933	1949-50	205	312	44	7518	207*	28.05	8	13488	677	19.92	8-38	40	7	157	
Pope, H.	1939	1946	10	16	3	81	24*	6.23	0	599	15	39.93	3-80	0	0	3	
Porter, G.	1881	1896	36	55	15	378	93	9.45	0	2760	129	21.40	7-49	7	1	24	
	1881	1896	37	56	15	386	93	9.41	0	2795	130	21.50	7-49	7	1	26	
Pratt, R.	1923	1924	5	10	1	73	17*	8.11	0	did	not	bowl				3	
Prince, W.	1898		1	1	1	2	2*	-	0	38	0					0	
Purdy, H.F.	1906	1919	16	30	4	170	21	6.54	0	661	26	25.42	6-84	1	0	5	
Purdy, J.H.	1896	1906	9	13	4	39	10	4.33	0	310	9	34.44	3-53	0	0	4	
Radford, H.W.	1920		3	6	2	23	14	5.75	0	86	4	21.50	2-18	0	0	0	
Ratcliffe, G.	1887		5	10	0	145	64	14.50	0	8	0					0	
Ratcliffe, G.	1919		1	2	1	8	5*	8.00	0	10	1	10.00	1-10	0	0	2	
Reader-Blackton, W.	1914	1921	8	15	1	107	31*	7.64	0	81	5	16.20	3-40	0	0	6	
Regan, C.	1877		5	10	0	90	22	9.00	0	did	not	bowl				1	
Revill, A.C.	1946	1957	321	537	42	13334	156*	26.94	15	1843	45	40.96	3-12	0	0	327	
	1946	1960	387	654	53	15917	156*	26.48	16	1924	49	39.27	3-12	0	0	396	
Revill, T.F.	1913	1920	11	20	4	231	65*	14.44	0	did	not	bowl				6	
Rhodes, A.E.G.	1937	1954	267	413	33	7195	127	18.93	4	18084	642	28.17	8-162	29	4	82	
	1937	1954	275	422	34	7363	127	18.98	4	18660	661	28.23	8-162	29	4	85	
Rhodes, H.J.	1953	1975	288	357	123	2197	48	9.39	0	18785	993	18.91	7-38	42	4	73	
	1953	1975	322	399	143	2427	48	9.48	0	21145	1073	19.71	7-38	42	4	86	
Richardson, A.W.	1928	1936	159	239	30	3982	90	19.05	0	34	0					58	
Richardson, B.H.	1950	1953	27	36	11	279	29	11.16	0	1003	33	30.39	4-39	0	0	14	

Name	From	To	M	I	NO	Runs	HS	Avge	100	Runs	Wkts	Avge	BB	5wi	10wm	c	s
Richardson, G.W.	1959	1965	62	94	13	1206	91	14.89	0	3712	134	27.70	8-54	5	2	11	
	1959	1965	69	107	15	1460	91	15.87	0	4072	147	27.70	8-54	5	2	12	
Richardson, J.	1878	1883	11	21	4	117	18	6.88	0	517	32	16.16	7176	1	0	9	
Richardson, S.	1871	1878	14	25	0	202	25	8.08	0	43	1	43.00	1-43	0	0	8	1
	1871	1878	15	27	0	202	25	7.48	0	43	1	43.00	1-43	0	0	8	1
Richardson, T.H.	1895		3	5	0	34	11	6.80	0	did	not	bowl				4	
	1888	1895	4	7	0	49	15	7.00	0	did	not	bowl				5	
Rickman, R.B.	1906	1911	65	118	8	1262	68	11.47	0	1967	62	31.73	5-80	1	0	7	
Rigley, W.	1873	1882	57	106	0	1312	69	12.38	0	30	3	10.00	2-10	0	0	20	
	1873	1882	62	115	0	1449	69	12.60	0	30	3	10.00	2-10	0	0	22	
Rimmer, J.	1949		3	3	2	1	1*	1.00	0	264	5	52.80	2-71	0	0	0	
Root, C.F.	1910	1920	57	94	10	927	55	11.04	0	1935	63	30.71	6-42	2	0	42	
	1910	1933	365	586	51	7911	107	14.79	1	31933	1512	21.12	9-23	125	33	243	
Rose, A.	1924		1	1	0	0	0	0.00	0	did	not	bowl				0	
Rowe, L.G.	1974		17	30	1	1059	94	36.52	0	84	1	84.00	1-22	0	0	15	
	1968-69	1980-81	134	219	12	8112	302	39.19	17	215	2	102.50	1-19	0	0	102	
Rumsey, F.E.	1970		1	1	1	2	2*	-	0	97	2	48.50	1-34	0	0	0	
	1960	1970	180	204	84	1015	45	8.46	0	11773	580	20.30	8-26	30	5	90	
Russell, P.E.	1965	1979	167	207	44	2015	72	12.36	0	10108	335	30.17	7-46	5	0	124	
Ryder, R.T.	1903		1	1	0	10	10	10.00	0	did	not	bowl				1	
Sale, R. sen.	1908	1912	23	43	2	570	69	13.90	0	273	5	54.60	2-25	0	0	3	
	1908	1912	39	70	2	961	69	14.13	0	471	10	47.10	2-25	0	0	12	
Sale, R. jun.	1949	1954	24	39	3	835	146	23.19	1	4	1	4.00	1-4	0	0	8	
	1939	1954	66	115	8	2923	157	27.32	3	4	1	4.00	1-4	0	0	27	
Selby, T.G.	1885		1	2	0	3	2	1.50	0	7	0					0	
Severn, A.	1919	1920	13	24	2	342	73	15.55	0	did	not	bowl				5	
Shacklock, F.J.	1884	1885	18	34	2	287	50	8.97	0	988	59	16.75	5-42	6	1	6	
	1883	1904-05	156	231	26	2438	71	11.89	0	9456	497	19.03	8-32	36	6	92	
Shardlow, W.	1925	1928	38	42	14	201	39*	7.18	0	1939	56	34.63	5-41	1	0	16	
Sharpe, P.J.	1975	1976	40	69	0	2031	228	29.43	4	29	1	29.00	1-11	0	0	47	
	1956	1976	493	811	78	22530	228	30.74	29	197	3	65.67	1-1	0	0	616	
Shaw, H.	1875	1884	14	25	7	121	22	6.72	0	158	10	15.80	5-34	1	0	5	
Shearwood, K.A.	1949		1	2	0	6	4	3.00	0	did	not	bowl				0	1
	1949	1951	5	6	1	45	28	9.00	0	did	not	bowl				5	4
Sherwin, A.W.	1908		11	21	2	152	24	8.00	0	did	not	bowl				4	
Sherwin, C.B.	1907		1	2	0	7	7	3.50	0	did	not	bowl				0	
Sherwin, H.	1937		1	2	2	12	9*	-	0	32	0					0	
Shipton, W.L.	1884		1	2	0	4	3	2.00	0	did	not	bowl				0	
Short, J.D.	1957	1960	11	19	0	271	86	14.26	0	11	0					6	
Shuker, A.	1874	1882	22	40	2	601	86	15.82	0	did	not	bowl				12	
Skinner, A.F.	1931	1938	83	136	7	3442	102	26.88	1	250	6	41.67	2-12	0	0	59	
	1931	1949	86	142	7	3537	102	26.20	1	250	6	41.67	2-12	0	0	60	
Skinner, D.A.	1947	1949	23	36	1	475	63	13.57	0	182	2	91.00	1-41	0	0	11	
Slater, A.G.	1911	1931	210	326	28	5933	105	19.91	1	10487	498	21.06	8-24	28	2	122	
	1911	1933	211	327	28	5943	105	19.88	1	10548	500	21.10	8-24	28	2	124	

Name	From	To	M	I	NO	Runs	HS	Avge	100	Runs	Wkts	Avge	BB	5iw	10wm	c	s
Slater, Henry	1882	1887	5	9	3	22	11	3.67	0	185	3	61.67	1-35	0	0	2	
Slater, Herbert	1907		5	9	2	39	21	5.57	0	38	2	19.00	2-15	0	0	0	
Smith, A.	1873	1880	49	86	30	243	22	4.34	0	7	0					63	9
	1867	1880	55	98	34	305	30	4.77	0	7	0					70	12
Smith, D.	1927	1952	420	711	58	20516	225	31.42	30	706	19	37.16	5-37	1	0	360	5
	1927	1952	443	753	63	21843	225	31.66	32	734	20	36.70	5-37	1	0	378	5
Smith, D.H.K.	1965	1970	112	198	14	4915	136	26.71	4	23	1	23.00	1-1	0	0	83	
	1965	1977-78	114	202	14	4995	136	26.57	4	23	1	23.00	1-1	0	0	84	
Smith, E.	1951	1971	497	667	143	6884	90	13.14	0	31189	1209	25.80	9-46	51	4	204	
	1951	1971	503	674	144	6998	90	13.02	0	31448	1217	25.84	9-46	51	4	207	
Smith, H.W.	1920		1	2	1	34	24*	34.00	0	did	not	bowl				0	
	1912	1920	2	3	1	49	24*	24.50	0	did	not	bowl				0	
Smith, J.	1871	1878	22	38	2	403	35	11.19	0	162	6	27.00	3-38	0	0	14	
Smith, L.S.T.	1909		2	3	0	9	5	3.00	0	did	not	bowl				1	
Smith, R.P.	1871	1884	90	167	3	2424	69	14.78	0	23	0					64	
	1871	1884	103	190	3	2719	87	14.54	0	23	0					74	
Smith, W.	1913		2	4	0	13	8	3.25	0	did	not	bowl				0	
Snape, M.D.	1949		2	3	1	0	0*	0.00	0	did	not	bowl				0	
Southern, J.D.	1919	1934	5	10	0	95	43	9.50	0	did	not	bowl				0	
Sowter, U.	1871	1876	7	11	1	128	47*	12.80	0	did	not	bowl				7	
Sparrow, G.R.	1905		2	4	0	75	64	18.75	0	did	not	bowl				0	
Spencer, H.	1895		1	1	0	0	0	0.00	0	did	not	bowl				0	
Stapleton, E.	1902		1	2	0	3	2	1.50	0	did	not	bowl				0	
Steele, D.S.	1979	1981	64	101	18	2790	137	33.62	3	3699	148	24.99	7-53	10	1	56	
	1963	1981	425	706	92	20285	140*	33.04	30	10105	424	23.83	8-29	16	2	469	
Steeples, A.	1899		1	2	0	18	16	9.00	0	21	0					0	
Steeples, R.	1897		3	5	0	20	16	4.00	0	214	9	23.78	4-73	0	0	1	
Stephenson, G.R.	1967	1968	9	14	0	215	64	15.36	0	did	not	bowl				14	2
	1967	1980	272	357	66	4781	100*	16.43	1	39	0					584	77
Stevenson, G.S.	1904		2	4	0	10	9	2.50	0	92	1	92.00	1-79	0	0	1	
Stevenson, K.	1974	1977	47	60	19	374	33	9.12	0	2997	98	30.58	7-68	4	0	15	
	1974	1981	138	158	55	969	33	9.41	0	9824	333	29.50	7-22	15	0	45	
Stevenson, M.H.	1950	1952	3	4	0	23	15	5.75	0	did	not	bowl				0	
	1949	1967	66	106	7	2467	122	25.73	4	1882	50	37.64	5-36	1	0	26	
Storer, H. sen.	1895		6	10	1	92	35	10.22	0	13	0					3	
Storer, H. jun	1920	1936	302	517	28	13513	232	27.63	18	7525	232	32.44	7-26	9	0	214	1
Storer, W.	1887	1905	209	351	29	9887	216*	30.70	15	7209	214	33.69	5-20	4	0	258	26
	1887	1905	289	490	41	12966	216*	28.88	17	7863	232	33.89	5-20	4	0	376	55
Street, H.	1887		2	4	1	24	15*	8.00	0	did	not	bowl				1	
Stubbings, J.	1880	1885	4	8	3	20	10*	4.00	0	142	7	20.29	5-51	1	0	1	
	1877	1885	5	10	3	26	10*	3.71	0	142	7	20.29	5-51	1	0	1	
Stubbings, W.	1900		1	2	1	9	9*	9.00	0	80	0					0	
Sugden, H.E.	1882		2	4	0	13	9	3.25	0	did	not	bowl				0	
Sugg, F.H.	1884	1886	33	64	2	1278	187	20.61	1	14	0					20	
	1883	1899	305	515	30	11859	220	24.45	16	273	10	27.30	2-12	0	0	167	1
Sugg, W.	1884	1902	128	217	16	3460	107	17.21	2	1560	50	31.20	4-61	0	0	64	
	1881	1902	129	218	16	3469	107	17.17	2	1560	50	31.20	4-61	0	0	64	

Name	From	To	M	I	NO	Runs	HS	Avge	100	Runs	Wkts	Avge	BB	5wi	10wm	c	s
Swallow, R.	1959	1963	37	66	2	1296	115	20.25	1	8	0					12	
	1957	1963	38	68	2	1323	115	20.05	1	8	0					13	
Swarbrook, F.W.	1967	1979	199	285	82	4125	90	20.32	0	12809	416	30.79	9-20	14	2	123	
	1967	1979-80	223	326	88	4902	90	20.60	0	13998	467	29.97	9-20	15	2	138	
Swindell, R.S.	1972	1977	23	32	11	242	38	11.52	0	1665	50	33.30	6-79	4	0	11	
Sykes, E.	1925	1932	5	10	1	105	50	11.67	0	2	0					0	
Tate, C.F.	1928		4	4	1	48	21	16.00	0	112	2	56.00	2-9	0	0	0	
	1928	1933	11	12	3	82	21	9.11	409	8	51.13	3-65	0	0	5		
	1928	1933	11	12	3	82	21	9.11	0	409	8	51.13	3-65	0	0	5	
Taylor, F.H.	1908	1911	8	16	1	95	18	6.33	0	did	not	bowl				3	
Taylor, R.W.	1961	1981	467	657	123	8956	100	16.77	1	46	0					1066	136
	1960	1981	551	760	140	10549	100	17.01	1	46	0					1284	162
Taylor, W.T.	1905	1910	4	8	1	53	11	7.57	0	56	2	28.00	1-9	0	0	2	
Thompson, W.H.	1908		1	2	0	17	17	8.50	0	did	not	bowl				0	
Thornhill, F.	1876		1	2	0	0	0	0.00	0	did	not	bowl				0	
Tilson, J.	1871	1876	3	5	0	26	14	5.20	0	did	not	bowl				0	
Todd, N.D.	1906	1908	2	4	0	6	6	1.50	0	did	not	bowl				0	
Tomlinson, J.D.W.	1946		1	1	0	2	2	2.00	0	did	not	bowl				1	
Tomlinson, W.J.V.	1920	1924	26	43	3	566	43	14.15	0	982	32	30.69	5-53	1	0	9	
	1920	1924	38	65	8	852	51	14.95	0	1870	58	32.24	5-53	1	0	10	
Topham, H.G.	1881		1	2	2	5	4*	-	0	49	1	49.00	1-49	0	0	0	
	1881	1884	16	28	12	95	12	5.94	0	1120	60	18.67	7-62	4	1	15	
Townsend, A.F.	1934	1950	116	198	13	4313	142*	23.31	5	39	0					30	
	1934	1950	117	200	13	4327	142*	23.14	5	39	0					30	
Townsend, L.F.	1922	1939	446	713	62	17667	233	27.14	22	20380	969	21.03	8-26	42	13	210	
	1922	1939	493	786	75	19555	233	27.50	22	22985	1088	21.13	8-26	51	16	234	
Tunnicliffe, C.J.	1973	1981	117	132	28	1358	82*	13.06	0	7680	243	31.60	7-36	5	0	54	
Turland, H.	1921		1	2	0	1	1	0.50	0	did	not	bowl				0	
	1921	1924	2	4	0	30	29	7.50	0	14	0					0	
Turner, A.	1920		2	4	0	4	2	1.00	0	138	6	23.00	3-66	0	0	1	
Tye, J.	1874		3	4	0	21	11	5.25	0	4	1	4.00	1-1	0	0	2	
	1874	1881	24	38	8	226	48	7.53	0	1102	45	24.49	5-41	2	0	20	
Vaulkhard, P.	1946	1952	65	103	5	2170	264	22.14	1	36	0					52	4
	1934	1952	77	122	7	2460	264	21.39	1	124	1	124.00	1-30	0	0	64	4
Venkataraghavan, S.	1973	1975	46	71	20	988	51*	19.37	0	4767	171	27.88	8-77	10	2	50	
	1973	1980-81	309	419	78	6296	137	18.46	1	30481	1263	24.42	9-93	75	18	288	
Walkden, G.G.	1905	1906	7	13	0	114	33	8.76	0	did	not	bowl				2	
Walker, G.G.	1881	1898	70	118	24	1028	66	10.94	0	4649	187	24.86	9-68	9	3	24	
	1881	1898	75	128	24	1141	66	10.97	0	5063	202	25.07	9-68	10	3	26	
Walker, N.A.M.	1931	1936	2	3	0	22	13	7.33	0	22	1	22.00	1-12	0	0	0	
	1923-24	1936	4	6	0	48	18	8.00	0	77	2	38.50	1-12	0	0	1	
Walker, S.G.	1932		1	2	0	8	7	4.00	0	6	1	6.00	1-6	0	0	0	
Wallis, W.A.	1906		1	2	0	17	11	8.50	0	did	not	bowl				1	

Name	From	To	M	I	NO	Runs	HS	Avge	100	Runs	Wkts	Avge	BB	5wi	10wm	c	s
Wallroth, C.A.	1879		3	5	0	39	26	7.80	0	did	not	bowl				2	
	1871	1879	21	36	1	586	109	16.74	1	did	not	bowl				7	
Walters, J.	1977	1980	58	80	15	1296	90	19.94	0	1935	47	41.17	4-100	0	0	26	
Walton, W.	1887		1	2	0	4	3	2.00	0	did	not	bowl				0	
Ward, A.	1966	1976	115	115	38	709	44	9.21	0	7504	348	21.56	7-42	14	4	34	
	1966	1978	163	157	47	928	44	8.44	0	10495	460	22.82	7-42	15	4	51	
Ward, J.M.	1973	1975	20	35	0	536	104	15.31	1	did	not	bowl				8	
	1970	1975	49	87	4	1743	104	21.00	1	did	not	bowl				24	
Ward, L.F.	1899		1	2	0	0	0	0.00	0	did	not	bowl				1	
Warren, A.	1897	1920	250	439	44	5449	123	13.79	1	22563	918	24.58	8-69	71	15	188	
	1897	1920	255	445	44	5507	123	13.73	1	23061	939	24.56	8-69	73	15	195	
Wass, H.	1929		1	1	0	9	9	9.00	0	did	not	bowl				0	
Watson, R.M.	1947		6	11	3	68	25*	8.50	0	did	not	bowl				3	
Webster, D.	1975		1	1	0	26	26	26.00	0	28	1	28.00	1-28	0	0	0	
Webster, F.	1906		1	2	0	11	10	5.50	0	65	1	65.00	1-65	0	0	0	
Webster, W.	1911		1	2	0	3	3	1.50	0	did	not	bowl				0	
Whyatt, C.	1976		1	1	0	6	6	6.00	0	did	not	bowl				2	
Wickstead, A.	1911	1912	14	26	3	385	68	16.74	0	2	0					3	
Widdowson, A.	1894		1	1	0	1	1	1.00	0	did	not	bowl				0	
Wild, H.	1913	1920	32	59	7	628	68	12.08	0	129	2	64.50	1-3	0	0	29	
Wilde, D.	1971	1972	13	15	5	31	12	3.10	0	860	23	37.39	3-27	0	0	1	
Wilkins, C.P.	1970	1972	71	126	12	4060	156	35.61	9	1615	47	34.36	4-21	0	0	65	
	1962-63	1980-81	187	336	20	10597	156	33.53	18	4910	141	34.82	4-19	0	0	202	6
Willatt, G.L.	1950	1956	125	199	10	5127	146	27.13	6	76	1	76.00	1-2	0	0	40	
	1938	1961	185	303	17	8325	146	29.11	13	135	3	45.00	2-18	0	0	51	
Wilmot, A.A.	1871		1	2	0	0	0	0.00	0	did	not	bowl				1	
Wilmot, W.	1897	1901	10	16	3	155	25*	11.92	0	did	not	bowl				11	1
Wilson, G.D.	1902	1905	2	4	0	19	9	4.75	0	15	0					0	
Wincer, R.C.	1978	1980	23	21	8	131	26	10.08	0	1653	46	35.93	4-42	0	0	8	
Wood, A.J.	1911	1912	13	19	1	264	52	14.66	0	64	0					5	
Wood, A.M.	1879		2	4	0	28	9	7.00	0	did	not	bowl				2	
	1879	1908	59	105	3	2038	132	19.98	2	43	0					72	
Wood, B.	1980	1981	39	67	9	2319	153	39.98	5	1179	27	43.67	3-22	0	0	37	
	1964	1981	333	551	71	16580	198	34.54	29	8396	288	29.15	7-52	8	0	263	
Wood, S.H.	1894	1902	34	54	11	758	81*	17.63	0	50	0					12	
Woodland, A.W.	1920		2	4	1	27	19*	9.00	0	69	0					1	
Wood-Sims, W.	1879	1886	23	42	1	461	46	11.24	0	43	1	43.00	1-16	0	0	12	
	1879	1886	25	45	2	518	46	12.05	0	70	5	14.00	3-22	0	0	13	
Woodward, K.A.	1909		2	4	1	12	7	4.00	0	did	not	bowl				0	
	1896	1909	3	6	1	23	7	4.60	0	did	not	bowl				0	
Worthington, T.S.	1924	1947	406	648	54	17000	238*	28.62	27	17979	624	28.81	8-29	16	2	307	
	1924	1947	453	720	59	19221	238*	29.08	31	19445	682	29.24	8-29	16	2	340	
Wright, F.	1899		1	2	0	4	4	2.00	0	37	0					0	
Wright, H.F.	1904	1905	9	16	3	298	55	22.92	0	did	not	bowl				4	
Wright, J.	1898	1906	6	10	1	93	53*	10.33	0	16	0					0	

Name	From	To	M	I	NO	Runs	HS	Avge	100	Runs	Wkts	Avge	BB	5wi	5wm	c	s
Wright, J.G.	1977	1981	85	146	12	5316	166*	39.67	14	8	1	8.00	1-4	0	0	46	
	1975-76	1981	153	273	19	9518	166*	37.47	19	23	1	23.00	1-4	0	0	90	
Wright, L.G.	1883	1909	317	577	12	14800	195	26.19	20	194	1	194.00	1-4	0	0	232	4
	1883	1909	325	593	12	15166	195	26.10	20	204	1	204.00	1-4	0	0	237	6
Wright, W.J.	1932		2	3	0	58	58	19.33	0	did	not	bowl				0	
Wyatt, G.	1954	1960	11	20	4	184	59	11.50	0	2	0					7	
Yates, G.	1883		1	1	0	0	0	0.00	0	9	0					0	
Young, J.H.	1899	1901	28	48	9	379	42*	9.72	0	996	28	37.57	5-65	1	0	3	
Young, J.W.	1894		2	2	0	0	0	0.00	0	did	not	bowl				0	

NOTES

1. The match Chesterfield with Barlow (or Derbyshire) v United North of England XI in 1875 is not included in the Derbyshire figures as it was not a match sanctioned by the County Club, but it is included, where appropriate in the figures for all matches.
2. Matches included as first-class are those published in the appropriate ACS Guide.
3. Pervez Mir's record is not complete as full scores of some matches in Pakistan in 1977-78 are not available. Summarised details of these matches have been used, and such information as is known has been included.
4. W.Bestwick's innings of 2 v Leicestershire (Chesterfield) in 1899 where he was not out overnight and arrived late the following day is included as a dismissal.
5. F.Davidson's innings of 5 v Yorkshire (Chesterfield) 1898 where he was not out overnight and withdrawn from the match by his club the following day is included as a dismissal.
6. The versions of the scores published in the ACS printed match score books have been used.

CORRECTIONS TO PREVIOUS BOOKLETS

Surrey

K.F.Barrington	Sy RC 4729, AM RC 8907
J.Beaumont	AM RC 7805
T.Box	AM 246-454-43-4908-c234
W.Clarke	AM 143-243-37-2130, 4144-409plus386, 5i 82, 10m 25, c 55
J.Cobbett	AM 100-172-17-1573
D.Day	AM 51-88-15-417, 1182-102plus157, 5i 22, c 36
M.W.Deane	AM c5
J.Dunn	Sy R 85, HS 38*; AM R 95, HS 38*
G.F.Elliott	AM 1874-80; 51-93-8-1163
W.J.Hammersley	AM 34-60-5-567, c23
R.Harman	Sy RC 8708; AM RC 8975
W.R.Hillyer	AM 229-410-68-2649, 4-48-376plus1090; 5i 147, 10m 54, BB 8-26; c 201
G.G.Jones	Sy R 1155, AM 1202
J.M.Lee	AM 36-57-6-678, c24
E.Macniven	AM 12-21-4-407
W.Martingell	AM 182-308-46-2401, c129
E.Mills	AM w 87
G.Parr	AM 207-358-30-6626, c126
E.H.Pickering	AM 26-3-274
F.Pilch	AM 229-416-32-7147, ow 136, 5i 3, c121
T.Sewell sr	AM 116-208-13-1931-66*, s4
J.Southerton	Sy mt 152, AM mt 286, Sy 5i 115
N.Wanostrocht	AM 148-264-13-4356-, c112

Scotland

First Class records for players who appeared in non-f-c-matches only for Scotland

Dharsi, S.K.	**1965-6-1973-4: 49-76-5-2288-149-32.19-4; 18-1-18.00-0-1-4 c 67 s 26**
Walker, S.G.	**1932: 1-2-0-8-7-4.00-0; 6-1-6.00-1/6, c0**

IRELAND

S.C.Corlett	AM RC 1722
M.Halliday	Ire c3
R.Harrison	Ire R 16, HS 12
M.Hoffman	DU RC 18 - delete line for Hoffman at foot of page.
T.O.Jameson	AM c97
S.W.Middleton	DU HS 0*
J.D.Monteith	Ire Av 14.57
B.A.O'Brien	Ire Av 18.66
J.F.Kempster	Career 1920-22
J.P.M.Pigot	Career 1924 to 1925-6
P.F.Quinton	Career ended 1928-29
S.T.A.Radcliffe	Career 1925 to 1926-7
J.F.Short	Ire av 39.82
F.Stedman	AM c266, s50
T.F.Ward	Ire HS 3*
P.M.Webb	Ire c3
A.Wallis	DU HS 5*